Best Sermons
Book Four

Edited with Introduction and Biographical Notes by

Joseph Fort Newton
(Litt.D., D.H.L.)

Memorial Church of St. Paul, Overbrook, Philadelphia.
Author of "Some Living Masters of the Pulpit,"
"The Truth and the Life," "God and the
Golden Rule," etc.

New York
Harcourt, Brace and Company

COPYRIGHT, 1927, BY
HARCOURT, BRACE AND COMPANY, INC.

PRINTED IN THE U. S. A. BY
QUINN & BODEN COMPANY, INC,
RAHWAY, N. J.

IN THE VESTRY

What do ye counsel, Brethren, what do ye commend? Shall I devote myself to prayer, or shall I go about preaching? Of a truth, I that am little, and simple, and rude in speech, have received more grace of prayer than of speaking. Now in prayer, there seemeth to be gain and heaping up of grace; in preaching, a certain giving out of the gifts received from heaven; in prayer, again, a cleansing of the inward feelings, and an union with the one, true, and highest good, together with a strengthening of virtue; in preaching, the spiritual feet wax dusty, and many things distract a man, and discipline is relaxed.

—St. Francis of Assisi.

So Bonaventura reports the dilemma of Francis, who felt that in prayer we talk with God and listen for His answer, whilst in preaching we think, say and hear such things as pertain to men. He consulted with Brother Silvester and Sister Clare, who agreed that the Herald should go forth to preach, though he might long to linger and listen. He obeyed, and at Cannara the whole population asked to be admitted to the Order, as if to teach us that the more closely prayer and preaching are linked together the more richly both are rewarding: as in the little Prayer Room of Wesley in City Road chapel. If the preaching of our day is hesitating and vague, lacking the

iii

mysticism which lies at the heart of all spiritual power, mayhap the story of Francis tells us why it is so.

After all, what is preaching? If we put the question to Beecher, he tells us that preaching is the making and mending of men. If we ask Phillips Brooks, he describes it as the revelation of truth through personality, truth shining through the prism of a human soul. William Law held that the end of preaching is so to strike all the outward senses of the soul that, from sleeping insensibility, it may be awakened to know God and live in Him. One of the greatest sermons in our language was that of Channing at the dedication of Divinity Hall in Boston, in 1826, and its subject was the Christian Ministry. In a series of majestic paragraphs he sets forth the secret of power in the pulpit, by which he meant a vivid sense of spiritual truth which enables the preacher to quicken a like sense in others. If we go further back and put the question to St. Paul, he tells us that preaching is persuasion. That is to say, they all agree with "Father" Taylor, the sailor evangelist, when he said that it is the business of the preacher "to take something hot out of his own heart and shove it into mine."

Let it be remembered that preaching, in the New Testament sense at least—as in the ministry of the mighty Hebrew prophets—is not the making of a homily; it is the urgent announcement of a Message. There is evidence of the delivery of sermons or homilies in the early Christian assemblies, but it is nowhere called preaching. St. Paul is not said to have preached at Troas, but to have discoursed—a very different thing. Three words in the Greek are properly rendered Preaching, but they identify the preacher as a Messenger, a Herald, a Courier telling momentous tidings. It is not an otiose addition when teaching is mentioned along with preaching, for these are very different functions, each useful after its kind. Other offices are also linked together, "preach the word, reprove, rebuke, exhort," edify; but it is clear that to preach the Gospel is to announce Christ to unbelievers, and to those who have not heard the news. The old Evangelicals used to divide their sermons into two parts: one addressed to believers, the other to the unconverted—as if they were aware that in the latter part alone they preached the Gospel. Useful as other offices may be, what we need today is to recapture and relearn the genius of preaching in its unique, urgent meaning; and those who have that gift ought to be set free to be persuaders and winners of men, after the manner of Francis and his friars.

My reason for inquiring into the nature of preaching is the feeling, so widespread today, not only that modern preaching is chaotic, anemic and lacking in power, but that the pulpit has become a useless thing. Laments of like kind have been heard in every age, even when the greatest voices were speaking. Why should it be so, unless it be that we have forgotten what it means to preach, or else we do not speak with the authority of insight and the verity of experience —mere apologists defending the Message, not heralds announcing the best news ever told among men? The human heart remains the same in its needs, its aspirations, its lonely, wistful yearnings, and its broodings on the dim hereafter never fade or die. Today, as in all the past, to any fresh or earnest word on these intimate and mysterious themes men listen with the eagerness which imagination ascribes to the Ages of Faith. Our Christian ministry today may be toiling in the twilight, uttering its message in a stammering tongue, but that is only temporary. Soon it will find once more the master key, and speak with the emphasis of insight and the accent of power, making "one music as before, but vaster."

When we look into the New Testament we are startled—and dismayed—by the contrast between its boundless wealth and our poverty of power. Indeed, if we ask ourselves what was the *motif* of the ministries of Jesus and His apostles we find it all summed up in the text which Channing chose for his sermon: "His word was with power." Twenty-five times, in the most important connections, this word appears in the first three Gospels. When we think of the New Testament preachers, and the irresistible power of the Gospel by which sin was shattered, we often feel that it was some special dispensation denied us today. So, strangely enough, Wesley thought only a month before his "strange warming of the heart," as we read in his *Journal:* "This, I grant, God wrought in the first stages of Christianity; but the times are changed. What reason have I to believe that He works in the same manner now?" Even when he asked the question the answer was at the door, and soon he was going all over England a herald of the Gospel. Surely the same sources of power are open to us today if we seek until we find, and show ourselves worthy of it.

Now, consider. If preaching is persuasion, the man in the pulpit must be utterly persuaded if he is to persuade any one else. No hesitation, no balancing of probabilities will do. "I am persuaded," said St. Paul, and there lies the secret of his magnificent and ceaseless evangel, to which we owe more than to anything else except the life of Jesus. Persuaded of what? He was persuaded in mind and heart and soul of the Love of God, its tenderness, its tenacity, and its final triumph—nothing else really matters. Once men are sure that there is Love hidden in the hardness of life, meaning in its mystery, purpose in its pitiful broken beauty, and something eternal in its evanescence, the rest is only a detail of interpretation and adaptation. Until the supreme reality of religious faith commands the intellect of the preacher and subdues his heart, no matter how learned or eloquent he may be, there is no power of persuasion. Never were men more aware of religious perplexities, and, by the same token, never was there a richer opportunity for wise and winsome leadership in the pulpit, if it be both intellectually and spiritually authentic. To that end the pulpit must be free, fearless, and utterly frank, evading no difficulty, if it is to make men see the truth that sets us free from haunting fear and dark fatality.

In the Vestry

Persuaded, how? No one would say that St. Paul reasoned or argued himself into the vivid and glowing faith that glorified his life, though he was a mind of the first order. Even in an age clamorous for clarity mere intellectual conviction is not enough. Logic is ice, religion is fire. Faith is not first a philosophy; it is a fellowship. In the order of experience, its philosophy follows its fellowship, and is an effort, imperfect at best, to interpret the depth and wonder of that life of God in the soul which is the supreme reality of mortal life. In the *Journal* of Wesley we read how, in early life, he was troubled by this question: "How can you preach to others, who have no faith yourself?" He asked Peter Bohler whether he should not leave off preaching, and Bohler advised against it. "But what can I preach?" asked Wesley. Bohler replied, "Preach faith till you have it; and then, because you have it, you will preach faith." At first glance that looks like an exhortation to hypocrisy, but it is not. Wesley had no intellectual difficulty in respect to the faith he was preaching; none at all, apparently. It commanded his intellect, but it did not fire his heart. Later, what had long been true to him as a theology became an inward experience, and his word was with power in one of the greatest ministries in the story of England.

Today, alas, the situation seems to be the other way round, and the pulpit is so vexed by misgiving that its gospel ceases to be an apostolate and becomes an apology; but that is to reverse the true order of faith. No man may hope to answer any vital question of life—much less the unasked questions of the human heart—until he has learned to know the Answerer, and then he discovers, as Newman did at the end of his agony, that a thousand intellectual difficulties do not make one spiritual doubt. No eloquence of tongue, no charm of manner, no artistry of homiletics can atone for a lack or loss of a vital inward experience of spiritual reality, to seek which is our quest and to find which is our crown and consecration. Without it the pulpit may be able and useful, at once instructive and entertaining, and in many ways valuable as a popular forum or an educational agency, its sermons ranging all the way from lectures on economics to essays stewed in cream; but it is bereft of that haunting music which breaks the heart —and mends it—lifting the life of man, troubled by sin and tormented by woe, above a beshadowed earth into the shadowless sky of vision and joy.

In the lives of the supreme preachers one nearly always finds a golden year, a shining day—sometimes a single luminous hour—which gives the key to their career: they ceased to stammer and their sermons moved with the lilt and lift of lyrics. An unknown layman asked Tauler if he knew in his heart what he taught in his words, and he had to admit that he did not. They went together into the silence, and when he returned men heard their own souls speak in his simple, healing words. Who does not remember that golden year in the life of Phillips Brooks when, as if at the kiss of God, his spirit bloomed, and a whiter light from a higher sky fell upon his letters and diaries. One night Bushnell leaped out of bed, caught up into a great joy, crying, "I have found it! I have found the Gospel!" Thereafter his preaching had a new dimension, and in prayer he was as a child climbing upon the knees of God and talking to Him face to face. On a spring day, under an apple tree, young Beecher lay musing, when a sense of the Love of God in Christ flooded him like the soft light sifting through the leaves, transfiguring all his days and fusing all his faith to a glow-point of vision which never faded.

From belief we must advance to faith—and from faith to faith—by a deep inward way which transcends logic and makes the truth our truth; as Luther did in his cell at Erfurt; as Wesley did in the chapel on that memorable evening in May; as Dale did when, of a sudden, he realized for the first time—though he had been preaching it for years—that Christ is *alive!* The great truths of faith, which are the themes of the pulpit, must be known by an immediate and profound personal sense of divine things, if we are to speak with power and persuade others; since it is not the business of the preacher to prove things, but to make men *see* the truth. What Milton said of the poet is equally true of his kinsman, the preacher: "He who would be a true poet ought himself to be a true poem—not presuming to sing high praises of what is worthy unless he have in himself the experience and practice of all that is praiseworthy." Always it comes back to the culture of the life of the spirit in the heart of the preacher, his in-

In the Vestry

ward insight and adventure; and as he lives in God, so will the power of God live and speak in his words.

For preaching—in spite of our pitiful confusions and inefficiencies—is the noblest vocation on earth. No other calling asks so much of the manhood of a man, no other offers so much to those who enter it. No career can compare with it in the rich and satisfying relations into which it brings a man with his fellow-men, the searching insight which it gives into the human heart, and the opportunity which it offers to serve the souls of men. Knowing the terror of evil-doing, the preacher seeks to persuade men to live righteously; suffering with them in their sorrows, he leads them to the Eternal Comforter; and at the end-time he bids them trust the Love that never faileth. Truth taken into the heart sanctifies the life, and life sanctified reveals the truth; in that paradox lies the secret of service, the character of the preacher lighting up like an altar lamp the teaching of his words. When his work is done it is tribute enough if men say of him not that he was learned, or eloquent, or profound, but that "his word was with power."

JOSEPH FORT NEWTON.

Memorial Church of St. Paul,
  Overbrook, Philadelphia.

CONTENTS

xiii

Contents

xiv

THE ETERNAL REALITY

The retirement of Dr. Gordon from the Old South Church in Boston marks the close of one of the most memorable ministries of our generation. For more than forty years, employing an authentic genius with single-hearted devotion in the service of God and man, he has made an historic pulpit a throne of power and an altar of vision. A philosopher with the soul of a poet, a vital and constructive thinker in an age of theological confusion, he has been an incomparable interpreter of faith. Judged by any test, it was a truly great ministry, worthy of thanksgiving in all the churches.

A sketch of Dr. Gordon appeared in *Best Sermons, 1924;* and since then, by a rare fortune—more rare than some of us had hoped for, despite our requests for it—he has given us his autobiography, *My Education and Religion*—a book radiant with personality, rich in wisdom and warm humanity, at once a record of struggle and a rosary of friendship. If he will only gather into a volume his fugitive essays—such as those on Emerson and Milton—he will add to our obligation and round out a ministry which, alike in its completeness and its fruitfulness, is hardly surpassed in the annals of the Church.

One cannot overestimate the worth, both in example and achievement, of a life of high, incessant toil in the service of an august opportunity, full of the peace of great thoughts and faithful service, undisturbed by a vulgar popularity, not only maintaining but magnifying the tradition of the Christian pulpit in a gay and giddy-paced age. Dr. Gordon will be followed into retirement with abounding gratitude: may the evening be long and gentle, and when "the dumb hour brings the dreams about his couch" may its shadow be lifted by the radiance of a prophet's reward.

THE ETERNAL REALITY

GEORGE A. GORDON, D.D.

OLD SOUTH CHURCH, BOSTON

And I saw no temple therein! for the Lord God the Almighty and the Lamb, are the temple thereof. Revelation 21: 22.

When I was in Harvard College, one day William James sent me to his father's house where the professor was then living—it was before his marriage, so long ago did I know him—to get a book from his library. I was a total stranger to the family. I was met at the door by Henry James, Sr., with blazing eyes and austere aspect, not unlike one of the Greek Furies. He admitted me, as I thought, with some reluctance, examined and cross-examined me, led me into the library, and finally being satisfied that I was human, fell into a friendly familiar conversation. He told me of a debate between his two sons, William and Henry, when they were boys, upon the Church. Henry was nimbler than William in argument; William was profounder and far more serious. Henry said, "I am willing to confess the reality of God, but as for the Church, it is a mere conventionality, made of stone and lime, and I have no respect for it." William replied, "Whoever confesses the reality of God thereby confesses the reality of the Church, for

3

George A. Gordon, D.D.

ultimately God is the Church." So we read in the text, "And I saw no temple therein; for the Lord God the Almighty, and the Lamb, are the temple thereof." Here we find a boys' debate leading to the heart of the profoundest things in the Christian faith.

From of old this world of ours has been divided into the passing and the permanent, the evanescent and the everlasting, and sometimes thinkers have held that one aspect, and again the other, was the total reality. The charm of the early Greek reflection is that it is the reflection of children of genius in the morning of time. As in the debate between those two James boys, we see our own puzzles, our own thoughts and our own difficulties reflected as in the face and speech of brilliant and charming children. One philosopher, the great Parmenides, whom Socrates met when he was a very young man and Parmenides a very old man, and of whom he said that he was venerable and awful and of glorious depth of mind, held that the All was one and forever at rest; that change and motion were an illusion; the All was one, immovable, immutable, always at rest. Later this contention was represented by an argument which interests young people in their studies today: Whatever moves must either move where it is or it must move where it is not. A thing cannot move where it is; it cannot move where it is not. There is therefore no such thing as motion. That is one side. The other side was represented by Heraclitus, who said there is no permanence; everything is motion. It is impossible to bathe twice in the

4

same stream; the stream has changed before you can return. His disciple, Cratylus, as our vernacular would have it, "went him one better." He said it was impossible to bathe once in the same stream; the stream is forever changing. Furthermore, it is impossible even to name your father and mother, for while you are naming them they change into something else. All that one can do is to sit in silence and point to the wonder of the mysterious movement of eternal change.

Science has within a century reconciled these two views, in the doctrine of the conservation of energy. The force in the universe is forever the same; it cannot be diminished; nor can any addition be made to it. There is permanence. This eternal force is forever finding new forms of expression; there is change. This story of philosophy is a prelude to what religion, great religion, has done. From of old it has united these two contrasted and sometimes seemingly antithetic, mutually exclusive aspects of our strange, mysterious world. Take that incomparable Psalm:

> Lord, thou hast been our dwelling-place
> In all generations.
> Before the mountains were brought forth,
> Or ever thou hadst formed the earth and the world,
> Even from everlasting to everlasting, thou art God.

There is the eternal. But here is the other side, told with a realism gritty, hard but austerely faithful to the facts of human existence:

George A. Gordon, D.D.

Thou turnest man to destruction,
And sayest, Return, ye children of men.
For a thousand years in thy sight
Are but as yesterday when it is past,
And as a watch in the night.
Thou carriest them away as with a flood; they as a sleep;
In the morning they are like grass which groweth up.
In the morning it flourisheth, and groweth up;
In the evening it is cut down, and withereth.
For we are consumed in thine anger,
And in thy wrath are we troubled.
The days of our years are threescore years and ten,
And if by reason of strength they be fourscore years,
Yet is their strength labor and sorrow;
For it is soon cut off, and we fly away.

Or, as the Scottish version has it, with infinite pathos and beauty, "Our days wear awa like the sough of a sang." These two aspects are finally blended in the great prayer, one of the noblest ever uttered: "Let the beauty of the Lord our God be upon us." Let the pervading Eternal Spirit sweep through our whole temporal world and give it meaning, faith, and hope in the future. Upon these contrasted aspects of life I have two remarks to make:

1. When these two aspects of life are reconciled by great religion, we see the meaning of the temporal part of our world. This passing show is not vanity; it is not a fugitive thing. It has real meaning. It is responsive to the ideal successively from beginning to end, and its meaning is in its responsiveness to the ideal. Take, for example, a civilized home preparing

6

for the advent of a new life; the tenderness, the dignity, the elevation of humanity in that home; all the preparations made as if they were to be permanent. In a few years the little boy or girl is no longer a nursling, but a bird on the wing, off with a new life of its own. Thus, though the nursery for a few years seems to be permanent, it is superseded; there is the primary school, the secondary school, the college; they all are phases representing an ideal speaking powerfully to these different periods of life; but ultimately all are transcended, and men and women are landed in the great world as a finality.

Is the great world a finality? Take government; is that a finality? What made government? What improves it? The power of public opinion. What creates public opinion? An ideal of human welfare. The ideal behind all the governments in the world, working through confusion, ignorance and sorrow, still is human welfare. The power of it all is in God, the home of ideals. Look at our courts of law, courts for the administration of justice between men and men. There is an ideal justice behind them, and to that ideal courts of law are slowly rising. Consider the difference between the law and justice today and that of five hundred years ago. Again, what a long way we have come from the rules of the Mohawk Indians to the principles in the Constitution of the United States; and how that instrument has changed since it was adopted in 1789. All things earthly that are good are in motion because of the ideal forces that are working upon them, through the better conceptions, better feelings and larger outreachings of the human mind and the human spirit. Our ideals are the shadow of God in our life, and to that our actual world is responding, trembling where it does not move, showing signs of life where it is stagnant and ugly.

Sometimes in traveling through Switzerland you have gone, have you not, by what power you could not tell, in an ascension car operated from the heights? You step into the car, take your seat, and upward the car goes. You pass this field and that, this hilltop and that, this height and that; the whole world seems passing, and by a power that you cannot discover. But when you come to your goal you see the power-house there and the hidden source of the whole movement. So it is with this world of ours. Religion relates it to the best ideals in the souls of men. They are the shadows of God in the human mind. They are the great moving power of our human world, and when we get to our goal we shall see the power by which our world is moving, to which it was responsive; we shall see that which gave meaning to the otherwise fugitive insignificance.

2. We must take this world—satisfactory to nobody, I believe, since the Armistice was signed—we must take this world, with all in it that creates despair, in conjunction with God. If we take this passing world as pervaded by the ideals that represent the Eternal Mind, we may gain a faith by which we shall live a joyous life. I am free to say that, taken by itself, apart from these ideals that are the shadows

The Eternal Reality

of God's presence in our world, the world is simply a horror, an inconsolable grief, an utter heartbreak. Two aspects of this tragic world press upon men's minds all the while. First, the brevity of the individual life in the family life, for if there were no family life none of us would care for the individual life. It is love that gives one the sense of the infinite sorrow of the brevity of existence. Individual life, family life, national life, racial life, the life of the planet, what is it when measured against astronomic time? The flash of a firefly, out as soon as seen; the dance of the aurora, gone before you can name it.

> Or, like the rainbow's lovely form
> Evanishing amid the storm.

O the brevity of it, and the sorrow-stricken face of love as it looks upon that inscrutable mystery!

The second tragic aspect is the defeated idealism of history. You read the Hebrew prophets. Have you never been troubled by the fact that their glorious sayings have been, apparently, not actually, all ruled out by the course of the world? "There shall be nothing to hurt nor destroy in all God's holy mountain; for the earth shall be full of the knowledge of the Lord, as the waters cover the sea." Did that prophecy ever come true? The time shall come, says another, when there shall be no need of saying, "Know ye the Lord for all shall know Him, from the least unto the greatest." Is that true? Jesus said "The kingdom of heaven is at hand." Where, will

9

you tell me? There is nothing more tremendous than the delayed realization of the incomparable idealism of the prophets, of Jesus the supreme prophet, and the defeat, the apparent defeat, of the best thought of mankind. The first Hebrew went out seeking the city whose builder and maker is God. He never found it. John in Patmos had his vision of the new Jerusalem coming down from above. It never came, it never landed in this earth. Augustine wrote his great book on the City of God over against the city of man, and lofty souls in all history have been prophesying a new heaven and a new earth in which shall dwell righteousness.

What are we to say to all this? There is not in existence on this earth today a single Christian city, a single Christian nation. There are parts of America as pagan as blackest Africa. Face the fact, and then apply your intelligence. This world was never meant to be complete and self-contained. No perfect human being is seen anywhere; only the beginnings of things we have under the sun. Do not look for completions, look for initiations. Do not cry out for the perfect realization in individual or family or city or society or race; look for the beginning of a great, living, effectual response to the glorious ideal which signifies the presence of God with men. Only get the thing started and keep it moving; keep the world alive to the ideal, and God will take care of the completions.

What is the final source of power today, so far as there is any power, in the unrealized plan for the individual, the unrealized program for the family, the unrealized scheme for the city, the nation, the world? The unrealized means the ideal in God, and it is the sovereign power of the world today, so far as the world is morally alive and full of hope. In the name of that unrealized City of God, we protest against crime, against sin, against brutality of every kind, against ignorance and distress and preventable sorrow, against inhumanity; in the name of that unrealized City of God we pray, we aspire, we work, we frame programs and we go forth together to improve the actual in the light of the ideal. We do not think about completions; we think about beginnings and about progress, and we leave the end with God.

What I should like to remain in your minds today is not a vision of the city of Boston become the City of God or the City of Christ, but a sense of the heavenly power which moves whatever is moved in the right direction in your soul and in my soul, in your home and my home and in all homes in this city; a sense of that sublime heavenly power; and the resolve to set things in motion this very day for better and better, leaving the best to God's time and place and manner. The great truth here in these words of my text, in the might and strength of which a generation went through everything, nameless suffering, persecution, pestilence, famine, and death itself, was simply that in the heavenly regions there was power that eventually would rule all things, material and spiritual, everywhere.

Young men and young women, commit to memory

those great words of Tennyson as the very law of your life. They are as subtle as spirit and as true as the presence of God with men; they sing of that which is the shadow of God in the mind of man.

> Not of the sunlight,
> Not of the moonlight,
> Not of the starlight!
> O young Mariner,
> Down to the haven,
> Call your companions,
> Launch your vessel
> And crowd your canvas,
> And, ere it vanishes
> Over the margin,
> After it, follow it,
> Follow the gleam.

Give me an individual, give me a family, give me a church, all crude, all in the beginning, but truly initiated into responsive living to the Eternal Ideal in God, and there you will find a beginning that means eventual perfection in some world, in some eon, in God. "And I saw no temple therein; for the Lord God the Almighty, and the Lamb, are the temple thereof." God the final sanctuary of the universe, God the final home of all souls, God the Eternal refuge and strength of our entire humanity; that is our faith.

DOES GOD CARE?

Dean Scarlett was born in Columbus, Ohio, in 1883; he was educated at Harvard and in the Episcopal Theological School, Cambridge; and was ordained Deacon in 1909, advancing to the priesthood the following year, while serving as assistant in St. George's Church, New York city. In 1911 he became Dean of Trinity Cathedral, Phœnix, Arizona, where he had an extraordinary ministry, both as preacher and citizen, taking a whole State for his parish and making his leadership felt throughout the commonwealth. After eleven happy years, he was made Dean of Christ Church Cathedral in St. Louis, and quickly won a place of influence and command in a staid, conservative city, making his Cathedral a shrine of vision and service.

The sermon here to be read reveals a sympathetic understanding of the perplexities of the modern soul, astray in its own life, and baffled by misgivings, both spiritual and practical, in respect to the basic issues of faith. Its original title was *Does God Care? Do You?* showing the urgent practical emphasis of a preacher who sees that the old individualism, for all its virtue and value, is not equal to the need of man caught in the intricacies of the new world; his willingness to listen to the wildest cries of the age, lest the Church repeat old errors and overlook vital truth for today, and fail both of comprehension and comprehensiveness.

It is at once a challenge and a consecration, the while it lifts vexed and bewildered minds into a sense of a Divine Love hidden in the hardness of life, a meaning in its mystery, a purpose in its pitiful, broken beauty, and an intimation of the Eternal in its pathetic evanescence.

DOES GOD CARE?

WILLIAM SCARLETT, LL.D.

DEAN, CHRIST CHURCH CATHEDRAL, ST. LOUIS

How much more shall your Heavenly Father . . . Matthew 7: 11.

Many of the divisions which have occurred in the Church were due, no doubt, to the fact that the Church had forgotten something. When the followers of John Wesley gathered together outside of the Church of England they were seeking a less formal, warmer method of worship, a more intimately personal religion than they found in the Church. It is said when they left they took what there was of the stove with them. It has not been altogether a bad thing for the Mother Church; it made her aware of her own chilliness and set her recreating and rekindling warmth and beauty. The reason so many people have gone over to the Christian Science Church is again perhaps because the Church had forgotten something. That phase of the message of Christ had been largely overlooked. Again, this has not been without its reaction on the Church. It has set her rethinking the whole question of healing. So whenever we find a great social heresy such as Communism, it is because something has been forgotten: but the people who rest under

15

that neglect can never forget. Why is it that Marxianism is stealing like fire through the veins of the workers of Europe, as it has already captured millions in Russia? Why is it that they attack the Church so bitterly? Why do they regard Religion as one of the chief enemies of humanity? Why are they associating Christ and Oppression: God and Capitalism? Why are they putting up in Russia anti-religious posters, such as the striking one entitled "The Triumph of Christianity," representing Christ walking serenely ahead, followed by a gigantic cross of gold flat on the backs of the toiling, struggling, bleeding masses; while seated comfortably on the cross is the leering figure of the Capitalist, driving the people forward under their staggering burden? Or another, in brilliant colors, picturing Christ, a beautiful and attractive figure, standing on the edge of a sheer precipice, reaching his hands towards a chalice, lifted above and beyond Him—while up the mesa behind struggles a vast multitude, their crosses lifted high, those in front pushed over the cliff by the pressure from the rear, to be swallowed as they fall by the huge, red, yawning mouth of Capitalism. And the poster is headed, "Follow me and my Father will give you Eternal Life."

Why is it that in this country of ours so many people are not simply alienated from, but thoroughly hostile to, the Church? Why is it? It sets us thinking, does it not? And reëxamining our Religion as we practice it. Have we too forgotten something? Are we too easy-going? Too complacent? "Oh, yes,

16

there is a God . . . *but* His orders will not work. . . . He will be quite satisfied with the respectful repetition of them. . . ." "The gods of the East," said some one, "are sitting gods"; they simply sit and sit and sit, in the face of evils which should bring them to their feet in flaming protest. And perhaps our Religion as we practice it has been too much of a "sitting" religion, too conciliatory, almost resigned, in certain iniquitous situations.

There are two parts to the Christian religion, and neither is valid without the other. On the one hand Christianity is the most intimately personal religion in the world; in this respect no other religion can compare with it. It tells us we can take the friendship which means more to us than anything else in the world, which gives the deepest meaning and the richest color to life, for which we would be glad to offer our lives if occasion arose—and we can read that into the very heart and center of the Universe and find there the same quality of comradeship; "the fellowship, the loyalty, the powerful response, the love, of which the finest friendships and loyalties of earth are the shadows and foretaste." The testimony on this point is so strong that it cannot be shaken, and millions there are who have found and still find in the Mystery which surrounds us a companionship with One, Who gives warmth and purpose and Beauty to life, and without Whom life would be unthinkable. That is one side of the Christian religion, but it is not the whole of it, and by itself it is apt to lack validity in the end. There is real truth in the old legend of the monk in his cell experiencing a moment of ineffable joy in the presence of a vision of his Master which had appeared to him; then came a rap at the door and a call for help outside; he hesitated, should he go or should he stay? He went, and when he returned the Vision was there still, saying "Hadst thou tarried, I had gone." If religion for us is largely a matter of personal comfort we are in real danger of losing it altogether.

For there is another side without which Christianity is incomplete. If the parable of the Prodigal Son, especially the figure of that Father waiting for his boy, represents the personal element of Christianity, then the parable of the Last Judgment expresses the other feature—the great King calling all the nations of the earth before Him, touching their misery and poverty and sickness, saying, "*I* was sick and *I* was an hungered and *I* was in prison"; trying to make them see that the whole body of humanity is one; that a blow at the circumference is a blow at the center; that injury to one *is* injury to all, that suffering anywhere is bound to be felt everywhere ultimately, and in the heart of God; and condemning those who had been unaware of this. The two pictures go together. And personal religion without a social conscience is a poor thing: and social vision without personal religion is apt to lag in enthusiasm and be wanting in color and beauty.

And so we come back, first, to the old, old question—What is God like anyway? What is the Soul of the Universe like? Is there any one or anything at

Does God Care?

the heart of things who cares, or do we meet there nothing but indifference to our most precious values? Well, in order to begin to discover the answer, we might go back to a saying of that very wise man, Aristotle, that "the 'nature' of anything is the best it can grow into." Not by what it is, but by what it can become; not by its past or present achievements, but by its highest capacities and promise. Take yourself, what is your true nature? Are you to judge yourself by your inferior moments, by your meanness, by your selfishness, by your lower desires? Is that your true nature? Is that your real self? The true nature of anything is the *best* it can grow into. Not by your unworthy, but by your exalted moments are you to judge yourself; when you are the most devoted, the most unselfish, when you are most aware of God and of the sheer beauty of life, and your heart beats in full sympathy with your suffering fellowmen; when some great Cause has touched you, saying, "You belong to me: you are mine: you find your real self only in following me." Not by your mediocre moments, but by your highest experiences—

Like tides on a crescent seabeach
When the moon is new and thin,
Into our hearts high yearnings
Come welling and surging in—
Come from the mystic ocean
Whose rim no foot has trod—
Some of us call it Longing,
And others call it God.

19

William Scarlett, LL.D.

These deeper insights mark out the course towards the goal which God has in mind for us. So that every one "lives constantly under the shadow of his own rebuke," the rebuke of those dear and noble memories when the angel of our better nature had taken possession of us and we saw ourselves the men God meant.

What is the "nature" of humanity? Again, are we to judge humanity, as many do, by its baser or even its ordinary character, by its brutality, by its wars, when it is shattering its own values? Not by its worst but by its best. The "nature" of anything is shown by the best it can grow into, and we never can forget *that once humanity grew into Christ.* What is the true nature and quality of the Universe? Are we to judge it on its lower levels, by the hurricane which comes sweeping across the country, leaving frightful destruction and misery and broken dreams behind it? Is that the true "nature" of the Universe? Or down out of the north comes a wandering iceberg, as seen in the morning sun as lovely a thing as was ever made. And into a great ocean liner it crashes—crippling beyond hope the vessel carrying its precious cargo of men, women and little children, persons of infinite value to the homes from which they came, and the society in which they live. And after a few moments of turmoil the great ocean is calm again and the lovely iceberg floats serenely away. It is the hideous indifference of it that appalls us. Is that the true nature of the Universe? The true nature of anything is the best it can grow into, and we can never forget that the Universe has produced humanity, and that out of humanity once came Christ.

What, then, is on the Altar of the Life of the Universe? Do we find there only the reflection of a soulless mechanism, or do we in times of insight catch a glimpse of a Beauty almost too bright for human eyes? Do we find there the Goddess of Reason, or Some One like Christ? Do we find there only indifference to the things we value most, or a Love of which our finest human love is only a faint and feeble reflection? What is in the chalice on the altar of the life of the universe? Is it a drug to still for a moment the anguish of the world? Or do we find that of which One said, "This is my blood, shed for you!" The "nature" of anything is the best it can grow into. And through the best we know we begin to imagine the "nature" of God. Was Christ right, then, when he said the key to the riddle of the Universe was to be found in the words "our Father," with all of the implications of that high conception— Some One Who cares, Some One Who values, Some One Who never forgets!

Let me borrow this illustration: [1] The first child of James Martineau and his wife died in infancy, and was laid away in a little French cemetery near the city of Dublin. And years passed, many years, until there were only two people in the world who remembered that little child, its father and its mother. More years passed and the mother died,

[1] From Dr. Newton, *The Sword of the Spirit*.

and there was then but one person who recollected
that once a life, like a lovely flower, had blessed their
home. More years passed, and at length at the age
of eighty-seven James Martineau returned to Dublin
to attend the Tercentenary of the University. And
one day the famous old man left a brilliant function
and slipped out to a little French cemetery on the
outskirts of Dublin, and baring his head he knelt
beside the grave of the little child buried there over
sixty years before.

Surely Fatherhood means this: that back of all
the flux of circumstance there is Some One Who loves,
Who values, Who cares, Who can never forget, Who
can never forget even the downmost man! One
Whose will is for Beauty, Goodness and Truth, for
all His children; One Who touches the sore spots of
human society and says, "*I* suffer here and here and
here." Then, *it is against that Background we have
to interpret our human world, with all its problems
and perplexities.* It is against that Background we
have to see war, with its destruction of our most precious values, and see how war looks there. It is
against that Background we have to explain the slums
of our great cities, in which men and women and little
children rot away, cut off from beauty and loveliness,
and see how that looks there. It is against that Background we have to read the horrid thing we call Race
Prejudice, and see how it looks there. And against
that Background we have to place the idea of the
class conflict, and see how it looks there. And it is
against that Background we have to interpret all of

the misery and exploitation and injustice and gross inequality, and the hatred and the unbrotherliness of our world, and see how they look against that Light and Beauty and Love. Don't you see that *all problems are religious problems!* And we cannot possibly separate Religion and Politics, or Religion and Social Questions? That we must place *all* the problems of our human world against that Background and see them in its light, because that Background is Reality, to which all things ultimately must conform? So it is always His face we see shining through the mists of human life. It is always His will for beauty, truth and goodness for all His children, which comes to us as a challenge and a summons.

If Russia means nothing to us, if Europe means nothing to us, if Mexico means nothing to us, if the slums mean nothing to us, and the misery and unbrotherliness of our human world mean nothing to us, *then we do not know Christ.* And the measure of our indifference is the direct measure of our separation from Him. But for one who has this vision of the real Background of human life, then to him "the world is his parish" and he is under bond to labor on endlessly, no matter at what cost to himself, until the dark places in his own life and in the world about him have been reclaimed for light and beauty and goodness, and human society organized according to the will of God.

We wonder at times about Christ's Invisible Church. Who are its members? What are its requirements? It is rather certain that its members would not agree on ritual. It is certain they would not agree on all points of a creed. What then? In our office of the holy communion we call them the "Blessed Company of all Faithful People." Faithful to what? Why, faithful to the will of God for all mankind. Loyal to that! "Who is my mother, or my brother? . . . Whosoever shall do the will of God, the same is my brother and my sister and mother." "And they shall come from the east and the west, the north and the south, and sit down together in the kingdom of Heaven." The blessed company of all faithful people, faithful to God's will of beauty and love for all mankind, who find in their lives that one underlying, overarching loyalty to which all the minor loyalties of life must conform; who approach all the problems of their day from that angle, and judge them in that light; who remind themselves, "God wants me, He needs me, my mind, my strength"; and who examine themselves constantly, "What am I doing for His cause? Where am I failing? What does that Will require of me?"; and who find in Christ the great Interpreter of that will.

If that is our attitude towards life, and that the loyalty towards which we direct our efforts, then Christianity is on its way to being complete in us, and not only have we a standard by which we judge our human world and its problems, but also in us there is gradually built up more intimately the personal side of Christianity, and deeper and finer and more conscious grows a companionship to which no

other comradeship in the world can compare, until
we "wonder with delight what it will grow to as the
years go on." And so these lines become true for us:

> He led us on
> By the paths we did not know.
> Upwards He led us, though our steps were slow,
> Though oft we'd faint and falter on the way,
> Though storm and darkness oft obscured the way:
> Yet when the clouds were gone
> We saw He led us on.
>
> Through all the unquiet years,
> Past all our dreamland hopes and doubts and fears
> He guides our steps; through all the tangled maze
> Of sin and sorrow and o'er-clouded days,
> We know His will is done
> As still He leads us on.
>
> After the weary strife
> And the restless fever we call life,
> After the dreariness, the aching pain,
> The wayward struggles which have proved in vain,
> The joys, the satisfactions, the sunlight and the rain,
> Oh, still He'll lead us on
> And on and on!

WHAT DOES IT MEAN TO LOVE GOD?

Born in Philadelphia in 1879, Dr. Holmes was educated at Harvard University, and ordained to the Unitarian ministry in 1904. Since 1907 he has been minister of the Church of the Messiah, New York City, which in 1917 he reorganized as the Community Church. As a preacher, as editor of *Unity*, as publicist and author, he has exercised a stimulating ministry, winning for himself a unique place in American religious life.

The first book by Dr. Holmes was entitled *The Revolutionary Function of the Modern Church*, and it set the key for all the rest, among which may be named *New Wars for Old, Religion for Today, Is Violence the Way Out? New Churches for Old*, and the *Life of Robert Collyer*, whose memory is a fragrance. A leader of radical thought, both political and religious, he is master of a vivid and lucid literary style—a power of luminous statement which has added greatly to his influence as a teacher.

As an example of the intellectual perception of spiritual truth, the following sermon is remarkable, albeit dealing, as the preacher confesses, with only one aspect of a truth so vast that it makes all men one in their littleness. It opens a long vista of vision, showing that the most commanded of virtues is one of the rarest among men, demanding, as it does, a thrilling adventure of the soul into the Unseen.

WHAT DOES IT MEAN TO LOVE GOD?

JOHN HAYNES HOLMES, D.D.

COMMUNITY CHURCH, NEW YORK CITY

If a man say, I love God, and hateth his brother, he is a liar; for he that loveth not his brother whom he hath seen, cannot love God whom he hath not seen. I John 4: 20.

Ever since I can remember, I have heard it said that the love of God is what distinguishes religion from every other experience of the human heart. The most familiar, and certainly the most impressive, passage in the New Testament writings is Jesus' formulation of the two commandments of the law, of which "the first and great commandment" is, "thou shalt love the Lord thy God with all thy heart, and with all thy soul, and with all thy mind." But how many of us know what this commandment really involves? How many of us have ever asked ourselves what it means to "love the Lord thy God"? We know what it means to love a child, or a woman, or a man, or even an institution or a cause. But how many of us know what it means, in the form of definite, concrete ideas, to love this divine spirit of all life which we call God? By most of us, I am forced to believe, this phrase is used not to express any clear idea at all, but only to convey a general impression,

29

or even to cover up an absence of all thought. Now I want to ask if "loving God" does not mean, or cannot be made to mean, something definite in our lives; and religion, therefore, be understood in ways that have never been understood by us before.

In entering upon this inquiry, I find an excellent starting point in a passage from the first Epistle of St. John. Speaking therein of our duty of love one for another, the Apostle lays down the proposition, "If a man say I love God, and hateth his brother, he is a liar; for he that loveth not his brother whom he hath seen, how can he love God whom he hath not seen?"

In this passage we find several important statements. First of all, it is declared that the love of man and the love of God are two entirely different things, to be distinguished one from the other in our thought. Secondly, it is declared that the love of man is the primary obligation of the soul, and that the love of God lies beyond, and is conditioned by, the love of man. Lastly, and most important of all, from our present point of view at least, it is intimated that the love of God transcends and thus surpasses the love of man, by reason of the fact that to love our brother is to love what we have seen, but to love God is to love what we have not seen. It is this third and last point which we must notice. The love of God, as distinguished from what we ordinarily accept and understand as the love of man, signifies the love of the invisible. It is the reaching out of our souls toward that which lies beyond the apprehension of

What Does It Mean to Love God?

our physical senses—the dedication of our lives to what we cannot know, but, in the absence of all knowledge, may "faintly trust." It is akin to faith, so nobly described in the book of Hebrews as "the substance of things not seen." It is what Tennyson so wonderfully unfolded, in the opening lines of his "In Memoriam"—

> Strong Son of God, immortal Love
> Whom we, *that have not seen thy face,*
> By faith, and faith alone embrace,
> Believing where we cannot prove.

In this suggestion that the love of God may mean, among other things, love of the invisible, or devotion to the invisible, we have a golden thread which may guide us through the labyrinth of this theological mystery. I propose to follow this thread, and see if it does not lead us to some central shrine. For if we find what is involved in the invisible, may we not find what is involved in the process of "seeing him who is invisible," and therefore of loving him?

In coming to this matter of the invisible, we find that we encounter it first of all in the realm of *space.* Here we are living from day to day on one little spot on the vast surface of the globe. All around us swings the circle of the horizon, beyond which it is impossible for us to see. Within this circle are the things which are visible; far away, beyond that encompassing rim of mountains or of ocean, there lie those things which are invisible, and hence unknown. In

31

the same way we are dwelling beneath this stupendous canopy of the skies. Looking out a few miles into the darkness, we see the stars which make the radiant company of our world. We number and name these hundreds of constellations which are visible to our gaze. But beyond those constellations lie unmeasured leagues of space which are as invisible to the telescope as to the naked eye. In the same way, again, we are living here in the midst of a little group of human beings. Our family, our friends, the members of our church and club, the citizens of our neighborhood and town, a few of our fellow countrymen from other states—these are all the persons that we ever see or know. All around us, however, in places near and far, are those hundreds of millions of men and women whom we never see, but who have an existence as real, and to themselves as important, as the lives that we are living. The world, in other words, from the standpoint of space, can be divided into two parts—the visible and the invisible. There is the part which exists because we see it, and there is the part which exists only because we have faith that it exists.

Now, the great majority of men are quite content to spend all their lives in the realm of the visible. They have no desire to explore strange lands or meet peculiar people. Men sailed the shores of Europe for hundreds of years without feeling any desire to steer the prows of their ships toward that strange blue line on the western verge of the horizon, which marked the limit of the Atlantic which they knew.

What Does It Mean to Love God?

Men lived for millions of years, gazing nightly upon the stars, without wondering what lay beyond the bounds of the farthest planet which they could see. Men live all their lives, even today, without knowing or seeing any people save those who live in their own particular neighborhood or country. We are an incurious lot, most of us. We are quite content to stay at home, amid familiar objects. Only within these latest days of human history have any considerable number of men developed an interest in the invisible, and dared to challenge the horizon which rims their lives.

There have always been a few men, however, to whom the invisible, as it presents itself in space, has had an irresistible attraction. They have cared nothing for the seen and the known, and everything for the unseen and the unknown. One such man was Christopher Columbus, the discoverer of America. How could this Genoese voyager be satisfied with sailing the familiar trade routes of the Mediterranean, or even coasting along the less familiar shores of Spain and France, when beyond him, to the west, there stretched the vast expanse of the Atlantic, on which no ship in living memory had sailed? What lay beyond that horizon? Where would he arrive, if he steered steadfastly toward the setting sun? What lands were hidden in that realm which was invisible only because no man had yet dared to see? This western skyline of the Atlantic became a passion with Columbus. Its breezes called him, as the voice of Jehovah called Moses unto Sinai. To cross that line,

and see what lay beyond, became the purpose of his
life. He lived for nothing else, cared for nothing else.
To this one quest he gave his all, and made it therefore his religion. In other words, he loved the invisible, in so far as this invisible was to be found beyond that western verge of rolling sea; and shall we
not say that, in this love of the invisible, he loved
God? Such at least is the judgment of Walt Whit-
man! In that great poem, called "The Prayer of
Columbus," do you remember the words which the
poet puts upon Columbus' lips?

All my emprises have been filled with Thee,
My speculations, plans, begun and carried on in thoughts
    of Thee,
Sailing the deep, or journeying the land for Thee . . .
O I am sure they really come from Thee!
The urge, the ardor, the unconquerable Will,
The potent, felt, interior command, stronger than words,
A message from the Heavens, whispering to me even in sleep,
These led me on.

The same passion which led Columbus to explore
the globe has led other dauntless souls to explore the
infinitely vaster spaces of the cosmic universe. As-
tronomers have swept the heavens night after night
with their telescopes, to catch some ray of light not
seen before. Chemists and physicists have labored
in their laboratories to penetrate those mysterious
realms of atomic life which have hitherto been unseen by mortal eyes. These men have found it as
impossible to remain within the borders of the known,

34

What Does It Mean to Love God?

as Christopher Columbus found it impossible to hug the shores of the Mediterranean. Beyond these borders, into these strange spaces of the unknown and the unguessed, is where they had to go. They must find what stars are walking these distant spaces of the skies, what elements are hidden in these minute particles of matter, what energies are waiting for the discovery and use of man. They must open doors, scatter darkness, see the unseen with telescope and microscope and test tube. These men, the scientists of ancient and modern times, have lived for the invisible; they have given to it their faculties, pledged to it their lives. With the result that in our time the laboratory has become an altar, the text-book a Bible, and science a religion! In worshiping, seeking and serving the invisible, our scientists have been worshiping, seeking and serving God. It was this fact which was so wonderfully expressed by the devout heart of the immortal Kepler, discoverer of the laws of planetary motion, one of the greatest of all the searchers of the stars. Gazing in rapture upon the mystic spaces of the skies, and seeing what no man had ever seen before, he fervently exclaimed, "O Lord, I am thinking Thy thoughts after Thee."

More important, however, than our relations with geographical space and cosmic space, are our relations with the men and women who populate this globe. Most of us are tribal creatures; we are interested only in those persons whom we can see and feel and know—the members of our family, the citizens of our town, our associates in business or in pleasure.

35

John Haynes Holmes, D.D.

The people who for any reason live beyond the borders of our experience, the multitudes whom we can not or do not see and therefore do not know, to these we are usually as indifferent as we are on occasion hostile. We have no concern for the man who belongs to another social class, lives in another section of the city, or is a member of an alien race or nation. We have not imagination enough to understand the aspirations of these people, or to sympathize with their difficulties and sufferings. If we think of them at all, it is usually to fear them or hate them, because they live in a different manner, use a different language, are loyal to different principles and ideas, from ourselves.

Every now and then, however, there appears a man whose human interests cannot be confined within the borders of his particular family or tribe. He loves men just because they are men. Barriers of sea and land, distinctions of race or creed or nationality, do not touch in the remotest degree the affections of his heart. If men are ignorant or unfortunate in any way, if they are bearing burdens or stumbling beneath oppressions, then immediately he is their brother in suffering, and especially their comrade in the struggle for deliverance. Men who are invisible, in other words, are as real and precious as those who are visible, especially if they have need of human sympathy. Thomas Paine was such a man, when he declared, "Where Liberty is not, there is my country." John Howard was such a man, when he hunted out the criminals of England, thrust away in noisome

36

prisons from the sight of men, and rescued them from degradation. William Lloyd Garrison was such a man, when he gave his life to the chattel slaves of the South, whom he had seen only in the sensitive imagination of his heart. Jane Addams was such a woman, when she broke through the barriers of the modern slum, and took up her life with the poor and outcast of our great cities. Rabindranath Tagore has told us of such a true lover of mankind. This man was a Swede, who one day chanced upon the writings of a famous teacher and prophet of India. Instantly this young northerner of Europe was touched with pity and affection for the dusky hordes of southern Asia. His heart went out to these millions of his fellow-beings, whom of course he had never seen or known. His soul could not rest until he had gone forth to find these people and serve them. And at last he went, and in due season laid down his life in the torrid sun of India. This man, like Abraham, "went out, not knowing whither he went." He deliberately moved himself from the realm of the visible to the realm of the invisible. He loved these people whom he had not seen, but whose needs were as real to him as the needs of his own flesh. And in loving these "who (were) invisible," he was loving God! Surely, this was what Jesus had in mind when he said, "Inasmuch as ye do it unto one of the least of these my brethren, ye do it unto me."

So much for the invisible as it reveals itself in space! This brings us to a second and deeper consideration—namely, the invisible as it reveals itself

John Haynes Holmes, D.D.

in *time*. From the standpoint of the living man, all time is divided, like Cæsar's Gaul, into three parts—the past, the present, and the future. Now the past and present can be classified together, for our purposes at least, as that portion of time which is visible; it has been seen, or is being seen, and is therefore a part of the definite experience of mankind. The future, however, is that portion of time which is invisible. We know that it is coming—we see it coming, as we watch that amazing process of one minute passing into another. But until it comes, it remains invisible in the sense that we do not know what it is, or what it may bring to us of happiness or ill. The most that we can do with the future, so far as vision is concerned, is to foresee it—to prophesy that when it comes, it will be so-and-so. But it is an old proverb that "hindsight is better than foresight," by which we mean that it is the past, after all, and not the future, which is really visible.

Now, in the realm of time, exactly as in the realm of space, most men prefer to live in the midst of things visible, and not invisible. We feel most contented when we are dwelling in the past, with its ancient traditions, its venerable institutions, its familiar ways and customs sanctified by the practice of generations. To accept what our fathers have taught us, to follow the example which they tried and set, is like sailing a sea which has been charted in every square mile of its area. In this kind of life there is nothing undiscovered or unexpected; we know everything that there is to be known, and therefore run as little risk of disaster as of adventure. Some men there are, of course, who feel the monotony and even deadness of such a life as this; and these men move up heroically from the past into the present. They live in the new experiences of their progenitors; but they still cling to things visible, as the medieval mariner, who timidly made his way out of the Mediterranean into the Atlantic, clinging fast to European shores. Only now and then do we find a man who puts both past and present deliberately behind him, and launches boldly out into the invisible reaches of the future. A few of these men appear in every generation; they comprise the "glorious company of the apostles, the goodly fellowship of the prophets, the noble army of martyrs," of which the prayer book speaks. And these men are all characterized by a single remarkable fact! They see within their souls a vision of a better world than has yet been established upon the earth. They behold as in a dream a future age when all men will be happy, when cold, starvation and disease will be no more, when justice will be done and peace established, when "love (will be) shining in every face, (and) there will be no more sin, no pain, no loss, no death." They see a society so new and wonderful that it can be described in no terms that are associated with the society that now exists. They see, as Isaiah saw, the coming of a time when men "shall build the old wastes, and raise up the former desolations . . . and everlasting joy shall be unto them. . . . For as the earth bringeth forth her bud, and as the garden causeth the things that are sown into it to spring forth, so the Lord will cause righteousness and praise to spring forth before all nations."

Now, these are the men, the chosen of every generation, who live in the future, as the great masses of other men live in the present and the past. They burst the barriers of time. They seek the invisible, in deliberate rejection and defiance of the visible, and they do this because to them there is no choice between the two. Not the inheritances of the past and the realities of the present, but the promises of the future, constitute the real world. The invisible ahead, and not the visible behind and around, alone truly exists. In this future, therefore, they must live; for it, if necessary, they must die. They will "endure" all things—persecution, outlawry, suffering, ignominy, martyrdom—if only they can hasten its coming upon the earth. This coming may not transpire in their own time—probably will not—but this can make no difference in their service. They must still live for it as the sole reality. Here is the very essence, as I see it, of heroism and devotion. To labor for no gains that can now be seen, to sacrifice for rewards which will be paid not to yourself but to your children or your children's children, to live and mayhap die for a happier day which you yourself can never hope to witness or enjoy—this, to my mind, is the crowning achievement of the soul. Thousands of men and women, with no hope even of later fame and glory in the world, have been content thus to sow their seeds of faith, and leave to later ages the reaping of the harvest. And they have done this because they have believed "with all their heart and mind and soul and strength" in this future which is invisible. And what is this, I ask you, but believing in and loving "him who is invisible"—namely, God? These prophets, martyrs, and reformers—these heroes, young and old, who have dreamed their dreams and seen their visions—they are simply those who walk in the footsteps of Abraham, of whom it was said that he "looked for a city which hath foundations, whose builder and maker is God." To live for the future and its promises, to seek the Kingdom among men—this is one way at least of loving God.

It should be obvious, by this time, that this clue of the invisible is leading us to some definite answers to the question as to what it means to love God "whom (we) have not seen." Taking this "invisible," first of all, as it appears in the realm of space, we found it suggested that a man loves God when he moves beyond the fixed horizon of his little world, and launches out upon some adventure of the soul, a quest of truth, or a quest of service and compassion for the outcast and unfortunate among his fellow-men. Secondly, taking this "invisible" as it appears in the realm of time, we found that a man may be said to love God when he emancipates himself from the bondage of past and present, and reaches forth into the future of a better world, and gives himself unstintingly not to the preservation of what has been and now is, but to the creation or fulfillment of what may and ought to be. But not yet have we sounded the depths of our problem, for there is another and more fundamental realm where the invisible appears—that realm, lying altogether outside the borders of time and space, which we call, for lack of a better word, perhaps, the realm of the *spirit*.

If we ask what is the difference between an animal and a man, we find it, among other things, in the fact that the animal lives exclusively in the field of physical or material things, whereas the man, if he be true to his own best self, lives only incidentally in this field. The life of the animal is concerned from birth to death with matters pertaining to physical sustenance and sensation. To get and beget marks the whole round of his existence. Everything that concerns him can be seen and felt and handled. His world is a material world, and he devotes every moment of his time to the satisfaction of material purposes.

A man, on the other hand, if he be in the true sense of the word a man, lives only incidentally and occasionally in the material realm. At bottom, of course, he is an animal in the sense that, as a condition of survival, he must respond to certain physical appetites and needs. But no man who is really a man is content to exist on this low plane of animal experience. Just to the extent that he is a man and not an animal, he finds himself concerned primarily with certain things which never enter into the life of the animal at all. What these things are, it is difficult to say. They seem to belong not to the outer world which we can see and touch, but to a myste-

What Does It Mean to Love God?

rious inner world which is quite beyond our reach. They relate themselves not to any functional sensations of the body, but to certain extraordinary processes of the soul which we call thought and emotion. In themselves they are imponderable, intangible, invisible—as unreal and baffling as the wind which "bloweth where it listeth, and thou hearest the sound thereof, but knowest not whence it cometh or whither it goeth." Their invisible quality is what is perhaps most distinctive of these things which characterize the man as contrasted with the animal. How often in life do we see a man who deliberately ignores or defies those things which make up the whole sum and substance of the animal's existence? Terence MacSwiney, for example, who did what no animal could do—go without food, until starvation killed the body. When we look for the objects for which such a man was living, the things which he was hoping to gain for himself or others, we seek them in vain. They cannot be seen, as the food may be seen, which is the be-all and end-all of the animal's existence. Of course, they exist—exist so surely that a man is willing to give all the material blessings which life can hold for their dear sake. But they exist in that world of the invisible, where eye hath not seen, nor ear heard, but where the heart of man hath none the less conceived!

Now, it is these realities, which are thus so distinctive of human beings, which constitute what we mean by the things of the spirit. They are those forces of the inner life of man which are so unreal

43

that they can be seen by no microscope and measured by no balances, and yet so real that men will surrender for them food, shelter, comfort, ease, everything that the world can give. The true man will go bankrupt rather than break his word or violate his conscience. He will starve rather than forsake his ideal or betray his love. He will die, on the battlefield or on the scaffold, rather than desert the cause to which he has pledged his faith. Regulus, the Roman, went back to a death of hideous torture in Carthage, rather than break his promise to his captors. Socrates chose deliberately to drink the hemlock, rather than escape through violation of the laws which he had sworn as a citizen to uphold. Jesus faced Calvary, and the ending of his work in tragic failure, rather than take up arms against those who came in arms against him. These, and thousands like them in every age, have been like Moses who chose "rather to suffer affliction with the people of God than to enjoy the pleasures of sin for a season." These afflictions were real in every material sense, but more real were virtue, honor, faith, righteousness, love. These things, invisible to every eye but the mind's eye, belong to the spirit and not to the flesh. Their rewards are "the fruits of the spirit," of which the animal is so unconscious and the unworthy man so contemptuous. But to the true man they are the only reality, and life a perpetual dedication to their service. It is this which we mean by the life of the spirit, and this also, I must believe, which we mean by the life of "him who is invisible." To love not the flesh but the spirit, this is to love God. For "God," said the Nazarene, "is spirit, and they that worship him must worship him in spirit and in truth."

These are some answers to our question as to what it means to love God—all of them suggested by the single idea that God may be described, among other things, as "him who is invisible," him therefore "whom (we have) not seen." That these answers are adequate, that they cover the whole ground, is of course not true; they represent only a single approach to a question which is as wide as the circle of experience. But they may be said, I believe, to give us at least some glimpse into the problem of the nature of God, and of that relationship between man and God which constitutes the essence of religion. Is it not possible to sum up this discussion, inadequate and one-sided as it has been, and present some conclusions to our thought which are fundamental?

In the first place, it is evident, is it not, that religion has nothing essentially to do with creed and ritual, with ceremonial practices of any kind. "If thou bring thy gift to the altar," said Jesus, "and there rememberest that thy brother hath aught against thee, leave there thy gift before the altar and go thy way; first be reconciled to thy brother, and then come and offer thy gift." Religion, in other words, is a matter not of outward observance but of inward dedication. Religion is love, as "God is love."

In the second place, this love which is the heart of religion, must express itself first of all in the per-

John Haynes Holmes, D.D.

sonal relation between man and man. "If a man say, I love God, and hateth his brother whom he hath seen, how can he love God whom he hath not seen?" So intimate and immediate is the love of man for man as the primary expression of religion, that Jesus used a still more vivid word than that of "brother" to describe his meaning. He talked always of "neighbor," and defined that neighbor as any man with whom we came in contact on the road of life.

But the love of man for man, in terms of personal relationship, does not exhaust our problem. Beyond the narrow reaches of our present experience, there is the vast area of the unseen and the unknown—this world of the infinite which hides the destiny of man, this world of the spiritual which hides the mystery and the secret of all life. It is here, in this realm of the unseen and the unknown, that God in all his wonder is to be found; and it is here that he is to be truly loved. To follow truth for its own sake, to do right because it is right, to love not merely men but man, to "seek first the Kingdom"—this it is to love God. On the human side, I would define the love of God as the service of man in his eternal quest of the True, the Beautiful, and the Good. On the divine side, I would define the love of God as the sublimation of man's soul unto the likeness of those infinite and eternal realities of the spirit which are God.

> Love, from its awful throne of patient power
> In the wise heart, from the last giddy hour

What Does It Mean to Love God?

Of dead endurance, from the slippery steep
And narrow verge of crag-like agony, springs
And folds over the world its healing wings . . .
To suffer woes that Hope thinks infinite;
To forgive wrongs darker than death or night;
To defy power, which seems omnipotent;
To love, and bear; to hope till Hope creates
From its own wreck the thing it contemplates;
Neither to change, nor falter, nor repent;
This . . . is to be
Good, great and joyous, beautiful and free;
This is alone Life, Joy, Empire and Victory.

CHRISTIANITY AND WISE MEN

Preacher, scholar, journalist, diplomat, Dr. Montgomery has had a career unusually rich in variety of interest and service. Born in Turkey in 1870, the son of a missionary, he was educated at Yale and the University of Berlin, entering the Congregational ministry in 1901. After a brief pastorate in Bridgeport, he became professor of philosophy in Carleton College, and in 1906 associate minister of the Madison Square Presbyterian Church of New York City, where he served for ten years with Dr. Parkhurst.

At the outbreak of the World War he was special assistant to the American Ambassador in Constantinople; in 1917 in the Air Service in Paris; in 1918 attached to the Peace Conference; and in 1919 he was technical adviser to the Commission on Mandates in Turkey. Returning to America as assistant professor of French at Yale in 1920, he did fine work as director of the Armenia America Society, and on the staff of the Federal Council of Churches. Again he was in the East as special writer for the London *Daily Graphic* in Turkey, serving as war correspondent for the London *Standard* during the Græco-Turkish War. Yet he has found time to write such books as *The Place of Values* and *The Unexplored Self*—a most rewarding book, as I can testify—as well as to translate Leibnitz's *Metaphysics*.

Out of a life of deep thought and practical action this extraordinary sermon has come, sweeping a large orbit, surveying the whole spiritual situation, and putting a fair proposition to the wise men of the Sect of Cynics: If Christian faith is to be rejected, are you intelligent enough to put a meaning into our days? Let them try it honestly, and they will come at last, inevitably, to something very like the faith they have cast aside.

CHRISTIANITY AND WISE MEN

GEORGE R. MONTGOMERY, D.D.

PRESBYTERIAN CHURCH, NOROTON, CONN.

They offered unto him gifts, gold, frankincense, and myrrh.
Matthew 2: 11.

The text, as you recognize, is from the story of
Jesus' earliest infancy. The wording accords with
our visions of the gorgeous East. There is a certain
pomp like that of a religious spectacle in the behavior
of these wise men who presented the gold, and the
frankincense, and the myrrh. The entrance and exit
of the alien astrologers is drama-like rather than real.
The description seems to be that of a pageant. It
may be that we have here the transcription of an
early Christian miracle play.

After bestowing their incongruous gifts, the wise
men of the East pass off the stage and never again
enter the scene. Their rôle is to pantomime a sort
of prologue. This prologue, however, is not of a
piece with the succeeding occurrences; nor in those
occurrences do they have any part assigned to them.
The ideal which they loyally pursued was separated
by a wide angle from the message of the cross. How
would it have been had they stayed on in Palestine
till the Child grew up and as a man began his minis-

51

try? The chances are that they would have been of those who turned back and followed him no more. Technically it was not Christ whom they worshiped, but the star. Those who came to Jesus because of miraculous portents were the least stable of his adherents. Their point of approach prevented them from catching the actual content of the faith.

I

The writer regards the entire incident as a splendid fulfillment of prophecy. Instead of being a fulfillment, however, the incident turned out to be but a continuation of prophecy. It was only a happy augury, this prompt recognition of Christianity by the wise men; and during Jesus' lifetime the augury was not fulfilled. The world's wise men were conspicuously absent from the group of his followers. He expressed a natural surprise when he said that his message, though revealed unto babes, was "hidden from the wise."

The same absence of the world's wise men, notable during Jesus' lifetime, is also notable in the rest of the New Testament narrative. The Apostle Paul pointed out that those who answered the Christian appeal included "not many wise after the flesh." If some should name the Apostle Paul as an exception to the general rule, the reply would be that while he was Saul he could not be counted among the world's wise men, because the wise man is tolerant and Saul was violently intolerant. We read that "Saul laid waste the Church, entering into every house, and dragging men and women, committed them to prison." His subsequent tolerance, as Paul, is remarkable tribute to this attribute of wisdom produced by true Christianity.

The notable variance from the early augury is continued in the history of Christendom. There was a period, even, when that Christianity where faith was held against reason was put highest. Faith and reason were for long regarded as in inverse ratio to one another. A distinguished scholar of a generation or so ago, in two volumes on *The Warfare Between Science and Theology in Christendom,* held the position that the warfare was inevitable.

II

For the prevalence in the past of this unexpected alienation between Christianity and the world's wise men, there are good and sufficient reasons. It is worth our while to look at some of these reasons. Politics, for one thing, has had its share in producing this alienation. Political maneuvers have demanded racial or national loyalty to traditions once accounted a part of the Christian faith, and such loyalty has often been put above loyalty to logic. Confusion of this sort where political loyalties blanket Christian truth, is interfering with the progress of Christianity in many countries even today.

For the estrangement between Christianity and the world's wise men, another reason has been the mistaken notion of ecclesiastics that to establish the antiquity of a doctrine was the easiest way of defending it. When the battle has shifted to new grounds many churchmen have continued to hurl their vain missiles from old fortifications. The mischief of such tactical blunders has been increased by their proof-text method of argumentation. A proof-text is an isolated verse taken without considering the spirit of the rest of the writing. In the New Testament where are contained the basic teachings of the Christian faith, the special polemic is directed against the Judaizers, and proof-texts selected out of such polemic have little value in later fields of battle. In somewhat the same way the polemic of the early Fathers was mainly against the Platonizers and their specific arguments have small effectiveness in the positive thought of today.

Another reason, and an important one, for the unnatural alienation between Christianity and the world's wise men is found in the centuries of effort on the part of the wise men to exclude ideas of benefit from their systems of truth. Expediency was so feared that all slightest hints of advantage were carefully sifted out. As it is in many universities today, it was the fashion to consider education and morality to be distinct enterprises. Truth for Truth's sake was the slogan. A sharp line was drawn between thinking and feeling; confidence was reposed in thinking, but feelings and emotions, which are integral elements in Christianity, were regarded as without reality and outside the pale of logical treatment. They were too entirely personal and individual.

In this effort to disclose truth unhampered by useful objectives is it that we find the explanation for the monstrous idea mentioned a moment ago. I refer to the idea that Christian faith was most acceptable if opposed to reasoning. When reasoning purposely shut out from its field every beneficial aim, it became abstract. It forgot that one test of truth is to try to see if any particular theory will work with constructive results. Some devotees of Christian faith found doctrines which worked well despite oppugnant reasoning; they, therefore, clung to them. They were willing to hold to a doctrine which was clearly constructive, even though its place in the general scheme of truth was not established. The significance for them of a doctrine increased with the increased contrast between its constructiveness and its "reasonableness."

Still another reason for the unfortunate alienation between Christianity and the world's wise men is to be found in the constant expectation of professional thinkers and of professional nature studiers that they were on the verge of discovering through their quests the real explanation for existence, its whence, why, and wherefore. Alluringly hopeful were in turn the vistas opened up by mathematics, by astronomy, by physics, by chemistry, by geology, and by biology. Tennyson gracefully expressed in one of his best-known poems the belief of men of science that by finding out all about "the flower in the crannied wall," they would "know what God and man is." The speculational modesty of the Gospel did not accord with the high hopes held out by those glorious sciences. These ambitious hopes have in each case proven vain, so that the atmosphere of humility in which the sciences are now content to describe without the expectation of explaining, makes the world's deep thinkers more sympathetic toward the positive method of Christianity. This positive method works out from men's personal experience. From the highest in humanity does this method pass to the meaning of the universe and of the flower in the crannied wall.

III

It is, however, a more definite change in the attitude of wisdom than mere caution or even disappointment that is bringing about today the fulfillment of the auspicious augury contained in the adoration of the Magi. Truth and righteousness are now met together for two outstanding reasons. The first of these outstanding reasons is the discovery that pleasures to be gained or pains to be avoided are an essential ingredient in every experience, and experience is the most real thing that we have. Philosophy finds feeling to be as real as thinking. Wisdom is growing a passion for things practical and is no longer satisfied with the passion for a cold system of truths. In fact, it finds many things that are true to be remote and unimportant. Wisdom is searching for an additional element of significance within the systems of truths. Some have suggested "Significs" as a good name for this new discipline. This discipline is new to philosophy, but is not new to Christianity which has always recognized the question, "What am I for?" as more fundamental than the question, "What am I?" The most essential thing just now is not to widen the horizon of knowledge, nor to complicate the classifications, but to lay bare this factor of compelling significance in the knowledge that is already gained. All this comes very close to the constraining love in life which, from the start, Christianity set as its point of departure and its goal. Thus the lines of interest are converging.

IV

The second and more striking reason for the change in the attitude of Wisdom is this. The wise man of the world finds himself face to face with the disconcerting fact that truth and error are united by the sign of equality unless he can demonstrate one way of living to be better than another way of living. There is no prospect that further mere widening of the horizon of knowledge will bring to view a *bonum* or a *summum bonum,* a good or a highest good. Wisdom must, therefore, on the basis of the knowledge and information which it already has, establish the usefulness of prolonging and of promoting the pulsing of the brain. In a vague way there has been

57

in the background of the philosopher's creed the idea of development, but now he sees that a complex and organized universe has no advantage over scattered star dust, unless existence itself be an advantage; and if there is no advantage in existence, there is none in accurate thinking about existence, except, perhaps, with the object of propaganda towards universal extinction. Here again Christianity is contributing its share to the converging of the lines of interest, because it is discovering that behind evangelistic appeals for morality must be convincing evidence that what men do counts tremendously for betterment or worsement.

Many of the world's wise men have complacently assumed that agnosticism, "I don't know," is a safe and sane creed. They have assumed that people's confidence in logical processes would remain while logic slowly manipulated its materials. They have seemed to expect human beings to abide in a state of suspended animation while the philosophers debated the pros and cons of that animation. They have, however, discovered that the necessity for action cannot be adjourned. Human beings are compelled to act "willy-nilly," and must, therefore, act either as though the kind of action makes a difference or does not make a difference. Time and tide wait for no man, nor is there any interruption in the flow or ebb of the digestive fluids. "Men must work, and women must weep." Choices cannot tarry till Truth has made its ultimate explanation. The more radical spirits are refusing to wait on the uncertainty of a metaphysician's verdict and are seeking every one his own answer.

The equivocal attitude of philosophy toward the question of a meaning in life has encouraged many radicals to deny any essential difference in the quality of thinking as well as to deny any essential difference in the quality of choices. The wise men of the world, accordingly, are being compelled to find in a prompt sanction for right living their sanction for right thinking. Christian preachers, also, who supposed it to be sufficient to portray vice and to praise virtue, are discovering that life itself must be validated to warrant a moving distinction between vice and virtue. It is no longer enough for the scholar to make his leisurely and modest contribution to the body of knowledge, nor for the exhorter to ridicule the pessimist. The more exacting students are demanding from their mentors that any preference of truth to falsehood be meshed at once into some valid motive for being; and to influence our sophisticated youth the moralist sees that he must link his appeals into the dominant instinct of "life, more life."

The skeptic of yesterday had already questioned, with Hamlet, the superiority of "to be" over "not to be." The skeptic of today goes on to draw the obvious conclusion and to question the superiority of fact over fiction, of well-reasoned over ill-reasoned. Even the absolute skeptic of yesterday had confidence in the reasonableness of his position and was calm; the skeptic of today is logical enough to be disturbed and distressed by the disastrous consequences of his deductions. The vague idea of *development* which was the stock in trade of the teachers of yesterday, the thinking youth of today, innoculated with the virus of the aimlessness in events, is likely to dismiss with rather shattering comments such as these: "Development does not necessarily imply improvement; a development that has not reached a goal in the infinitude of years behind us has no likelihood of reaching one in any finite number of years ahead of us; your development to be consummated eternities hence means nothing in my young life." The teacher and the preacher may regret the difficult terrain into which the battle has been brought. In this terrain, however, is it that at least for the present the battle must be fought, defeat averted, and victory made possible. The preacher is certain that, if the youth can be brought to think and to think without prejudice, the final victory of right living and right thinking will be an overwhelming one.

V

For those teachers of wisdom who do not expect such a victory, who make what they deem a careful survey of the Christian faith and yet come to the sorry conclusion that neither here nor in heaven is there any meaning of worth further than appears in the fact of death and extinction, we have a fair proposition to offer. Our proposal to them is that instead of accepting the futility of things with the consequent futility of knowing about things, they make a concerted effort to prevent the plunge into the chaos of the nothing-matters doctrine. Is it necessary that they give up in despair, either with the advice to their pupils that they eat, drink and be merry, for tomorrow comes death, or with the counsel that piercing the heart with a bare bodkin is the easiest way out?

The fair proposition results from this question: Is it not possible that the human mind is intelligent enough to put a meaning into our days? The fair proposition which we would make, then, is this: Let the skeptic wise men set to work to see if they cannot construct a worth out of the materials found at hand. After all, they and their fellow men and women are bewilderingly intelligent and capable. The natural and human universe offers a bewilderingly wonderful medium. There are bewilderingly utilitarian tools at their service. Bewildering is the word to describe the world of which they are a part. If blind chance has wrought by accident such continuous and bewildering improvement from the original star dust, is it not possible that by skillful and earnest planning, by directed research, by previsioned invention, and by united application, they shall be able to advance life into something really worth while? In this fair proposition we are not, like Pascal, asking the skeptic to take a chance on the existence of a directing Personality behind the visible order of things, although we feel ourselves compelled by our share of experience to believe in such a Personality. We are inviting the skeptic to coöperate with other wise

61

men and to become a directing personality within the visible order of things.

If, instead of resigning himself to the religion of indifference which when consistently practiced becomes the religion of despair, the modern skeptic is willing to undertake the fair proposition and will set to work to try and invent and produce a worth in life, he will find himself making the same appeals to himself and others now being made in behalf of the Christian faith. He may indeed find himself coming to be stirred by the same optimism and cheer.

VI

The fight is on now for the very value of Wisdom. In the past Wisdom has stood aloof as a sort of umpire without any direct interest in the issues of life. Many investigators, moved by scientific zeal, have again and again proclaimed the inanity of all things. For the first time it is being generally seen that if life is not worth living, then all scientific zeal is silly; the false is in no whit inferior to the true since both are vanity. The truth-lover, if he is to continue his faith in his sciences and his truth, is driven to defending the position that being is an infinitely precious legacy; and lo, this emerges as Christianity's central theme.

Thus has come about the fulfillment of that initial augury when the wise men worshiped the infant Christ. The fact of an adequate value in human effort and in the human mind or soul has become the common foundation both for Christianity and for the wise men of the world. Science and religion are allies and associates in a warfare to maintain this fundamental fact. The common belief of every one who has faith in truth and in endeavor is that, with the issue clearly seen, the victory will be a triumphant one for an inestimable preciousness in the individual man.

CHRISTIAN PRINCIPLES OF WAR AND PEACE

Father Ryan is a great churchman and a great citizen, known and beloved far beyond the boundary of his own religious communion. Born on a farm in Minnesota in 1869, educated in St. Thomas Seminary, St. Paul, Dr. Ryan was ordained to the priesthood of the Roman Catholic Church in 1898, and did graduate work in the Catholic University, Washington City, where, since 1915, he has been professor of moral theology and industrial ethics. In the same year he became Director of the Social Action Department of the National Catholic Welfare Council.

Among many books by Dr. Ryan, one remembers vividly his famous debate with Morris Hillquit on *Socialism, Promise or Menace; Distributive Justice, Social Reconstruction, The Church and Labor, The State and the Church;* and his latest book of essays, *Declining Liberty,* which ought to be read by every citizen in the land, especially the chapter entitled "If I Were President." The present sermon appeared as a chapter in that volume, and brings home to us how little we have done in a practical way to build up a peace-mind; as witness the survey of school text-books, and the space devoted to peace and war respectively.

The trouble is that we have been peace-talkers, not peace-makers; and Dr. Ryan here shows us that something more practical and fundamental must be done, if we are to avert the perils of a narrow nationalism and a bigoted jingoism. All religious teachers must not simply declare, but expound, interpret, and make concrete the commandment of Christ, making its obligation not only implicit but explicit. Until we create a mind for peace, leagues and pacts will be of little avail.

CHRISTIAN PRINCIPLES OF WAR AND PEACE

JOHN A. RYAN, D.D.

CATHOLIC UNIVERSITY OF AMERICA, WASHINGTON, D. C.

Blessed are the peacemakers; for they shall be called the sons of God. Matthew 5: 8.

Christian principles would make peace secure and war impossible. For Catholics this is a truism. We recommend it unceasingly to statesmen and peoples. Not infrequently, however, our manner of stating this proposition suggests the inference that we expect Christian principles to operate automatically. We seem to attribute to the phrase, "Christian principles," something like the intrinsic efficacy which the magician pretends to ascribe to his words of incantation. We speak as though a formal profession of Christian principles in the abstract would of itself bring in a reign of peace.

Obviously, no intelligent Catholic intends to convey this impression. The Christian principles of international conduct are not self-operating, any more than the Christian principles which relate to the family or to industry. A husband may think that he loves his wife and yet put upon her uncharitable burdens; an employer may think that he is just to his

67

employees and yet deny them the rights proclaimed by Pope Leo XIII. Peoples and their rulers may assume that they are observing the precepts of justice and charity in their intercourse with foreigners, all the while they are violating both.

Two conditions are prerequisite to the efficacious working of Christian principles in the promotion of international peace. The first is specific and detailed application of the principles; the second is such long-continued inculcation that they will have become imbedded in man's emotional as well as his intellectual nature. The general principles must be brought down from the lofty abstract regions of the mind and made a part of the individual's practical thinking; and they must become an integral element in his training, a part of that mental furniture which is readily available for use in everyday life.

How can we perform this task of specific and persistent application of Christian principles? Let us first examine to what extent our authoritative teachers have in the comparatively recent past fulfilled the duty of enunciating and applying the Christian principles which relate to peace and war.

The Supreme Pontiffs have during the last half century repeatedly proclaimed the moral obligations of the nations to one another. Pope Leo XIII expounded the Christian doctrine of international relations in more than one majestic encyclical. One of the last acts of Pius X was to warn and rebuke the Emperor of Austria on account of his government's treatment of Serbia. At the outset of his pontificate

Christian Principles of War and Peace

Benedict XV recalled to the minds of the belligerents the principles of international justice; later on he offered them a practical program for ending the war and setting up a stable peace. Pius XI condemned the French invasion of the Ruhr and on other occasions has urged the nations of Europe to abandon force in favor of the methods of Christianity.

None of the subordinate exponents or teachers has an equally creditable record. Our text books of moral theology and moral philosophy are lamentably inadequate in their exposition of the ethical principles of peace and war. My examination of these manuals has brought to light only one which states clearly the very important moral truth that any and every war, taken as a whole, as a two-sided process, is always immoral. At least one of the belligerents is always in the wrong. In his *Institutiones Juris Naturalis,* Theodore Meyer, S.J., declares: *Bellum nequit esse, objective loquendo, ex utraque parte formaliter et materialiter justum.* In substantially all the other moral texts that I have consulted, the emphasis is placed upon the lawfulness of war and the duty of opposing unjust aggression, rather than upon the immorality of war and the duty of averting it by negotiation and conciliation. War is represented as more or less natural, normal and inevitable. With the exception of Meyer and Cathrein none of the authors adequately stresses the obligation of exhausting all peaceful methods before resorting even to a war of defense. Scarcely any of them calls attention to the obvious fact that if states gave due atten-

John A. Ryan, D.D.

tion to this duty of exploring methods of conciliation, wars would be rare occurrences. Had all the involved states sincerely observed this condition in 1914, there would have been no Great War.

Of lamentable significance is the fact that none of the manuals contains in its index the word "peace." The word does not occur in the indices because the subject receives no formal treatment in the text. Neither the blessings of peace nor the Christian principles concerning it are submitted to systematic discussion.

In other fields of instruction, the situation is no better. In schools, in religious periodicals and occasionally in the pulpit, a doctrine of patriotism is taught which is profoundly unbalanced. The declaration of the pagan poet, *Dulce et decorum est pro patria mori,* is quoted without qualification and generally with complete approval. Seldom is it pointed out either to pupils in the schools or to audiences that to die for one's country is neither sweet nor becoming if one's country is engaged upon a war of aggression. Indeed, the virtue of patriotism is frequently taught in such a way as to convey the impression that it is identical with willingness to fight and die for one's country. Undue emphasis is placed upon the lawfulness of supporting just war and opposing unjust aggression.

Not long ago a study was made by three American college professors of twenty-four history texts and twenty-four supplementary readers, in order to ascertain the extent to which war is emphasized in these school manuals. The investigation showed an excessive amount of space devoted to war; the amount devoted to peace almost negligible; the discussion of war nationalistic, biased, and in many cases flamboyant; the war illustrations reflecting only the glorified imaginings of the artists; very little telling of the real truths about war; and the great military leaders receiving vastly more attention than the conspicuous leaders in the arts of peace. An examination which I have made of eight history texts widely used in Catholic parochial schools discloses the same perverse emphasis. The proportion of space given to war varies from 16 per cent. to 35 per cent., while the number of pages devoted to peace describe a descending scale from four to none.

In consequence of the excessive emphasis upon narrow patriotism in the schools, in the newspapers and on public platforms, and owing to the absence of specific and systematic instruction concerning the rights and claims of foreign peoples, the majority of persons, Catholics as well as non-Catholics, are disposed to assume that their own country is always in the right when it engages in war and that there is no other effective method of defending national welfare. The few courageous souls that now and again undertake to point out the violations of justice or of charity committed in the name of their country are commonly denounced as unpatriotic. This applies even to national wars which are so far in the past that they ought no longer to arouse patriotic emotions. For example, the American war against Spain in 1898 was utterly unjust and immoral, inasmuch as the latter country had conceded everything for which America was contending. Although in full possession of this fact, President McKinley went before Congress and asked for a declaration of war. The documents which prove this disgraceful transaction have been known to historians and certain other persons for more than twenty years. The story is set forth in more than one standard work on United States history. Nevertheless, it is probably not known by one American in one thousand. The few who are aware of the facts hesitate to mention them from fear of being condemned as disloyal to our glorious military traditions.

Although the Catholic Church is international, the inculcation of Catholic principles on international relations has been so inadequate and so faulty that the masses of Catholics in every country are almost, if not quite, as greatly misled as their non-Catholic neighbors by the false theories of one-sided patriotism and excessive nationalism. "They drink in the false doctrines of the jingo press; they are misled by the fallacy of abstraction into conceiving vast nations as single entities; they do not realize that to hate or malign a whole people is just as sinful as to hate or malign an individual. Their patriotism has lost sight of the necessary limits imposed by their Christianity."

In a word, the excesses and defects of our actual instruction on international affairs have exposed us to the imminent danger of accepting the creed of modern nationalism. Now modern nationalism has in more than one country assumed many of the characters of a religion. "Nationalism as a religion inculcates neither charity nor justice; it is proud, not humble; and it signally fails to universalize human aims. It repudiates the revolutionary messages of St. Paul and proclaims anew the primitive doctrine that there shall be Jew and Greek, only that now there shall be Jew and Greek more quintessentially than ever. Nationalism's kingdom is frankly of this world, and its attainment involves tribal selfishness and vainglory, a particularly ignorant and tyrannical intolerance—and war."

While I have made no formal investigation of the subject, I feel safe in asserting that the number of pastorals on peace published by European bishops in the critical years and months before the Great War might be counted on the fingers of one hand. Although the peoples of many European countries greatly feared and dreaded the coming of war during a quarter of a century before 1914, no international Catholic peace organization was established as an effort to prevent that great catastrophe.

It is not an easy or a simple task to apply the moral principles of Christianity to international affairs. There must be both individual instruction and political instruction. Under the first head the religious teacher must declare, expound, interpret, illustrate and make concrete Christ's commandment of love and the divine precept of justice. This teaching must be imparted to all groups and classes; in theological seminaries, in colleges and schools; in the pulpit and in catechetical instruction; in religious books and periodicals. The individual must be taught a right attitude of mind toward all foreigners. It is not enough to declare that "every human being is my neighbor." The obligations which are implicit in this phrase must be made explicit. They must be set forth in detail with regard to foreign races and nations. Men must be reminded that "every human being" includes Frenchmen, Germans, Italians, Englishmen, Japanese, Chinese, and all other divisions of the human family. And this doctrine should be repeated and reiterated. Effective teaching and adequate assimilation depend largely upon the simple process of repetition. The duties of patriotism must be expounded in a more restrained and balanced way than that which has been followed heretofore. Men must be taught that it is not "sweet and becoming to die for one's country" if one's country is fighting for that which is unjust. Without denying or weakening the sentiment of national patriotism, we can set forth that wider and higher patriotism which takes in all the peoples of the earth. And we should bring about a profound shifting of emphasis in explaining the conditions which justify war. Instead of laying stress upon the lawfulness of engaging in war, we should clearly and continuously point out that all the conditions which are necessary to make war morally lawful have rarely existed together in history. We should strive to concentrate attention upon the obligation of preventing war through negotiation and conciliation, rather than upon its lawfulness.

The mental attitude of the people must likewise be changed and reformed with regard to the possibility of establishing permanent peace. One of the greatest obstacles to peace has always been the lazy assumption that wars must come, that there will always be war while men are men. So long as this pessimism prevails, the majority of persons will not assert themselves in the cause of peace. World peace is largely, if not mainly, a matter of human faith. If the majority of people believe that peace can be established and secured, peace will be established and secured. Therefore, we must strive to make the people think peace and talk peace. We must incessantly declare the feasibility of a reign of peace until this idea and this faith become a dominating and effective element in the habitual thinking of the average man and woman. To be sure, no human being knows whether war can be forever banished from the earth. Only God knows. What we do know is that war may be made more and more remote through human action aided by the grace of God. To make war remote, to push it into the indefinite future, is a practical and a sufficient program.

So much for the specific application of right principles with regard to individuals. Were this achieved to the extent that is readily possible, it would not be sufficient. It must be supplemented by effective political action. In its final stage the process of attaining world peace must be carried through by states and governments. In that field also Christian principles must find specific and detailed application.

A fundamental method is adequate preaching of the principles of international morality. The grossly immoral doctrine that states are above the moral law is not so frequently uttered or defended today as it was before the Great War. Nevertheless, it is still implicitly or explicitly accepted and acted upon by statesmen in more than one country. Even where it is not held, there is need of outspoken and frequent declaration of the truth that nations, as well as individuals, are subject to the moral law, particularly to the precepts of justice and charity.

Besides the general preaching of the doctrine that political and international actions are governed by the moral law, its precepts must be applied to particular events, policies and proposals. Moral teaching of this sort must be addressed not only to the people but in an especial manner to statesmen. This is, indeed, a difficult task. It is not easy to determine how far contemporary international actions or policies are contrary to either justice or charity. Even when the moral aspect of the situation is clear, the question may arise whether religious teachers are not bound to remain silent from motives of Christian prudence.

As we now realize, many features of the Triple Alliance and of the Triple Entente, and many of the policies adopted under these agreements, were contrary to the principles of Christian morality. Should the authoritative religious teachers of Germany,

Austria and Italy, of England, France and Russia have denounced these things at the time they occurred? Should they have condemned the war-provoking policy of competitive armaments? Obviously this was a very delicate situation. Nevertheless, it does seem to us now that the religious teachers in all these countries could have done something to check these disastrous courses.

Whatever we may think about the past, we can see some duties fairly clear in the present. All the leading states of the world are morally bound to labor earnestly for the establishment of peace. The methods which seem likely to promote the attainment of this end should command the active interest and approval of all religious authorities. We should oppose the doctrine of indefinite preparedness as a means of preventing war. Mindful of what competitive armaments have done to provoke war, we ought to emphasize that fact and to point out its moral implications. With entire propriety we can urge the people to study deeply and faithfully all the positive proposals that have been brought forward in recent years for the prevention of war. These are the League of Nations, the World Court, the outlawry of war, compulsory international arbitration and universal disarmament. One or more of these methods do not appeal to all of us, but that is to be expected. All of them are deserving of study and consideration and the ideals underlying them are in harmony with the principles of Christianity.

Indeed, the Catholics of the world, both the clergy

77

and the laity, have received specific and authoritative guidance concerning practical measures for the establishment of peace. In his address to the belligerents, August 1, 1917, Pope Benedict XV proposed that:

Moral right be substituted for the material force of arms in the reciprocal dealings of nations; the nations enter upon a just agreement for the simultaneous and reciprocal reduction of armaments; armed force be replaced by "the noble and peaceful institution of arbitration," with the provision that penalties be imposed upon any state which should refuse either to submit a national question to such a tribunal, or to accept the arbitral decision.

In his letter to the American people on the last day of 1918, the same Pontiff expressed a fervent desire for an international organization which "by abolishing conscription will reduce armaments; by establishing international tribunals will eliminate or settle disputes; and by placing peace on a solid foundation will guarantee to all independence and equality of rights."

It is worth noting that all these recommendations of Pope Benedict XV became embodied in the Protocol for the Pacific Settlement of International Disputes, adopted by the League of Nations Assembly at Geneva, in October, 1924. They likewise constitute the essence of the treaties concluded at Locarno. Therefore, any Catholic who desires to accept and advocate the essential provisions of the Protocol or of the Locarno agreements, can obtain comfort and encouragement from the reflection that he is in accord with the mind of the Holy See. He can properly favor universal disarmament, the abolition of compulsory military service, the adoption of compulsory and complete international arbitration, the outlawry of war, the World Court, and the League of Nations. Any Catholic who opposes any of these things on grounds of selfish nationalism or international hatred is out of harmony with the mind of the Holy See. To be sure, a good Catholic is justified in rejecting any or all of these proposals and institutions, if he honestly thinks that they are or would be harmful to legitimate national welfare or to any other important legitimate cause or interest. But he should take this stand only after careful and impartial consideration and after he has cleared his mind of all jingoism and all hatred of foreign nations. In a word, he should examine the whole situation in the light of objective evidence and in the spirit of Christian charity which knows neither Jew nor Gentile, neither barbarian nor Greek.

In the movement for world peace, American Catholics have, moreover, the active leadership of their own bishops. In the Pastoral Letter issued by the Archbishops and Bishops of the United States assembled in conference at the Catholic University of America, September 26, 1919, we find these sentences:

"One of the most effective means by which States can assist one another is the organization of inter-

John A. Ryan, D.D.

national peace. The need of this is more generally felt at the present time when the meaning of war is so plainly before us."

On February 2, 1922, the Administrative Committee of the National Catholic Welfare Council declared:

"As Catholics—brothers of the Prince of Peace—and as Americans, we have the spiritual responsibility of promoting peace not only in our own country but throughout the world."

On May 2, 1924, the Administrative Committee of the National Catholic Welfare Conference gave out another statement on peace which included the following sentences:

"We should, individually and through organizations, earnestly study to preserve the peace of the world. Our thoughts, our aims, should be in the path of peace. Peace should be our goal."

HAVE WE LOST THE POWER OF VENTURE?

In my diary of *Preaching in New York* I ventured to describe Dr. Lynch as "a *liaison* officer in the service of Christ, whose life is a ministry of reconciliation, interpretation, and strategic good-will"; and those words tell the truth. Perhaps no man among us has done more in behalf of a closer fellowship between Churches, and in the larger field in the service of international understanding—as tireless as he is tactful in his labors.

Born in Rhode Island in 1867, educated at Yale, Dr. Lynch was ordained to the Congregational ministry in 1899; serving first as assistant pastor in the United Church in New Haven, and later as pastor of Pilgrim Church in New York City. Later he became editor of *Christian Work*, recently merged with the *Christian Century;* the while he has for many years been educational secretary of the Church Peace Union. Among his many books one may name two favorites, *One Great Society* and *Personal Recollections of Andrew Carnegie*, his friend and fellow-worker in the cause of peace.

If, in the sermon following, Dr. Lynch seems to be depressed by the untoward aspects of a time of reaction, in which idealism seems obsolete and the spirit of adventure in abeyance, it is in fact only seeming. Above the apathy and timidity of the time a prophet-voice here calls to the soul of America to lead the way toward a just and wiser world order.

HAVE WE LOST THE POWER OF VENTURE?

FREDERICK LYNCH, D.D.

CHURCH PEACE UNION, NEW YORK CITY

Now when he had left speaking, he said unto Simon, Launch out into the deep, and let down your nets for a draught. Luke 5: 4.

Launch out into the deep! Try the unknown! Take great ventures! Dare the impossible! Have faith in new and untried worlds! Forever the voice of Jesus calls to us and we are afraid. It is only one man out of a thousand who dares think or do anything new. We content ourselves with conformity, smug contentedness, stupid respectability, the safety of the crowd. We have no courage to fulfill even though the ideal dawns upon us and calls. Respectability, contentedness, fear of the new thought and deed, very well sums up our world, even the world of the churches.

Yes, it is true, you will say, but we must look to youth. They are on fire with new enthusiasms; they have caught visions of the promised land and will lead us into it; they will build a new world for us; they have the courage to dare the untried tasks; they will go forth to do shining things. Well, where are youth flaming with great enthusiasms, throwing in

83

their lot with the prophets and explorers, seeking the city of God, even interesting themselves in the new things the courageous of the world are doing, the new orders the brave are trying to build?

I

Not in our colleges. It is my lot to visit many colleges. I meet the men in chapel, in conferences, in discussion groups, in clubs, in social gatherings, and I have much contact with them after graduation. I never visit a college without coming away depressed and asking myself, "Has youth lost all power of venture?" I know of no place in America or England, or on the Continent for that matter, where one finds less courage to dare the new thing, less enthusiasm for the new order we are trying to build, less faith in a redeemed society, less fine frenzy for the ideal than on the college campus. I know you will say: "But look at our student gatherings at Milwaukee, at Indianapolis, and elsewhere. See the idealism manifested, the shaking off of shackles; the facing new tasks, the courageous consecration to prophetic leadership, the pledges to dare the unknown deeps." Yes, this is splendid. But these thousand boys are the exceptions among the hundred thousand and they are often laughed at, on the very campus from which they came, for professing an ideal or conviction different from that held by the campus, and sometimes ridiculed and even ill-treated for daring to break away from the old thought conventions. Thank God there are these exceptions—this thousand, and of course more—but most of our campuses are the strongholds of convention and conservatism. One would think that college boys would rebel against this old, age-long process of standardization, which takes every particle of individualism out of their nature. But they do not. Instead, they uphold it, they believe in it, they ostracize any boy who thinks differently and of course they have no interest in the attempts being made all over the world to get out of a political order based on force into one based on good will and mutual confidence. The trouble is they are fearful of the new. They dare not try it. I have met with them again and again and they are afraid to leave their guns and try the new way. They dare not leave the old shores and launch out onto the deep. They have none of the Columbus in their natures.

It is pathetic, for one would, of all places, expect to find in colleges boys wild with enthusiasm over the great experiments the world is trying—Leagues of Nations, World Courts, Locarnos, Disarmament Conferences, above all the outlawry of war movement which challenges the faith and courage as nothing else in our time. Instead one finds the colleges the very seat of the old nationalism. The ideals of patriotism are those held by the mob in general. Seldom have I found in a college group that enlarged and idealized ideal of patriotism which has all the promise of the future in it. One finds respectability, one finds goodness, one finds conformity both in dress and morals, one finds good manners, one finds trained minds with ability to succeed in the professions, in politics and business. But it is all passionless intelligence. There is so little of the spirit of adventure, so little of that discontent with old, imperfect things, that has always driven the prophets, the crusaders and the explorers to try new worlds. They even become cynical of new things. I have never found such cynicism, such scorn of enthusiasm, such blasé attitudes toward a redeemed society, such distrust of idealism as I have found on the college campus, both among students and professors—found it in the very place where one expects high courage, daring ventures, faith in the untried vision, prophetic leading.

What would happen, I wonder, if a revival of real Christianity—that is, trust in the leadership of Jesus, his words, his ideals, all he stood for—should suddenly sweep through our colleges and through the hearts of all youth, everywhere? What would happen if suddenly three hundred thousand young people should rise up and say, "The past belongs to you, old people, and what a mess you have made of it. The future is ours and we propose to take it and make it new. We propose to follow the Christ who said, 'Behold, I make all things new.' We propose to cast aside all fear and try that new world with him, launch out into the deep with him"? What would happen, I say, if our youth should turn with disgust from all this old, conventional, worn-out, timid respectability, this trust in age-long institutions that are powerless to bring either security, brotherhood or peace; that

are as powerless as the Jewish Church out of which
Jesus had to rise into a new world; and catch again
the sublime courage of the young Christ who dared
the unseen with a cheer, and with his courage in their
hearts throw in their lot with those brave men who
are trying to reconstruct the world on the high principles of the gospel, who dare believe in the Christian
world order and throw in their lot with it, who have
the courage of a great faith in the ideal as the one
practical thing in a world ruled by God, who welcome with a beautiful enthusiasm any attempt,
whether at Geneva or The Hague or Locarno or
Washington or anywhere else, such great experiments as the brave are trying there, and shout, "My
place is there where men are making all things new"?
Again I ask what might happen if our youth should
catch the vision of the new patriotism which leaps all
boundaries of states and embraces all the family of
God, and dare to believe in it, and stand for it, in
the face of all this pagan gospel of isolation and
nationalism? I do not know, but I have a feeling
that if the youth of the world would recover that fine
frenzy of the Christ, that daring of the impossible
which has marked all leaders, that love of venture
that would commit them to great enterprise, the
world of even the old might catch the contagion and
lose its fear and move out of its walled cities of convention, to try the unexplored wonder of God's new
worlds.

87

Frederick Lynch, D.D.

II

Has the Church lost the power of venture? The creation of the Christian Church was a great venture. It was an act of sublime and surpassing faith. A young man was born into an age of convention, religious formalism and theological fixity. He dreamed a dream of a new kingdom—a kingdom of the freedom of the spirit. He called together twelve men—it was the greatest venture ever made—and established a Church which was as far removed from the existing Church as socialism is from feudalism. It was its daring that saved it. The Church would not have lived had it been only a little way removed from the Jewish Church, only one step beyond or above. It was because it was so revolutionary, so radical, so impossible, that it lived and attracted the attention of the world. It arrested men. It put before men a new, glorious, alluring ideal; a living, spiritual state, an opportunity fit for gods. As a result, it won prophetic souls, and these prophetic souls banded themselves together, held by the inspiration of a great venture and by devotion to their Lord—the great Adventurer of history.

The primitive Church was a weak affair. When Christ died, there were probably not more than a hundred real church members in existence. It was a little group of men and women, none powerful, none famous, set in the midst of a great Jewish religion and a Roman civilization. The first discus-

sion which agitated this new Church was whether
it should not conform to the Jewish faith, merely
grafting on to it a faith in Jesus as the Messiah.
Everybody knows now that had the counsel of the
conservative Jewish members prevailed, there would
have been no Christian Church. Fortunately, it did
not prevail. The prophetic members had their way.
The primitive Church decided to make a great venture. It broke with Judaism in one great bound. It
broke with contemporary ethics. It broke absolutely with Roman civilization. It broke with the
current Greek philosophy, which at its core was
simply that life existed for self-protection, self-de-
velopment, self-security. To see how great this
break was, one has only to read the sermons of the
first missionaries as recorded in the Acts of the Apostles, the Epistles of Paul and John, and the sermons
and treatises of the Church Fathers. The gospel
offered by the early Church was as far removed from
the ordinary conventional religion as were the stars
from the haunts of men. It had nothing in common
with the ideals or ethics of the crowd. Its idols had
nothing in common with the idols of the market
place. In a world that believed in revenge, it
preached love. To a society engrossed in pleasure, it
preached duty and purity. To a civilization based
on force, it preached good will. To a civilization in
which war was the accepted and normal life, it made
direct protest against war. Practically every one of
the Church Fathers said, "Christians must not bear
arms against each other."

Frederick Lynch, D.D.

In a social order where caste was fixed and accepted, the Church said all men were equal. In an autocracy, it preached democracy. In a world that put nationalism above everything else, it placed humanity first, and put citizenship in the kingdom above allegiance to the state. In a world which idolized forcefulness, physical prowess, lordship over others, triumph in arms, it proclaimed meekness, gentleness, forbearance, and the spirit of lowly service as the most admirable qualities of manhood. With a sublime and unequaled confidence in its message, it went out into the world with it. It was a great venture, and because it was a great venture the Church soon commanded the attention of the Greek and Roman world. It was the very impossibles of the early Church that assured its life and growth. It not only drew the prophetic souls of the ancient world into its fold, but it commanded the admiration of the crowd in due time simply because it had a message. A church without a new, transcendent gospel would never have made any progress in either Greece or Rome. But the great thing is that it dared make the great venture. By its very flight toward the stars it made itself seen of all men. Only that which is lifted up can draw men to it. The Church can lead only when it is far ahead of the people— only when it dares make the great venture.

Many are wondering today if the Church has lost this power of venture. Does it dare make the venture with Peter across the stormy sea to meet the Lord where he stands? One has only even carelessly to read the secular press of both Europe and America, together with the many books that are being written, to see how widespread the feeling is that the Church, as an institution, has neither any vision in this moment of a perplexed and distressed world, nor any faith to make again the great venture, even if she had the vision. One turns in vain to the utterance of either Catholic or Protestant Church in Europe for any prophetic word. The Vatican has issued two or three encyclicals praising peace and deploring war, but it has no great, new, commanding word for stricken Europe; the churches of Germany and Great Britain, nine years after the war, have no new word to say. There is yet no intimation that they are planning any great venture, formulating any new, prophetic word to speak to a world still building armies and navies and still in the grip of the war system. To be sure, some of the churches have passed resolutions deploring war. Some of the British churches have stood behind the League of Nations; but there is no sign of the British Church excommunicating the whole war system.

But what shall we say of the Church in the United States? What is happening in this favored land, where, far from the scenes of the late war, we can contemplate it in right perspective, view all its terrible calamity, study causes and effects, and speak some great healing word? Here is the greatest apostasy the world has ever witnessed—War! Here is a denial of everything for which Christ stood. Here are millions of Christians bending all their energies, resources and genius to slaughtering each other, stopping at no diabolical method. Here are millions of women and little children, who will be starved and driven crazy should another 1914 or worse—and it would be worse—come upon us. War and the preparation for war puts fearful burdens upon the shoulders of the poor for succeeding centuries. Institutions, social organizations, charities, philanthropies that have taken years to form are brushed aside through war. Missions are set back for centuries. Cities are devastated. But, worst of all, hatreds among the Christians are engendered that must make even the far-seeing Christ despair of his kingdom of goodwill ever coming in the earth.

It is true that the national assemblies of the various communions have—and sometimes in the face of much opposition—passed resolutions putting their communions on record as furthering all attempts at the substitution of judicial processes and peaceable methods for war in the settlement of international disputes. Some have gone further and condemned all war except defensive war. Many leaders of the churches have become thoroughly convinced that Christianity and war are as antipodal in a Christian civilization as Christianity and slavery, and are saying so; but as yet no great, compelling word, new—new like the words the early Church spoke—has fallen on our ears, no condemnation of war, in voice heard to the ends of the world, as an unholy, unchristian thing having no part with Christ or Christ's Church. In 1925 when all the churches of the world, save one, met in Stockholm all they would say about war was that it was futile as a means of settling international disputes.

Often I wonder what might happen if the Church in America were to make a great venture and say the big, new, healing word, were to condemn forever with one unanimous voice the whole outworn, incapable, toppled, unchristian war system that preceded this war; were to proclaim the new gospel of love of the enemy, goodwill, forgiveness, redemption of other peoples as the only mission of a nation, as the primitive Church took a great venture and proclaimed it as the only mission of a Christian man; were to proclaim that the time has come for the nation to bend all its energies to establishing a kingdom of goodwill among nations as the early Church proclaimed this as the mission of every soul; were to demand that patriotism be broadened to include all the Kingdom of God and that love of country be for the republic of God, the city of God, the home of all God's children; were to demand that national boundaries shall mean no more to nations than local boundaries mean to Christians; were to reaffirm Jesus' great teaching of real brotherhood, a closer tie than citizenship in the same country; were to proclaim the unity of all the sons of God, and that the time has come for the Church to take Jesus by the arm and have faith in his teachings, and go forth bravely to apply them to the world. I say, I often wonder what might happen if the Church should have the courage to do this, to trust her own Master, to dare believe her own gospel and announce it. Sometimes I think that should she do it the tired and weary world, the world which now looks for the healing word in vain, would rise in one great shout of acclamation and hail her again as the bride of heaven, the voice of God, the vicar of Christ, the prophet of the Lord. I really believe that should she dare to do this holy, apostolic act, she would find the peoples of the world with her and war put into the limbo of unholy things.

III

Finally, a great multitude today are asking: Has our nation lost the power of venture? Certainly she had it once, for the sailing of the founders from Plymouth in the *Mayflower* was one of the sublimest and most courageous adventures in all history. It was so daring an emprise that all but a handful were afraid. Recall that great passage in the immortal Æneid, John Robinson's *Journal*, where he relates the debate of the Pilgrims in Leyden just before undertaking their great venture of seeking a new world, and there you have the spirit of venture out of which America was born. That little band of pilgrims had the courage of those who went from Jerusalem to Greece and Rome and carried the gospel into the pagan world. They dared the untried seas; they were not daunted by devastating winters and savage peoples, but remained to found a new world; they dared the impossible and believed that God was faithful to his promises.

Later when in the exigencies of history the time came to break away from England and found the republic, they were not afraid. The republic was a great venture, how great we cannot realize today. Many of the timid counseled against it, but the brave prevailed and the republic was born. The early years were full of discouragement and conflicting ideals but never did the fathers lose courage. Often they were groping in the dark, but they persevered and laid the firm foundations of the greatest experiment in democracy the world has ever seen. When the question arose as to whether the gates of the nation should be open to all the world, again the timid counseled against it. It was an impossible thing to weld all peoples into a united society. Again the brave won the day and the gates were opened to all comers. They came by the millions—every nation, every kindred, every race, every tongue—bringing their varied traditions and opposing ideals. It was a great venture of faith, but who will say it was not justified, for in spite of the immensity and the newness of the venture, there is no nation more united than our own.

Again, when the conscience of the few came to see that slavery had no part in a Christian civilization they rose to smite it. Again there were many who shouted: "It cannot be done. Slavery is as old as time. It is embedded in the constitution of the world." But the Lincolns, the Garrisons, the Sumners, the Beechers and the rest of the Gideons knew that the truth could always be done and with a glorious courage and holy zeal they proceeded to make a nation where all men should be free, while all the world wondered at their divine audacity. When in 1918 we believed—whether rightly or wrongly matters not now—that democracy was imperiled and the weak were being crushed to earth again, we dared the new thing, namely, to forget self and give of our men and resource to serve a cause that was not our own and serve other peoples that had no claim upon us except that they were imperiled. It was a new thing in history for a great nation to risk all in the service, not of self, but of the world. But we rose to it. We dared the new thing. We said with our great leader: "There have been other nations as rich as we; there have been other nations as spirited; but I hope we shall never forget that we created this Nation, not to serve ourselves, but to serve mankind."

Then came the peace, and all the world looked to us to lead it into some new and untried order. For a while it looked as though the nation was going to rise to the great opportunity to lead the world into a new and Christian world order, but we suddenly lost courage and became afraid of the new thing. The United States could have gone to Geneva and made the League of Nations whatever it desired. There is not the slightest doubt in the world that had we kept our courage and dared forget ourselves, we could have made it a democratic association of nations whose sanctions would have been the public opinion of mankind. What held America back? It was timidity, the fear of the new thing, fear we might lose our time-honored and traditional rights to do what we planned, fear to trust ourselves to the justice of the world. A great European statesman said to me not long ago: "Had your country been at Geneva behind the Protocol, I believe it would have gone through and the entrance into war been made a crime for every nation." We did not go. We were afraid to try the unknown deeps, to risk a great venture of whose outcome we were not quite certain.

I often wonder what might happen if the United States again recovered her old daring, her matchless courage, her spirit of adventure, her forgetfulness of self or safety, her crusading spirit, her prophetic gifts, and again took her place at the head of the nations calling them to new world orders, to untried heights of promise. What would happen should a president arise who would challenge the nation to lead the world? What would happen should a president come who had the vision of the new world and who feared nothing but the smug contentment in old things, and who had the courage to forget shibboleths, parties, old ways of thought, yes, to forget his own fortunes and suddenly to say:

" 'The old order changeth, giving place to new.' Let us, as a nation, rise and go forth. We care nothing about your covenants at Geneva, but we will join you and make those covenants what they ought to be. We don't approve of your World Court altogether but we will come over and make it the strong and only tribunal of the nations. We are not interested in all you are doing, but we are interested in the one, great, fundamental thing, and if we come we shall give you no peace night or day until you have accomplished it, namely, the putting of war where once we put slavery, among the unpardonable sins. And if you are not willing to receive us on these terms, then we propose to go about it ourselves. We are going to be rid of war. It has no place in a civilization worthy of the name, it is an anachronism in our time, it belongs with slavery and torture in the limbo of forgotten things, it violates all decency, all morality, all fine, human instincts. As a nation we propose to have nothing more to do with it and we call upon all other nations to join with us in this banishing of it from the earth forever."

What might happen if such a president should arise? Sometimes I think that should such an one come to Washington, rise majestically from his chair and forget safe cabinets and safe congresses and tradition-ridden senates, and parties and personal fortunes, and speak such words to the people and throw himself upon their impulses, they would rise to him in one great shout of acclamation that would drown out the snarlings of the fearful, the respectable, and the timid—hail him their prophet and their deliverer. I know the people. I know how they yearn for deliverance, but there is no deliverer. Were he to come to Washington and dare this great thing

Have We Lost the Power of Venture?

I believe the people would follow anywhere he led them. I think he would find himself another Lincoln. I believe, too, that all the other nations are ready to make the great venture should we lead.

CHRIST AND THE CREEDS

Bishop Mouzon was born in South Carolina in 1869, educated at Wofford College in his native State, and entered the Methodist ministry in 1889 in the Texas Conference. After several pastorates in Texas, he was called to the Central Church, Kansas City, and later to the professorship of theology in the Southwestern University, Georgetown, Texas. Elected Bishop in 1910, he assisted in the founding of the Southern Methodist University at Dallas, and in many ways has shown himself to be a leader, alike in Christian thought and enterprise. His best known books are, *Does God Care? The Program of Jesus,* and *The Missionary Evangel,* the last two being the Cole and the Fondren lectures.

To read this sermon on Christ and the Creeds is to learn why Bishop Mouzon is honored and beloved not only in his own Church, but by men of all communions in the South. It finds the secret and center of Christianity in the inner experience of God in Christ; a radiant and creative mysticism of which theology is but the prose exposition. It sets forth the eternal orthodoxy of the heart, to interpret which each theology uses the imagery and dialect of its age: the living truth abides and grows while theologies come and go.

CHRIST AND THE CREEDS

EDWIN D. MOUZON, D.D.

BISHOP, METHODIST EPISCOPAL CHURCH SOUTH,
CHARLOTTE, N. C.

Come unto me, all ye that labor and are heavy laden, and I will give you rest. Take my yoke upon you, and learn of me; for I am meek and lowly in heart; and ye shall find rest unto your souls. Matthew 11: 28, 29.

If any man would come after me, let him deny himself, and take up his cross, and follow me. Matthew 16: 24.

If any man willeth to do his will, he shall know of the teaching, whether it is of God, or whether I speak from myself. John 7: 17.

These three passages of Scripture set before us, in the simplest and plainest manner possible, exactly what Christ's one condition of discipleship is. With such explicit language as this before our eyes, how can it be possible to misunderstand what it is to be a Christian? Learning of Jesus, following Jesus, doing the will of God—this is the sum and substance of it. Whosoever meets this condition is a Christian. Whosoever does not meet Christ's one condition of discipleship is not a Christian.

103

Edwin D. Mouzon, D.D.

I

And how the simplicity of this one condition does contrast with certain conditions which have sometimes been imposed upon us as prerequisites to the beginning of our discipleship to Jesus!

1. From very early times, and possibly never quite so insistently as now, it has been urged that the first and foremost condition of discipleship is a correct creed. Now I, for one, do believe in the value and importance of a correct creed. There cannot possibly be any value in loose and superficial thinking. Undoubtedly creed, character, and conduct are vitally related each to the other. But it is not one's attitude toward an intellectual system that determines one's Christian character; it is always one's moral attitude toward Christ and the teachings of Christ that decides whether or not one is a Christian.

When a man says that he believes a creed, he may mean one of several things. *He may mean that he does not disbelieve.* I suspect that this is about all that some mean when they say that they believe. They simply accept what has been handed down to them from their fathers. They do not wish to be disturbed. They want to be let alone. With true spiritual insight another has said that there are men who have never believed enough to doubt. Faith has never meant enough to them to venture out upon it and feel for the solid rock beneath their feet. It was of doubt of this kind that Tennyson wrote:

104

Christ and the Creeds

There lives more faith in honest doubt,
Believe me, than in half the creeds.

Or when a man says he believes, *he may mean that he accepts the intellectual interpretation of reality to which the creeds seek to give expression.* We have the highest respect for the great philosophers and theologians who have sought to interpret in terms of the world's best thought the significance of the everlasting realities of our holy religion. But Christianity is much more than a system of theology, and being a Christian is vastly more than yielding intellectual assent to a creed, no matter how correct and comprehensive that creed may be. That kind of faith cannot possibly save a man. All *that* is purely intellectual; there is nothing ethical in it. Only metaphysicians can have that kind of faith.

Or when a man says he believes, he may mean something other and better than this; *he may mean that the language of the creed interprets the experience of his soul,* and that only the language of the great creeds is adequate to the expression of the things he has made real to himself in his own experience. We shall find that the great creeds of the church were born out of the experience of Christians. But men are not theologians first and Christians afterwards. Men are Christians first of all, and then theologians—if, indeed, they ever do become theologians.

Take, by way of illustration, the Apostles' Creed which, as Dr. Schaff says, is the creed of creeds just as the Lord's Prayer is the prayer of prayers. It will not do to make the intellectual acceptance of even so simple a summary of the facts of Christianity as is contained in that creed a condition prerequisite to the beginning of discipleship to Jesus. For when did Peter and James and John become Jesus' disciples? Certainly not when they gave assent to any formal statement of things to be believed, but when they began to follow Jesus. They came to Jesus; they denied themselves and took up the cross; they were willing to do his will. By meeting Christ's one condition of discipleship they became his disciples. Or take our little children. Surely it is easy for a child to become a follower of Jesus. Heaven does lie round about us in our infancy. A child brought up in a Christian home finds it natural and easy to love Jesus and follow him. And whosoever loves Jesus and follows him is a disciple of Jesus. Or consider the average busy man of affairs. He is no philosopher; he cannot settle for himself questions of science and metaphysics. But he is a human being with human wants and weaknesses and sins and sorrows; and Christ does forever speak directly to his soul. The call of Christ finds him: "Come unto me all ye that labor and are heavy laden. Take my yoke upon you and learn of me." "Deny yourselves and follow me." "Will to do God's will, and you shall know the truth of my teaching." Christ's one condition of discipleship every man can meet.

We conclude, therefore, that the acceptance of a correct creed cannot possibly be laid down as a condition previously required of those who seek to become Christians.

2. Here in America, where our evangelical churches have always stressed the necessity of an experience of conversion, we often find men taking the position that before one can begin the Christian life one must first have a definite experience of religion.

Now, the importance of Christian experience can hardly be overstated. All religion grows out of experience. The fact of conversion is one of the most significant facts in human experience. The disciple does come into an experience of communion with God. The fact of the forgiveness of sins is a personal fact, the restoration of personal relationship between us and God. It must be admitted, however, that our evangelical churches have, to too great an extent, sought to standardize Christian experience. We have presented the experience of Saul of Tarsus as typical, or the experience of Augustine, or the experience of John Wesley. Now Paul's experience was the experience of a converted Pharisee, and Augustine's experience was the experience of a converted libertine, and Wesley's experience was the experience of a converted High Churchman of the eighteenth century. A man's experience will be determined by a number of things—by his education, his temperament, his past manner of life, his associations. To try to bring all men into the same sort of Christian experience is a capital mistake. And then to go on and insist that a certain kind of experience is necessary as a condition of entering upon a life of discipleship to Jesus, is to make a twofold blunder—the blunder of holding that experience must antedate life, and the blunder of insisting that all men pass through precisely the same sort of emotional crisis.

Definite, clear-cut Christian experience is greatly to be desired. It brings new power to the soul; it brings new buoyancy into the life; it brings clarity of vision; it gives rest to the weary and heavy laden. But experience is not, and cannot possibly be, a condition of entering on the Christian life. That is to put the cart before the horse. Experience is a *consequence* of living the Christian life. We must come to Christ before we find rest to our souls. We must deny ourselves and follow Christ in order to become his disciples. We must will to do his will if we are to come into the experience of Christian certitude. Men ought, therefore, never to be urged to seek an *experience* of religion. This leads to a self-centered kind of life which cannot possibly be happy. It ends in a subjectivity which upsets the very purpose of the Christian religion, namely, to lead men to live for others and think of others. No! It is not an *experience* that we should seek; it is *religion* itself, right adjustment to God and to our fellow-men, fellowship with Christ and obedience to his teachings. When this true end of religion is attained, then the *experience* of religion will take care of itself.

Christ and the Creeds

II

Set over against such conditions as have been suggested, how simple and yet how exacting is Christ's one condition of discipleship. I say it is simple. Anybody can understand it. Non-Christian people beyond the seas, the little children of our own household, untaught men on the street who know nothing about philosophy and science, men also who have heard many doctrines and read all sorts of books and who are all at the four winds in their thinking—all these can come to Jesus and follow Jesus.

And I say also that it is an exacting condition. It is far more exacting than if it were nothing more than an affair of agreeing to a theology or signing a creed. For it is moral and spiritual. It touches men where they really live. It has to do with the manner in which they behave in their families and in their daily business, as members of society and as citizens of the state. I suspect that just here lies the reason why so many rich men nowadays are putting their money into propaganda in the interest of a type of religion that lays stress on things to be believed rather than on a life in Christ to be lived. They deceive themselves into thinking that they are religiously safe and sound, if only their creed is correct. But according to the teaching of Jesus what counts eternally is one's personal relation to Christ and one's obedience to the message of the Master.

Studying, then, the implications of the great passages from the lips of Jesus which we read at the opening of this discussion, we see that two things are involved: (1) Whosoever would be Christ's disciple must take him as his Teacher; and (2) he must do more than this, he must take him as the Lord of his life.

1. The true disciple must take Christ as the Master of his thinking. This ought to go without saying. For the word "disciple" in the New Testament is just the Greek that means *learner;* and the word "master" is just the word that means *teacher.* If we are Christians, Christ is Teacher and we are learners in the school of Jesus. And what a teacher Jesus is! He did not say many things, but he said much. He did not lay down minute rules for the guidance of life, but he enunciated great principles and taught comprehensive truths. God is our Father and the Father of all men. All men are the children of God and all men are our brothers. True religion lies not without, in form and ceremony, nor in legal obedience, but it lies within, in the heart that loves God and loves all men as the children of one common father. It is found among those who are poor in spirit, and meek, and hungry for righteousness, and merciful toward the sinful and unworthy, and pure in heart and clean in mind, and among the peace-loving and peace-making disciples of Jesus. The great end and aim of Christ's disciples must be the building of the Kingdom of Heaven here on earth, the bringing in of that new order of society which Jesus came to establish, in which God is loved and

served as Father and men are loved and served as brothers. This is the kingdom we are commanded to seek. It is for this that we pray when we say, "Thy kingdom come, Thy will be done on earth as it is in heaven."

And the teachings of Jesus are sun-clear. They make their appeal immediately to the soul. To see their beauty, to confess their authority, it is only necessary to be a human being with mind and heart lying open toward God and the truth. One does not need to argue for the beauty of a rose, or for the compelling power of a sonata, or for the grandeur of a sunrise. Beauty, music, sunlight—all make their direct and immediate appeal to all normal men and women. And just so with the teachings of Jesus. All men bow before them. They speak a universal language. As John Stuart Mill said, "Nor would it be possible, even for an unbeliever, to find a better translation of the rule of virtue from the abstract into the concrete than to endeavor so to live that Jesus would approve his life."

2. The true disciple must do more than this, he must take Christ as the Lord of his life. Just here we touch a point that is essential to true Christianity. For Christianity is more than obedience to a teaching; it is love and loyalty to Jesus as living Lord. Here, as has often been observed, lies an important distinction between Christianity and all other religions. Other religions offer a teaching; Christianity presents Christ. The religion of the Old Testament offers the teaching of Moses and the prophets.

111

Buddhism offers the method of Buddha. Confucianism offers the teachings of Confucius. But Jesus offers himself. Browning comes exactly to this point:

> What is the point where himself lays stress?
> Does the precept run, "Believe in good,
> In justice, truth, now understood
> For the first time"?—or, "Believe in me,
> Who lived and died, yet essentially
> Am Lord of Life"?

It is exactly here that Christ does lay stress. His claims are the most exalted. His demands are the most exacting imaginable. "Come unto me. Take my yoke upon you. Learn of me." No other teacher, nor any founder of religion, ever made such claims as these. And again, "Deny yourselves. Take up the cross and follow me." The condemned criminal, sentenced to die, was made to take up his cross and carry it out to the place of execution. Christ, it will be remembered, had his cross to carry, but fainted under it. To follow Christ, carrying the cross, is to follow Christ with the rope about our neck, as we should say today, ready to die for Him at any time if need be.

When Christ speaks, we must obey. It is nothing short of marvelous how Jesus lays upon men his compelling power, the power of his masterful personality. Matthew leaves his tables as a collector of taxes, and Peter forsakes his trade as a fisherman, and the rest give up all and follow him—and still they followed him when the way led to prison and scourging and torture and death. He declared that all authority was his, and they rejoiced in calling themselves the bond-slaves of Jesus. It was not because they had become convinced that he was divine, that they did this. It was not because he had first taught them that he was the Son of God. Rather in discovering his authority they found out that he was divine. He had made himself the Lord and Master of their lives, and thus they came to see and know that he was indeed the Son of God. And precisely so does Christ win his way to our hearts and lives, exactly in this way does he come to his dominion over our lives in this twentieth century. To use the words of Dr. Dale, "It is not because we first believe that he is divine that we acknowledge his authority over our moral religious life; it would be truer to say that in discovering his authority we discover that he is divine."

III

If now we have accepted Christ's one condition of discipleship, there will follow certain blessed consequences. There will come to us a satisfying Christian experience, and there will come also a spiritual understanding of the fundamental realities of our religion.

1. This is the assurance brought us in the words from the lips of the Master which we have been quoting again and again, the assurance of a satisfying

Christian experience. He who meets Christ's one condition shall have the experience.

It will reward us carefully to study the great paragraph with which the eleventh chapter of Matthew concludes: "At that season Jesus answered and said, I thank thee, O Father, Lord of heaven and earth, that thou didst hide these things"—these spiritual truths concerning the Kingdom of Heaven—"from the wise and understanding"—from men wise with the wisdom of this world and versed in the lore of the scribes—"and didst reveal them unto babes"—these simple, childlike disciples, whose ignorance was their salvation as thereby they escaped mental preoccupation—"yea, Father, for so it was well pleasing in thy sight. All things have been delivered unto me of my Father; and no one knoweth the Son save the Father; neither doth any know the Father, save the Son, and he to whomsoever the Son willeth to reveal him." And then follow the words of the gracious invitation, "Come unto me all ye that labor and are heavy laden, and I will give you rest."

Note carefully that this is not first of all a message to the sorrow-laden, not first of all a message to those to whom sickness and loss and death have come. Jesus has been talking about the knowledge of God and assurance of spiritual realities—things hid from the scribes and Pharisees and revealed to the open mind of childlike obedience. He goes on to show that there is perfect knowledge of the Son on the part of the Father and perfect knowledge of the Father on the part of the Son. It is the knowledge of the Father made manifest in and through the Son that has been revealed to Christ's obedient disciples. It is for the want of this that men "labor and are heavy laden." For there is no burden so heavy as the burden of truth sought and not found—God sought and not found. There is perfect knowledge between the Father and the Son because there is perfect moral sympathy between the Father and the Son. Moral affinity is always necessary to the understanding of personality. Only the holy can know the holy. Only through the door of moral kinship can we come to the knowledge of God. On the basis of this great spiritual law, Jesus calls to men laboring and groping in the darkness and heavy laden with substitutes for the inner experience of reality, "Come unto me. Take my yoke upon you. Adopt my principle of living. Put your life in harmony with mine as I am in harmony with the Father and the Father in harmony with me. And ye shall find rest unto your souls. As I know the Father, so shall you come to know the Father. And with that knowledge shall come abiding peace."

In different language, the same principle is set forth in the words quoted from the Fourth Gospel, "If any man willeth to do his will he shall know of the teaching." There is no other way. *"Obedience is the organ of spiritual knowledge."* I say, there is no other way. Forms and ceremonies may assist, but they assist only as they help to bring us into harmony with the divine, into moral sympathy with God. Credal statements may help, but they are of service

115

only as they lead to action which enables us to surrender to him who is beyond the creeds. And often forms and ceremonies sadly hinder—we may wear ourselves out substituting form for reality. And creeds, too, often stand in the way—we may fall into the fatal error of supposing that Christianity is an intellectual system to be accepted, rather than a moral and spiritual life to be lived in harmony with Christ. When two musical instruments are in one room, when they have been put in harmony the one with the other, if then the musician touches the chords of one of them, from the chords of the other music made by unseen fingers may be heard softly flowing. And even so, when our lives and hearts have been put in tune with the spirit and teaching of Jesus, then within ourselves will be heard the same music which filled his soul with peace—the peace of God which passeth understanding.

2. And another consequence will follow the life of obedience. We shall come into possession of a creed which is at bottom correct.

To demand a correct creed as a condition prerequisite to the beginning of a life of Christian discipleship, is manifestly to demand an impossible thing. For in a truly Christian sense, *no man can be said to believe a thing until he has interpreted its significance by experiencing its power.* "No man can say that Jesus is Lord but by the Holy Spirit." As soon, however, as the soul comes into touch with Jesus, he is always called "Lord." All creeds of lasting value and power have been born out of Christian experience. "The deity of Christ cannot be proved either to the man on the streets or to the sage in the chair—but only to the evangelical experience."

A story out of the life of Horace Bushnell is instructive just here. He had been converted from almost universal skepticism. He had resolved to do God's will, and the knowledge of God had come to him in the way of personal experience. But still there were many things that remained dark. On one occasion, after returning from church, he came into a room and throwing himself into a seat with an air of abandonment, and thrusting both his hands through his black, bushy hair, he cried out: "O men! what shall I do with these arrant doubts I have been nursing for years? When the preacher touches the Trinity and when logic shatters it all to pieces, I am all at the four winds. But I am glad I have a heart as well as a head. My heart wants the Father; my heart wants the Son; my heart wants the Holy Ghost —and one just as much as the other. My heart says the Bible has a Trinity for me, *and I mean to hold by my heart*." Exactly so! The great truths of religion are primarily truths of the heart.

And in just this way did the first followers of Jesus come to their understanding and interpretation of their Master. Simon Peter followed him as a disciple. He took him as his teacher. He was to him the greatest man he had ever known; his teachings were to him the words of eternal life; his works were the manifestation of the mightiest personality he had ever been associated with. Gradually there grew in

Peter such a passionate devotion to Jesus as was never given to a man. Thus it came about that Peter saw God in him. And when, after a while, Jesus asked, "Who say ye that I am?" Peter was ready to answer, "Thou art the Christ." And John, who had been a disciple of the Baptist, had felt strangely drawn to Jesus. Through his devotion to him and a spiritual kinship which drew him to the center of the inner circle, John became the Beloved Disciple. In that closer intimacy Christ was so revealed to him that in later years when he would tell what he thought of him, he took over the best language that Greek philosophy had and wrote, "In the beginning was the Word, and the Word was with God, and the Word was God. And the Word became flesh, and tabernacled among us, and we beheld his glory, glory as of the only begotten from the Father, full of grace and truth."

The theology of Saint Paul also is the theology of Christian experience. It was as the spiritual and heavenly Christ that Jesus revealed himself to Paul on the Damascus road, and it is always as the spiritual and heavenly Christ that Paul thinks of him. Paul's great Trinitarian benediction, "The grace of our Lord Jesus Christ, and the love of God, and the communion of the Holy Ghost be with you all," is distinctly a formula that came out of his experience. The history of the progress of revelation through a growing experience of God, is seen in the "grace of our Lord Jesus Christ" who was the gift of "God's

118

love" and through whom there comes our conscious "fellowship with the Holy Spirit."

It has become the fashion nowadays to discount and discredit the great creeds of Christendom. We have been told that they are nothing more than Greek metaphysics imposed upon the simple Christianity of the primitive Church. As a matter of fact, the great creeds of Christendom came out of the great experience of early Christians. Men think in terms of a great theology when men greatly experience the things of the spirit and when men greatly believe. That the theologians wrote in terms which we find hard now to understand, need not surprise us. They were speaking the language of their own time, and the early creeds of the Church are just the setting forth of the realities of religion in the profoundest philosophy of the day in which they were written. In the light and under the power of a profound Christian experience, these men were giving intelligent interpretation of the facts of divine revelation in terms of the best thought of their times. There is nothing fixed and final about the language of creeds. The *truth* that is in them is final; the experience that they seek to set forth is an experience open to Christians today. James Denney speaks profoundly when he says that "they ought to be *sung* rather than *signed*." They were born out of Christian experience, and they are of lasting value to us only when with true feeling we are able to sing about the spiritual realities to which they bear witness.

119

But the point which I had wished to make is, that just as the creeds were born out of experience in the early centuries, so today a genuine experience of religion will lead men truly to interpret the things of the spirit; and while we may fail entirely to make men religious by insisting that they shall first of all become orthodox, we shall never cease to have a church orthodox in all essential particulars, if now and always we seek first to make men religious. Religion does not necessarily flow out of strict orthodoxy; but essential orthodoxy always comes out of the evangelical experience of salvation through Christ.

Coming back for a moment to the point of our departure—the one condition of discipleship which Christ lays down, how simple it is and how plain, especially after we have listened to the confused and confusing voices of the age we live in! The element of emotion is not to be overlooked in religion. But emotionalists have presented a type of religion which cannot appeal to men interested chiefly in things ethical. It is to be feared that in many instances men brought up under the influence of this type of religion, have either delayed beginning the Christian life, waiting for some tide of emotion to sweep them in; or have turned away from religion as not interesting itself profoundly in the way human beings must live in this world. On the other hand, there are those who have presented Christianity as primarily an intellectual system. With them believing in Christ has been made to mean the acceptance of a theology concerning him. And honest men have hesitated because they could not accept the theology. Over against all this, how simple and appealing are the words of Jesus, "Come unto me all ye that labor and are heavy laden and I will give you rest." "If any man would come after me, let him deny himself and take up his cross, and follow me." "If any man willeth to do his will he shall know of the teaching." Surely no Christian church and no Christian teacher should lay down any condition other than Christ's one condition of discipleship! We say, then, with our Quaker poet:

> Our Friend, our Brother, and our Lord,
>   What may thy service be?
> Nor name, nor form, nor ritual word;
>   But simply following thee.

CAN THE CHURCHES UNITE?

Dean Ritchie is a native of Scotland, born in 1864, trained in Edinburgh University and in the University Divinity Hall for Theology. Ordained to the Congregational ministry in 1890, his first pastorate was at Dumferline, whence he was called, after six years, to be successor to Dr. Jowett at St. James' Church at Newcastle-on-Tyne; a church of which I have happy memories. In 1903 he became Principal of Nottingham Theological College, where he labored for seventeen years as teacher, author, and executive.

After the World War—during which he served as special lecturer for the University Commission of the Y. M. C. A. in France—Dr. Ritchie came to Canada, drawn by the hope of Church union, and by the fact that four colleges, Anglican, Congregational, Methodist and Presbyterian, were working together as one. He is now Dean of the United Theological College of Montreal, where his genius as teacher and preacher is dedicated to the service of a united Church, in whose fellowship he rejoices and whose spirit he seeks to interpret in the sermon here to be read.

Can the Churches unite? The answer is that in Canada they have actually done so, working together not upon the basis of a dogma to be argued about, but in a fellowship in which the riches of each become the spiritual inheritance and treasure of all. It is a demonstration, to which America cannot remain indifferent, that the brotherhood of religion is the first step toward the religion of brotherhood.

CAN THE CHURCHES UNITE?

D. L. RITCHIE, D.D.

DEAN, UNITED THEOLOGICAL COLLEGE, MONTREAL

Till we all attain unto the unity of the faith, and of the knowledge of the Son of God, unto the measure of the stature of the fullness of Christ. Ephesians 4: 13.

I

A Church, or the divine society, is native to Christianity. Where the Christian life is, we expect to find the Church as we expect to see heather in Scotland, palms in Egypt, or maples in Canada; it is indigenous to the soil.

First, Then, Note Clearly That the Christian Faith Implies a Church. I am not unmindful that scholars have raised the question whether the Lord ever used the word "church," or whether the thing itself ever came within His purview. Certainly, it is not thinkable that any of our modern ecclesiasticisms ever did. But for practical purposes, none of these things matter. The divine society is contained in the seed of the Christian life, and just as assuredly as human life means a social order of some kind, so a Christian personality presupposes a Christian fellowship—a Church—in some form or another. Society is necessary to personality. Moreover, the wealthier we

125

would have a personality become, the richer in the true things of life must his society be. All these things are plainly written in our modern thought and may now be regarded as elementary truth.

The people who think that they can have the abundant life of which our Lord speaks and at the same time be heedless of Christian fellowship in worship and work are talking foolishly. They can have given no serious thought to the things of which they speak so glibly, as they criticize existing churches, and dream that the Church is an effete institution. If churches as they exist are unworthy, Christian people have no choice but to set about and make them better, or fashion other and better forms of a Christian society; and the sooner they learn the fact the better for themselves and the churches.

Moreover, if our Lord did not use the word "church" or utter its commission as set forth in St. Matthew's narrative of the Cæsarea Philippi incident, he did something more significant, he called to himself a band of disciples and lived with them in holy fellowship that they might know and receive the divine life, and have wherewith to witness and communicate to others. That was one of our Lord's originalities. He chose a circle of companionship; He founded a Christian college; in short, He instituted a Christian society—a Church—so that He might do His work of bringing them, and, through them, other men, into the unity of the faith, to the knowledge of the Son of God, to be as one man in Himself. We must have done with playing with

words and trifling with quibbles; we must handle the
substance and abiding reality of Christian things.
The main question here is not a matter of words
spoken or written, but the vital question of the inevitable issues and the abiding authority of the Christian life and its facts. The Christian life carries in
it the idea and power of a Church. The Church is an
inevitable outgrowth of the Christian life.

II

*In the Second Place, Consider St. Paul's Concep-
tion of the Christian Church.* The Pauline conception of the Church is that of a body vitalized by
Christ's spirit. It is an organism created and sustained by life; without life we cannot have it. Men
work with organizations which they build and into
which they put power; God works with organisms
that have power inherent in them. We cannot know
spirit apart from body; we do not know life except
in, and through an organism that expresses it. We
cannot even think of spirit, or life as disembodied.
But a body may be diversity in unity; not a phantom-
unity, invisible and unrealizable as some suppose
when they speak of Christian Unity, for the New
Testament knows nothing of a unity that is not realized and seen; it is unity in a body of which St.
Paul speaks. True, it is not a uniformity, not even
mere oneness, but a fellowship, an active relationship
of divers members, seen working harmoniously as a
corporate unity. To use St. Paul's own beautiful

word the sound of which seems to carry with it its
sense of a harmony in living relationships, it is a
"koinonia." And surely, Paul's teaching here is
a photograph of Christian experience. Wherever
Christian life is energetically at work, the Christian
Church is a corporate fellowship.

It has to be acknowledged that when St. Paul
comes to the thought of the Church as the embodi-
ment of the Spirit, he takes to himself eagle's wings
and soars into the empyrean of spiritual truth, where
with undazzled eye he sweeps vast horizons and gazes
steadily at them in the white light of God. The
great human unity already exists in Christ, he says;
but it is growing and being enriched all the time. It
is at once a fact and a prophecy, an existence and a
process; a gift and a goal. But even now, it is the
commonwealth of the redeemed that bears the true
witness to the unity of all mankind. That will be
completed only when the unity of the faith is realized in the knowledge of the Son of God, and the perfect man has come.

True it is, that "the perfect man" of St. Paul—
"the measure of the stature of the fullness of Christ,"
in his own exuberant phrase, tries the somewhat
clogged and maimed wings of most of us, for we are
such inveterate individualists, self-sufficient in our
isolation, that we cannot readily grasp that corporate
oneness of men in Christ, and of Christ with His people. But the meaning, if hard to realize, is clear
enough. Christ is incomplete until His Church, a
corporate unity, is united to Him, the Head, by the

one life, as in one man. That is the "far-off divine event to which the whole creation moves" and which the Spirit of God would hasten, so that the Kingdom may come. Our individualized Christianity, in a measure true, quickly becomes an impoverished thing, and arrogant in its poverty, when, in self-sufficiency as persons or sects, we isolate ourselves from the other members of the body and fail to draw life through the wealth of the corporate whole. A limb with a structure impeding the full tide of life in the body, cannot fail to atrophy and wither into palsied uselessness. That is the fate which, sooner or later, overtakes all mere sects. But there are also the results on the body as a whole. And the Church of God in the world today is proof of how alarming these results can be. The Church is divided and the Kingdom of God among men is checked and stunted in its growth. It lumbers along and tarries.

III

Mark Therefore the Contrast to St. Paul's Vision in Churches Today. In the light of all this, with its appealing truth and glowing vision, what about the divided Church of Christ in the world today; especially what about our Protestantism, shattered and dismembered into powerlessness with its gaping wounds crying aloud for healing? What about the sects which, in the blindness of spiritual and social arrogance, un-church one another as if God's sunshine took any notice of their barbed fences, or God's gracious rain was restricted to their exclusive ecclesiastical paddocks? In the light of New Testament teaching, and of vital Christian experience, and of the one thing that matters—the manifestation of Christian life among men—can there be anything more ridiculously futile, and, if it were not so calamitous, more utterly preposterous and laughable than the assumed superiority of the sectarian spirit even unto un-churching one another in the name of Christ. It is a comfort to think that He that sits in the heavens can laugh; otherwise, in impatience, He might destroy us all. His endless mercy is abundantly seen in that He bears with, and waits for, the repentance of his silly children. What we all need to learn is, that ecclesiastical posturing and strutting is not Christianity. It is not enough to say that it is at least conscientiously done, for men, especially Christians, are responsible for an enlightened conscience. "If men, being evil, know how to give gifts unto their children, how much more will the Heavenly Father give His Holy Spirit to them that ask Him." But our divisions and bickerings are proof of the absence of that Spirit of Christ. Born of human pride and ecclesiastical folly, they are evidences of human littleness, and only give occasion to the unsanctified to blaspheme and for the saints to mourn.

Granted that for the most part the sects once had significance, for one cannot forget that some of them are witnesses to neglected, vital truth, which, failing to find room for expression within the wider Church, broke away to find place to live and work; yet, where

130

today is the need for their continuance in town and village and even scattered countryside? Is there one living issue that separates the majority of them? Is there one vital truth that would suffer if they were to merge their forces into one Protestant Church? Is there one necessary witness concerning Christ that would not be borne if they were to seek a unity of faith in one body? Considering the needs of the world, is not the plain call of Christ that they should do it? Not faith, but tradition; not truth, but stubbornness; not principle, but prejudice and personal idiosyncrasy are keeping them apart. With a little of that humility and brotherly love which the Apostle teaches as necessary to the life of the body, the barriers would disappear and the "isms" of self-assertion, if not of a willful pride, fade into insignificance.

The tendency today as taught by the Spirit is manifestly away from the musty ecclesiologies inherited from the past and kept alive largely by traditional sentiment—to the central reality in Christ Jesus, in whom men find life and God through brotherhood. Men want the Gospel that quickens, sustains, and enriches personality and society with the divine life; not a creed to be argued about, but a reality that meets the needs of daily experience, and which is a living power in thought and life. More and more, they refuse as Christian men to parade in the dead issues of yesterday. They want a Christian life and a Church that are the surest things they know and the greatest treasures they possess. So, that for them, the best Church—the Holy Church—

is that which most worthily expresses that life and ministers that treasure.

Of course in this regard, there are other things to be taken into account: temperament, tradition, early religious training, social contacts, personal predilection for a type of building or service, or, even the attraction of a minister. These things determine for many people their attachment to a church; and the whole situation raises the question whether there can be a Comprehensive Church inclusive of a variety of Church "order" and services. Rome, with her usual skill, within her unity has much variety to meet the needs of her children. Why should not Quakers and Ritualists be able to live in the same church, if not in the same congregation? Both of them are ritualists in their own ways. Cannot Congregationalists and Episcopalians merge their differences to serve their Lord? If fixed on a common center—the Lord, the Life-giver—why cannot they permit differences like spokes from the hub of a wheel to run out to meet a variety of temperament and training in the one circle of truth and life? Such a proposal may be too much for human nature, especially for some types of Protestant nature, but is it too high for the Christian spirit? Is it not the duty of Christian men to come to the unity of the faith in an increasing knowledge of the Son of God. Dare they rest content with present conditions while so many are straying from the way and missing the gate of life? Whence comes our own impoverished life? From our divisions. Whence come our futilities in service?

From our divisions. Whence comes our failure to win the world? From our divisions, rending Christ's body, so that the world cannot see and know him as Saviour. Why cannot we have the unity of the faith in a Comprehensive Church that excludes no one that calls Jesus "Lord"; so that we might give the purpose of God a chance in the world.

IV

Now Note the Chief Causes of Division. When we come to the idea of a Comprehensive Church, the questions that are at once raised are those of "faith and order"; and experience abundantly proves that more insuperable difficulties arise in regard to the second than to the first. The central things of faith can be held together, but on the outposts of "order" we squabble and disagree, and part company. The pity of it! For at the highest, "order" is the second, not the first. Before the disorder in regard to "order" can be removed, Churches must learn to be loyal to truth. Christian scholarship must no longer be used to underpin and buttress the tottering theories of yesterday, and with ecclesiastical logic to maintain manifest error; it must be used to build Christ's Church on the bed-rock of faith, truth and fact. Only yesterday, the churches with strange and contradictory theories of inspiration, on Biblical authority wrote and spoke of "order" as if it were fashioned on the pattern made on the Mount. Today, we see that Church Governments at best are Divine Utilities

133

and Divine Expediences—Divine, in so far as they express Christ's spirit and do the work of the Kingdom of God, expediences, in that they have grown up in the midst of the ages fashioned after the pattern of things round about them. Scriptural authority can no longer be claimed for any of them; to say so is to deceive the unlearned, and that is a base, as it is a cruel thing to do.

We all, doubtless, but our Episcopal brethren especially, must awake to the truth; for their best scholarship from Alford through Lightfoot and Hatch to Gwatkin, Headlam and Inge, has fearlessly told us the facts. The last, for example, declares that their doctrine of Apostolical Succession, one of the greatest barriers to unity, is a mythical theory. Of course that is saying nothing against Episcopacy as a Divine Utility, a *bene esse*—a help to the well-being of the Church, through which God makes his will prevail. But in the New Testament, it is not, and cannot in common sense be, the *esse*—being or essence—of a Church. There have been, and are, other Divine Utilities in the form of Church Governments, which so plainly have done and are doing Christ's work in the world that their abundant fruits of the Spirit, demonstrating that they have in them the sap of the true vine, are ocular contradictions of any theory of only one specifically and divinely ordained channel of the Holy Spirit? So clearly is it so that all talk about covenanted and uncovenanted mercies, regular and irregular "orders," the specifically appointed and the mercifully recognized methods of work, is trifling in the presence of God's urgencies speaking in facts. Cannot these Church governments get together, first acknowledge one another, rejoicing that Christ has deigned to use any one of them, and all of them, to express his life and build up his Kingdom, and then see what can be done without hurt to anything but tradition, and prejudice born of sentiment, to unite them in one Comprehensive Church?

Is not the Conference to be held at Lausanne prophetic of the fact that God's Holy Spirit is moving his Church towards that goal? Surely two of the great hopes of the world are the League of Nations and the Lausanne Conference of Churches, both of them seeking unity and good-will among men, and, in the long issue, both of them born of the Spirit of Christ. Why? ask non-Christian peoples, why among Christ's brethren should there be so much disorder over the question of "order"? Can it be because the mistaken ambition of the sons of Zebedee still lives? When the tide recedes from a rocky shore, it leaves behind many pools, rock-girt in isolation; but, when it flows, all pools and barriers are blotted out in the leaping, laughing, conquering waters. The greatest need of the Churches is a tide of the Spirit.

In different parts of the world, and repeatedly in tense circumstances, I have seen how differences of race, nationality, and church "order" all disappear like ice in the sun when Christian men gather in the glowing presence of their Lord. Men generally discover unity when humbled at his feet. There, Christian men of different races and nations will be more to one another than even non-Christian men of their own nationality or race can be, for there is a unity of the faith in the knowledge of the Son of God in whom all middle walls of partition are broken down. At such times hearts run together as one in Christ Jesus; and are not these the great hours of revelation and of life, when questions of "order" all disappear and the glow and unity of faith alone remain. On the other hand, I can never forget after a long day's conference on matters of "faith and order" at Lambeth Palace, in the waning light of evening I put to a distinguished and greatly revered bishop the question: "Is there then not a common faith?" only to receive the discouraging answer: "Yes, and no! On nine points we agree, but the tenth is vital." To him all the others evidently depended on that one and were construed through it. To me it was only a matter of "order"; and one left feeling how near to and yet how far from one another Christian men can be at the end of a discussion. But in all charity was not that answer building a great wall of separation that is not of faith? Was not that erecting barriers that the sunlight of grace refuses to recognize? Is not that to straiten the Holy Spirit of truth and love? In the light of Christian experience, surely "order" is the second, not the first; and, moreover, is it not of the same experience that the second should serve the first, and not the first the second? "Order" is for the good of faith; faith is manifestly not de-

pendent on "order" but on the Holy Spirit that uses
many members for the good of the body.

v

Lastly, Consider the Healing of Christ's Body.
The first step to be taken is that in every Christian
Church Holy Communion at the Lord's Table should
be thrown open to all who devoutly seek to show
forth their Lord's death and have vital fellowship
with him in the communion of saints. Who in the
name of their "ism" has a right to exclude a disciple
from that feast of love? To what a miserable sect
such exclusiveness reduces a church! If it is the
Lord's Table every Christian has a right to be there;
of course, if it be only a sect's table, presence or absence does not matter. Then there should be exchange of pulpits among churches with duly ac-
credited and fittingly trained ministers. Exclusiveness here should be only on grounds of personal
fitness and not of ecclesiastical "order."

Even in the matter of faith's confession must we
not go back to simplicity of expression before we
can realize and restore unity? Has the Faith in coming down the centuries and through the generations,
like a great snowball, not gathered in its course many
things—mere débris—that are not of itself? Does
not the history of doctrine prove it to be so? Must
it be said that it is impossible now to get rid of such
accretions? Some say that for a basis of unity we
must get back to the creeds of the first six centuries,

others would be content with the formulated faith
of the first four centuries. But why stop at the Sixth
Century or even at the Fourth, in seeking ground for
unity? Why make creeds coffins of the Holy Spirit?
To be a Christian and a Churchman is it not enough
to have the Spirit of Christ? Even the Apostles'
Creed is a growth in the midst of controversies from
its beginnings in the Christian Benediction. Cannot we get back to the latter as the necessary expression of faith? Is it impossible for Churches to
agree to work together on a creed as short and as
sufficient as: "I believe in God the Father Almighty,
and in Jesus Christ his only Son our Lord, and in
the Holy Spirit of truth and love"? Is not that the
vital faith of a Christian, expressing the life that he
knows in the Lord?

Certainly it was by getting things into their true
perspective that the Churches in Canada with separate standards and traditions—Congregationalist,
Methodist, Presbyterian—were able to unite happily in one great Communion. Through necessity as
well as by choice they had worked together, only to
discover that the things that divided them were not
of abiding faith, but were concerned only with old
controversies and matters of order out of which all
sap of life had gone. Most of their differences, fit
only for a historical museum, were being kept in use
at great cost by sentiment or controversy. They
soon discovered that in things vital to faith they were
not far from one another, and set themselves to prepare a "Basis of Union." True it is that the sub-

stance of the Catholic Creeds are embodied in that document, but the demand made on members and teachers of the United Church is, that they should be "in essential agreement" with its doctrine. There it stops. "In things essential, unity; in things doubtful, liberty; in all things, charity," is the spirit of the new Church; and so it moves happily forward to conquest in the things of the Spirit. Its only peril at present is that it should fall into the hands of leaders without the grace of mental flexibility in things secondary, or that even do not matter.

So far, in questions of "order," there is liberty in local congregations, coöperation in Presbyteries and authority through the Council. The United Church of Canada rests on loyalties rather than on legalities, on the Christian conscience rather than on ecclesiastical compulsions; on the presence of the Spirit, and not on the pressure of the letter of its legislation. Its members rejoice in that they are members of a Christian Church, unshackled by any of the old "isms" and free to venture forth with its Lord to find treasures in things both new and old. Cannot the great experiment be repeated and extended? Among many diversities Christians can find a unity of faith in the knowledge of the Son of God. Why do they not show ostensibly to the world that they can? Is that not the urgent duty of the hour?

One thing is as clear as sunlight can make it in the teaching of the New Testament: unless the eyes of men and churches are turned to the unity of the faith, to the knowledge of the Son of God, they are not in the way of the Spirit; they are turned from the purpose of their Lord; they are thwarting the end for which he lived and died and lives for evermore. The vision that St. Paul had of Christ and his people as the Head and the Body—manifesting one corporate life, is surely a purpose worthy of God in creation and redemption. It is the incarnation of himself in a perfected humanity, the filling to the full with the harmony of life all that has known human breath and has aspired to the full reach and measure of humanity's stature. That has been the dream of all the saints; it is the purpose of God in Jesus Christ; it is the work of the Holy Spirit in and through the Church; it is the Kingdom of God for which all creation groans. "O Lord, how long, how long?"

In these spacious, gracious days, ministers go from one Church to another as from room to room in one House of God; and that is as it should be. Sectarian walls are so broken down as to permit the passage of a tourist elephant with baggage, for which let us give thanks. When Dr. Nixon left a professorship in the Baptist Theological Seminary in Rochester—the chair honored by the genius of the late Walter Rauschenbusch, of blessed memory—to take the pulpit of the Brick Presbyterian Church in the same city, no one thought it unusual, much less revolutionary.

To a great and noble Church—rich in lovely friends and happy memories, as I can testify—Dr. Nixon brought gifts and training of an unusual kind, and his ministry has been a triumph. No man among us is more searching in his insight, and none more forthright in his speech, as witness his sermons on *A Modern Christian Creed,* as well as his articles in the *Atlantic Monthly*—such as "The Dilemma of an Evangelical" —in the *Christian Century,* and other journals. Few men of the American pulpit promise more for the leadership of faith in a difficult time.

The sermon here to be read appeared as an article in the *New Republic,* and is a plea for the adoption of the spirit of intellectual inquiry as a Christian virtue; at the same time asking the intellect not to disregard the inner vision, too often put aside as "mystical stuff," remembering the wise word of one of old, that "God may be gotten and holden by thought never, but by the sharp dart of longing love." As a survey of the religious situation, both in its assets and its liabilities, the sermon is worthy of a long and deep pondering.

BRAINS IN RELIGION

JUSTIN WROE NIXON, D.D.

BRICK PRESBYTERIAN CHURCH, ROCHESTER

Thou shalt love the Lord thy God with all . . . thy mind.
Matthew 22: 37.

I

All religions face a judgment day. Confronted by
the challenge of novel situations they either die or
change and grow. A vital religion thrives on crises.
The dead elements of its tradition disintegrate, but
the living elements unite with creative aspirations in
the soil of a new age to produce a harvest of faith.
The situation of Protestant Christianity today is
critical enough to determine whether in truth it is
a vital religion. To the eye of the historian, the
decline of ecclesiastical instutions in western civilization has been apparent since the religious wars
of the seventeenth century. The metaphysics of the
Church is alien and forlorn in the new universe of
science. Its ethical precepts, adapted to a handicraft
culture, give us few clews to the solution of large
scale problems in an industrial era.

European Protestantism has settled down into a
rather precarious status as an inherited cult. In

143

England, the subjection of the working people to the factory system has been accompanied by their estrangement from the Church. In America, the grip of Protestantism is most tenuous where the influence of science and industry has been most profound—upon the intellectual class and the urban proletariat. Even the farming population, the stronghold of Protestantism, reveals, according to Fry's sample studies, a decline in church attendance of fifty per cent. during the last generation. The churches are disturbed about the situation. They federate in local and national unions. They make alliances with education and entertainment to attract the masses. They stir up controversies in the effort to find the theological Jonah, whose elimination will take the curse off the ship. Certainly as far as Protestantism is concerned the decision whether it shall become a plastic organization of growing life or remain the hardened deposit of a spent enthusiasm cannot be indefinitely postponed. Something fateful is happening.

When a difficulty is as deep seated as the one which threatens the future of Protestant Christianity, it can hardly be removed by external adjustments. No campaigns or revivals of the usual type, no gestures of good-will exchanged by scientists and religious leaders; no compromises by the custodians of tradition will resolve this crisis, for it originates within the souls of men. It is the very substance of religion that is changing. What is the nature of this change? The answer to this question leads us directly into an inquiry concerning the nature of re-

144

ligion. We hazard no definition when we say that religion is a very ancient and amorphous experience of the race. Its earliest manifestations were perhaps those feelings of curious and fearful wonder which came over primitive man in the presence of inscrutable power. With these original emotions, emphasized by Goldenweiser, Marett and Söderblom, have been blended in transient and permanent union many others.

The essence of religious evolution has been the changing variety and strength of the impulses of human nature which function within the religious "complex." Economic want, sex hunger, national ambition, racial hatred and human sympathy have in turn been organizing forces among the "sacred" moods of the soul. The most salutary change in the history of religion was that wrought by the Hebrew prophets when under the stress of a precarious national existence they were able to introduce the higher moral aspirations into an area hitherto preempted by ceremony and tribal custom.

The transformation in the nature of religion which is taking place in our time is hardly less significant than that which occurred in the days of the prophets. The characteristic and constant factor in this transformation is the growing coöperation of religion with the eager and curious energies of the mind. The intellectual revolution which began near the close of the Middle Ages, after conquering other areas has swept over the barriers which divided reason from faith and knowledge from revelation. Not since the eighth century B.C. has religion faced the possibilities of so radical a change. Then, confronted by the peril of national disaster, the Hebrew prophets were able to bring the higher morality under the egis of religion. Today, religious leaders are trying to bring intellectual creativity under the same sanction. As religion was remade once by the intrusion of the ethical it may be remade again by the intrusion of the intellectual. The discovery of divine implications in the humane spirit saved religion once. The discovery of a sacramental meaning in the scientific spirit may save religion now.

Whatever the outcome either for the mind or religion, their conjunction in our time makes vivid and unmistakable the most fateful question in our present spiritual situation: Shall the impulse of intellectual inquiry be accorded religious recognition?

II

The issue we have just raised appears everywhere in the activities of religious men. They cannot meet the problems of their lives, personal or institutional, without the methods of intellectual inquiry. Haltingly, but inevitably, the Church invites the coöperation of the psychiatrist in her cure of souls. She suborns the educator for the instruction of her youth. She maintains her institutions by employing the most effective financial technique. Even when passion runs high as it does on the question of Prohibition, the Church cannot refrain from asking,

Brains in Religion

"What are the facts?" The report of the Federal Council of Churches is the answer. In theology, morals and management, the Church betrays an open or secret collaboration with the spirit of research characteristic of our age. Will she now bring this spirit within the chancel and invest it with sacrosanct authority?

The answer to this question is sufficiently doubtful to divide the opinions of the most intelligent as well as the most religious men. There are leaders of science who believe that the intellect offers religion a shirt of Nessus in which the faith of mankind will wrap itself to its doom. There are religious scholars who confirm this view by asserting that religion in the past has been able to maintain itself only by keeping the intellect at a distance. In the Cathedral of Durham there is a spot in the floor which marks the point beyond which women might not advance as they approached the shrine of St. Cuthbert. So with the inquiries of the mind as they approach the subject of religion. The sphere of the intellect is limited within the edifice of a faith which enshrines an ultimate mystery. But the mind is not satisfied with this subservient rôle. One hundred and fifty years of success in securing for man control of the forces of nature have made it aggressive and revolutionary. Once admitted to the scene of man's spiritual drama, it seeks the center of the stage, recasts the plot and criticizes freely all the other impulses of human nature which have a part in the play. Man himself does not know whether the entrance of the intellect upon this dramatic spectacle brings promise or peril. It would seem to bring both.

The promise which the intellect makes to the soul of man in return for being allowed to deal with the problems of his moral and spiritual destiny is the promise of progress. It says in effect: "I will install the principle of progress in the very heart of religion. See what I have done in other realms. Medicine, technology and education were static until I came. Wherever I go progress follows. Without my coöperation religion tends to petrify in conservatism. Its changes are merely reactions to change in the aspects of life where I am at work. The trouble with religion is that only rarely does it obey its own injunction to love God 'with all thy mind.' When religion followed the prophet of Galilee who invited all men 'to come and see,' it moved forward with the step of youth. Its eyes greeted a wondrous dawn. The great moments for religion have been just those moments when religion has come back to the raw experiences of life and has surveyed them in company with a free mind. Then religion has imparted the contagion of that 'early morning feeling' which Zimmern says was the secret of the Greek genius. Then the mind has cut back the dead branches of tradition and the sap of spiritual desire has flowed out into fresh green forms. Youth has flocked to the standard of an imperial adventure. But fear has gotten the better of faith and religion has ended by exchanging the word 'inquire,' which was the message of Jesus, for the word 'accept,' the symbol of ecclesiastical bondage. Is it any wonder that 'the shades of the prison-house began to close' and that 'the vision splendid' dies away 'into the light of common day'?"

Can any one doubt the poignant and alluring character of this appeal? No one doubts it who knows anything about the temper of youth. Only a moving, purposeful, growing and adventurous religion can have any sway over spirits that dare the untried ways of a new and better world. For such men the only choice that remains is a progressive religion or none at all. The future of the Church in its relationship to those who will soon be responsible for the development of our culture is dependent upon its answer to this appeal of the mind. Why not close with this appeal? Why not invite the mind to prospect freely in the realm of religious experience? Suppose it does stop work in areas where men are taking out the low-grade ores of superstition, it will open up veins of truth far richer in the promise of righteousness and joy. The advantages seem obvious, why hesitate?

With great issues of our civilization at stake on the venture, it would be a tragedy if religious aspiration and intellectual research should fail to achieve an understanding. For past failures in this critical adjustment religion has borne the major portion of the blame. The sins of its history are numerous and glaring. But does the intellect come off scot-free of all responsibility for dividing the soul of man? If its self-confidence is not wholly invulnerable may it not profit by a few suggestions?

The mind, for instance, as it operates in this area should be aware that it incurs the very obligation it seeks to impose upon religion—the obligation of growth. It will have to face many paradoxes. It will have to reconcile many anomalous moods. It must be synthetic as well as analytic. It must adapt its tools to its materials. Its methods cannot be taken over without change from other realms of investigation. Measurements, for instance, will be valuable, providing the student knows what he is measuring. But let him first ask himself if he understands that word of the great English mystic, "By love he may be gotten and holden, by thought never." Let him wrestle with the meaning in that confession of Rabindranath Tagore's: "I saw God, not with fleshly eyes but with the inner vision from those Himalayan hills, the holy land of Brahma." If Tagore is too Oriental, we submit the conviction of a western intelligence, that of Beatrice Webb, who assures us that "it is by prayer, by communion with an all-pervading spiritual force that the soul of man discovers the purpose or goal of human endeavor." If our student turns impatiently from this "mystical stuff" and says, "Let us get down to questions and hard facts," may we remind him that it was Socrates, the greatest questioner of history, who stood in a trance for twenty-four hours on the field of Potidæa and who found in that experience the hard fact upon which he built a career of purifying and saving the souls of men. It would certainly be one of "life's little ironies" if the effort of the intellect to explore religion were defeated by a zeal which is "not according to knowledge."

We may urge also that the intellectual approach to religion ought to be motivated by sincerity. The student of music ought really to enjoy music and the student of religion ought really to believe that there is something precious in the spiritual experience of man. Mere intellectual curiosity devoid of sincerity does not distinguish between cargo and ballast. A devotee of spiritual nudity, it gives sardonic advice concerning the apparel of the soul. It laughs at the toppling shares in the market of the world's faith because it has no investments at stake. The impulses in human nature, moreover, which urge on scientific effort are marvelous in their promise, but when they are at the mercy of others which express hatred and political aggression, you have such a catastrophe as the recent slaughter of mankind. There are no "pure" instincts, and the value of any impulse depends upon the context of motives in which it appears. If the impulse of intellectual curiosity and invention coöperates with a healthy love of activity, with a desire for experimentation in the concrete and with a decent respect for ordinary human nature, it may greatly enhance the richness of religious experience. On the other hand, a distaste for action, a religious interest which is limited to the esoteric and the bizarre and a contempt for the human "herd" may create out of the questionings of the intellectuals

151

a flight from reality as marked as anything in the pages of Freud and Jung.

Another aspect of the situation which the mind faces in its contact with religion may be stated in a somewhat allegorical form. Under the stress of a precarious civilized existence the spirit of intellectual curiosity and invention has come to sit in on the councils of the soul. It finds there many impulses of man's nature. There are ancient fears as old as man himself, born with him in the darkness of the primeval forest, suckled on its mysterious silences and fed through the ages by shadowy hands reaching from the unseen and the unknown. The soul often ignores them but in the hour of crisis they reassert themselves. They are difficult to understand and to control. There are old loyalties at the council board, bred of primitive conflicts, the pressure of the huddling herd, the feuds of family and clan. There are the humane aspirations of mankind, the children of the prophets. The great hopes and deathless longings of the race are there as well as the forebodings, the craven wishes, the fantasies whose spells lure the soul into the false security of a world of dreams.

Into this council chamber of religion where so many impulses of human nature have found a place for weal or woe, comes in our day the impulse of intellectual inquiry. For ages it has been shouting through the windows at the councilors, mocking their ignorance, disturbing their judgments and occasionally offering them sage advice. Now this spirit, angel or demon, according to your point of view, has won its way within the sacred pale. What will it do there? Will it despise the runic wisdom of those who have been long at the council board because they cannot speak in a modern tongue? Will it strike dumb the old loyalties which clung to the soul and saved it alive when all others had forsaken it? With ribald laughter will it slaughter, along with the ancient fears and fantasies, the hopes and longings by which the soul has held its own thus far in its conflict with fate? Will it, in a final act of treachery, open the citadel of man's soul to the pagan lusts and vast despairs which a sterner morality and a cruder faith have for generations held without the gate? Or will the spirit of intellectual inquiry come in to appreciate the old as well as to make a place for the new? Will it seek his best gift from each of the councilors at the board so that no values may be lost, no rich experience filched from the hard won treasury of spiritual achievement?

Upon the manners as well as upon the methods and the motives of this spirit of curiosity and invention depends the fate of the ancient council chamber of Mansoul and of the civilization whose arch of security rests upon the twin pillars of religious aspiration and intellectual research.

III

The pivotal fact, accordingly, in the present critical situation of Protestant Christianity is the intrusion of the spirit of intellectual inquiry into the deepest moods and purposes of the religious life. If the intellect is cast out from the councils of the soul organized religion has a doubtful future. It may continue as the source of compensatory experiences, supported in static communities by tradition, and in more dynamic communities by extraneous attractions. It will not organize our culture or give it perspective. The main currents of spiritual life will flow outside its rigid forms. The dysgenic influence of its creeds will operate with increasing certainty to isolate and displace from leadership the very men who could integrate religion with the nobler quests of our civilization.

If the intellectual spirit remains within the scope of the religious interest, if it is viewed as an expression of the divine, if "the ardor of the thought" becomes "one of the Christian virtues," risks worthy of the venture may be incurred, but religion will be fertilized by "the powers of the endless life." Many abortive and sterile forms will come from this union. Liberalisms, non-propagating and dilettante, will arise to make their proud boast of enlightenment and then to perish. Ultimately a hardy and prolific type of religion must emerge, carrying in its seeds both the precious inheritance of the past and the promise of variation and progress in the future. It may be as early Christianity was, least among the herbs of the field, but in the end its leaves "shall be for the healing of the nations." To live for the coming of such a religion is to participate in the messianic hope of our time.

WILL MEN EVER FOLLOW JESUS?

A Japanese student said recently that the strange thing about Jesus is that one cannot get away from him. Something in him pursues us, haunts us, demanding a decision, one way or the other, as to his teaching and his way of living. No one of us but feels ill at ease if he feels that Jesus is on the other side of any issue: he will not let us go. He is here, in the world, like leaven in a loaf; once there, always there—nobody can get it out. Either the way of Jesus is the one way to go, or his gospel is a fiction too fair ever to have been true in the past, and too frail ever to come true in the future.

Such is the challenge of Jesus to our generation, felt more keenly by the young men of the pulpit today than ever before in the history of the Church; and by no one more keenly than by Dr. Tittle. In the first book of *Best Sermons, 1924*, he dealt with the tragedy of clashing loyalties, in which the universalism of Jesus stood over against the tide of narrow nationalism running in the wake of world war. Here, again, in a sermon as pitiless in its insight as it is passionate in its faith—searching us like a white flame—he flings the challenge of Christ in the face of our acrid orthodoxies and elusive liberalisms, as a rebuke to both.

God be thanked for a clarity of vision and a courage of heart to bring us back from futile debate about irrelevancies to the actual issue before our age. Two ways are set before us, either we must follow Christ or turn away from him. Both ways are difficult, but one is hopeless, and we dare not follow it unless we wish to resign ourselves to endless feud and final chaos.

WILL MEN EVER FOLLOW JESUS?

ERNEST FREMONT TITTLE, D.D.

FIRST METHODIST CHURCH, EVANSTON

Follow thou me. John 21: 22.

There are three great needs of which thoughtful persons today are more or less acutely conscious. One is the need of faith in God. There are many things in this world which we could get along fairly well without. Indeed, the number of these unessential things is probably far greater than most of us imagine. We think we could not be happy without a certain annual income, and a certain domestic establishment, and a certain social position. But we probably could be, and would be, even in circumstances greatly different from those in which we find ourselves today, provided only that we could keep alive our faith in God.

But when faith in God goes, how vastly much goes with it. The thought that one is not alone in the world; the belief that there is, at the heart of things, an eternal goodness; the conviction that the universe is on the side of the angels, that there is "one far-off divine event to which the whole creation moves"; the hope that life does not end at the grave, but that

157

gallant spirits fare on ever there as here—all this goes when faith in God goes.

If, then, some man strikes an attitude and says that he, for his part, feels no very urgent need of faith in God, must we not write him down as one who has never deeply thought, and never greatly loved, and never dangerously lived for noble ends? The great skeptics have not struck any such attitude. They have rather said with Professor Clifford, "We have seen the spring sun shine out of an empty heaven, and felt the utter loneliness that the Great Companion is dead."

The second great need is the need of light on the question, How may we hope to make the most of our chance of life? Did not Tennyson give voice to the inarticulate longings of a multitude such as no man could number when he said,

> 'Tis life whereof our nerves are scant;
> More life and fuller that we want.

More life and fuller is what we want. But many of us do not seem to know how to get it.

Some years ago, Dr. R. J. Campbell, then pastor of London's City Temple, shocked a lot of pious persons by suggesting that even a poor, besotted drunkard is, in reality, seeking God. But would these same pious persons have subscribed to the statement that what a poor inebriate is seeking is the very devil? Does anybody consciously and deliberately seek the very devil? Does anybody do wrong because it is wrong? Does he not rather do wrong because, to his clouded and deluded brain, something that is evil wears for the moment the guise of a good?

It is good that men want, not evil. It is truth they want, not lies. It is beauty they want, not ashes. It is life they want, not death. The poor fellow who drinks his fifth whiskey and soda is not seeking a drunkard's grave. The poor girl who accepts the cheap and awful substitute for a good man's love is not seeking the ashes of a burnt-out heart. The conscienceless profiteer who grows fat on the misery of his fellows is not seeking the hell of loneliness that will inevitably be his. People who let themselves hate other people are not seeking the bitterness that hate involves. And it is, I suppose, only right to assume that people who by their economic or political policies bring on wars are not seeking to destroy their fellows. Certainly they are not seeking to destroy their own sons.

It is life we want, "more life and fuller." But we need to have some one tell us how to get it—some one who really knows.

A third great need is the need of power. Huxley is reported to have said that "it doesn't take very much of a man to be a Christian, but it takes all of him there is." Well, is it not a part of the glory of Christianity that it doesn't take much of a man to be a Christian—that "whosoever will may come"? The Christian movement began with some very humble peasants who, when they came to Jerusalem, were profoundly impressed by the tall buildings which they saw there, and could not believe that a day would ever come when these proud buildings would be left without one stone upon another. And never since the beginning has any great Christian movement hesitated to sweep into itself the humblest of the humble or the lowest of the low.

> Drabs from the alleyways and drug fiends pale,
> Minds still passion-ridden, soul powers frail!
> Vermin-eaten saints with moldy breath,
> Unwashed legions with the ways of death.

Christianity has never disdained to take them, provided only they wanted to be saved. It doesn't take very much of a man to be a Christian. But it takes all of him there is. And is not this, too, a part of the glory of Christianity?

There are, it is true, certain diluted forms of Christianity which ask of their adherents little more than the formal recitation of religious creeds and the formal performance of religious rites. Having said your prayers, you may find consolation in a little game of poker. Having been to church on Sunday, you may begin again on Monday to look out for number one. But the Christianity of Christ—what tremendous demands that makes! Not merely a right act, but a right motive. Not merely a clean record, but a clean heart. Not merely the first mile which the law requires and society expects, but the second mile which only an undiscourageable idealism will take you. Not safety first, but safety last, and adventure first—adventure for a better, kindlier world in which cruelty

160

and injustice shall be no more, neither shall there be oppression any more, nor hopeless poverty, nor preventable disease, nor industrial friction, nor international strife; for age-old wrongs and miseries shall have passed away. It takes all of a man there is to be a Christian, as every one knows who, in some luminous hour, has caught a glimpse of the total moral meaning of the Christian way of life. And so, a man's final need is the need of power.

Here, then, are three great needs of which many of us are acutely conscious. In the presence of heavy responsibilities, and occasional sorrows, and disappointments, and disillusionments, we need something to live on. We cannot live on bread alone. Can we live on anything less than faith in God? We crave life. O God, how we crave it—a little real happiness and warmth and color and beauty and peace! But many of us do not seem to know how to get it. We need light on the question, How may we hope to make the most of our chance of life? Nor is it light alone that we need. For many of us are not living in accordance with the light that we now have. We see the better—and do the worse. We become afraid of our own selves. We dread to think of what we might do under certain circumstances which may, almost any day, arise. We need moral reënforcement; not light only, but power.

And now, alongside of these three great needs, I want to place those words of the Master, spoken to a warm-hearted and impulsive, but weak and timid disciple, "Follow thou me." One of our living seers

has said, "When we go back to the headwaters of
the mighty stream of Christianity, we find, not the
formation of a set of doctrines, but the founding of a
new ecclesiastical organization, not the forging of a
new body of commandments, not the formation of a
new ritual, but a radiant and illuminating personality
who made God mean more than he had ever meant
before, and who exhibited a new quality of life altogether." Does not the salvation of modern civilization lie in the hope that men and women the world
around may be brought into sympathetic contact with
that "radiant and illuminating personality."

I

Here we are with our simply tremendous need of
faith in God. And here is Jesus saying, "Follow
thou me." If only we should follow him, would we
not become sure of God. In his thrilling little
volume, *On the Edge of the Primeval Forest*, Albert
Schweitzer describes the effect which Christianity has
on the mind of the native in Central Africa! "Christianity is for him the light that shines amid the darkness of his fears; it assures him that he is not in the
power of nature-spirits, ancestral spirits, or fetishes,
and that no human being has any sinister power over
another, since the will of God really controls everything that goes on in the world." If Christianity is
able to do that for black Africa, is it not also able to
do that for white America? May not Jesus Christ
become for us "the light which shines amid the dark-

162

ness of (our) fears"? May he not assure us that we are not in the hands of vast, impersonal, non-rational, non-moral forces which know not nor care when a good man dies, or a dear woman is tortured by cancer, or a little child is crushed beneath the wheels of a speeding car, or a defeated people are driven by vindictive and oppressive measures to despair?

Jesus certainly was no ordinary man. Judge him by that severest of all judgments—the judgment of time. Has he managed to live in the memory of the race? Aye, for nearly two thousand years! Has the advancing experience of the race outgrown him? No, it has not yet caught up with him. In some respects he was, inevitably, a child of his time. And he never claimed omniscience. But the accumulating experience of mankind bears ever more witness to the eternal truth of his moral intuitions and spiritual insights. He was—to say the least about him—incomparably the greatest spiritual genius whom the race of man has produced. His testimony in the world of spirit must be conceded to possess at least as much authority as the testimony of Beethoven in the world of music or the testimony of Michael Angelo in the world of art. Is it possible, then, that Jesus was mistaken when he said, "He that hath seen me hath seen the Father"? Is it possible that he who saw, with such astonishing clearness, the immutable laws of life, was the victim of a gigantic illusion as to the innermost meaning of life?

"Follow thou me," he challenges. And surely, in

our search for the living God, we can afford to follow him as we can afford to follow no other guide in all the world. And there is still another reason why, by following Jesus, we may hope to become sure of God. Tyndall, the great physicist, once frankly acknowledged that the hours when he doubted the possibility of immortality were not his best hours. It would, I think, be true to the experience of every one of us to say that the hours when we become unsure of God are not our best hours. It is not to be wondered at that many people today are unsure of God, living as they do, almost continuously, in the atmosphere of a cabaret, or of a stock exchange. What chance have spiritual values to reveal themselves to a man whose imagination is continually befouled, or whose main interest in life is self-interest?

No, when men live on some low plane where the lust of the flesh or selfish ambition blinds their eyes to life's greatest and most significant facts, God and immortality, if they think of them at all, may appear to be but the imaginary creations of a groundless hope. But when men climb to a higher plane where truth and beauty and goodness stand out clear and compelling; when they begin to care supremely, not for material goods, but for spiritual goods; when they begin to keep spiritual company with the best and bravest souls of the ages, then they know that Tennyson spoke truly when, summing up his own personal faith, he said, "There's a Something that watches over us, and our individuality endures."

Here you and I stand, with our imperative need

of faith in God. And here stands Jesus with his inescapable challenge "Follow thou me." What better could we do than climb with him those mounts of vision where life's greatest and most significant facts have a chance to reveal themselves?

II

Here, too, we stand with our eager desire to make the most of our chance of life—to extract from life every grain of its sweetness, every petal of its beauty, every drop of its joy. And here, too, stands Jesus, saying "Follow thou me." "What!" cries the timidity in us, "follow one who threw away his chance of personal preferment; who chose a course that alienated all the 'best people' of his country; who made himself of no reputation, and got in bad with the authorities, and died the death of a felon on a cross? Follow him in your quest of life? Never!"

But once in a while another voice gets a chance to speak to us, and says to us something very different. "Was Jesus a fool?" it asks, and answers, "No, it is you who are a fool; a fool to think that a selfish life will ever turn out to be a happy life; a fool to suppose that material goods are life's supreme goods, that what really matters is the kind of house you live in, not the kind of man who lives in your house; a fool to imagine that to exploit your fellows will give you greater satisfaction than to serve your fellows; a fool to conclude that the way to avoid tragedy is to avoid the cross."

Ernest Fremont Tittle, D.D.

In all our sanest moments, do we not know perfectly well that it is this second voice which is telling us the truth? To look out always for number one; to play safe, to run no risks even in the name of an ideal; to let one's course be guided, not by principle, but always by expediency; to turn back from the cross the moment it looms above the horizon; to live selfishly, safely, softly—that is not the way to make the most of one's chance of life. That is the way to miss every great experience which life has to offer. But to follow after Christ even when the path leads through some Garden of Gethsemane, and becomes a Via Dolorosa, and takes you to Golgotha—that is the way into the permanent riches of life!

And if one thinks, not only of his own happiness, but of the world's happiness, how urgent becomes the appeal of those haunting words "Follow thou me." Is there for the world at large any slightest hope for prosperity or of peace unless it becomes willing to follow him? If, for instance, Frenchmen and Germans go on hating one another, what hope is there for the economic recovery of Europe? What hope of peace in Europe? What hope of permanent peace anywhere in the world?

Hate is an atheist. It does not believe in God who is Love. It believes only in force, physical force—handcuffs and halters and gallows and guns. "String him up!" cries hate; or "Shoot him down!" And what happens? Under treatment dictated by hate, the criminal individual becomes only more of a criminal. When he leaves prison, if he is permitted to leave it, he goes out as Jean Valjean went, with his hand against every man. And, under treatment dictated by hate, a guilty and beaten nation merely nurses its rage until it becomes physically strong enough to stand up and strike back. All that hate does is to wreak vengeance upon the body, leaving the heart untouched and unchanged. Hate is not only an atheist. It is a fool!

But love! Sometimes it, too, fails. Jesus himself loved supremely twelve men—and one of them betrayed him. But love is the only method that has any chance of success. One might paraphrase a remark of Gilbert Chesterton's concerning Christianity, and say of love that it has not been tried and found wanting, it has been found difficult and not tried. In dealing with bad boys and bad men and bad nations, in how many cases has love been found difficult and not tried! But in the relatively few cases where it has been tried, it has worked wonders. Love, said Jesus, even your enemies. And a skeptical world has said, It can't be done. But now and then some Abraham Lincoln appears and does it. Then we know that what Jesus plead for is possible. Do we not also know that, at this present moment, it is the one thing supremely needed to put an end to misunderstanding and fear and strife, to heal wounds, restore confidence, create faith and give us a better, happier world?

Here stands a world in fear and want and sorrow and unrest. And here stands Jesus saying, "Follow thou me." Will it follow him? Is there any thoughtful person who does not feel bound to reply, It had better do so?

III

Here, once more, stand you and I with our undeniable need of moral reënforcement. And here stands the Lord of Life, saying, "Follow thou me." If we do follow him, will moral reënforcement be given us? Has the love of Christ given men power for overcoming? It has. It has turned drunkards into sober men, thieves into honest men, Pharisees into humble men, and domestic tyrants into kind husbands and fathers. It has enabled literally millions of human beings to climb out of mud and slime and selfishness onto glorious sunlit heights where their souls were washed clean by the winds of God, and their eyes were opened to the beauty of the world, and their hearts were sustained by deathless hopes.

And I, for one, do not believe that the love of Christ has become, in our day, a spent force. On the contrary, I am confidently expecting that it will become a more powerful force than it has yet been. When the full meaning of his gospel is made known to the world; when the good news of social salvation is proclaimed with as much passion and contagious enthusiasm as was the good news of individual salvation; when men begin to sing about the new Chicago as men once sang about the new Jerusalem; when they begin to pray for the coming of the city of God with as much earnestness as they once prayed for the

168

salvation of their own souls, then, I believe, the love
of Christ will become in human hearts a passion so
powerful that the gates of hell will not be able to
prevail against it!

THE CHRIST MEN CAN FOLLOW

Dr. Landone is a scientifically trained, spiritually minded layman, educated by private tutors and in European schools and colleges, who has devoted himself to research and service of many kinds. Fellow of the Royal Economic Society of London, he was lecturer at the Sorbonne in Paris, 1915-16, and was appointed the following year Envoyé Spécial des Amitiés Françaises to the United States by President Poincaré.

But his chief labor in life has to do with the higher economies of the soul, seeking to interpret people to themselves, that those who do not understand their own hearts may be happy and free. Such books as *Deep Down in Your Heart*, *How to Turn Ideals into Realities*, and his larger work, *The Success Process*, outline and expound his method of leading people to physical health and personal efficiency through culture of the spiritual life; whereof we have more than a hint in the sermon following.

Such a sermon will be richly helpful to many bewildered folk, confused by the criss-cross currents of religious tradition in our age. It is as practical as it is picturesque, and a layman in the pulpit evidently does not think it a sin to be interesting, the while he shows us a Christ we can follow and not a visionary Preacher of moral impossibilities.

THE CHRIST MEN CAN FOLLOW

BROWN LANDONE, F.R.E.S.

HACKENSACK, N. J.

I am the way . . . no man cometh unto the Father, but by me. Matthew 11: 10.

When Christ was teaching men how to live aright, did his prescience vision our modern conditions and the problems of our life; and in spiritually guiding us now, does he *expect* us to follow his teachings of two thousand years ago?

Would he, this morning, ask you to lay up no treasure on earth—to provide nothing for the morrow, to decline life insurance, to open no savings account, and to invest in no lands of increasing value? Would he enjoin you not to bother about earning money with which to buy clothes, but to trust God to clothe you as God clothes the lily? Or, if a burglar last night took seven dollars from the top of your dressing table, would Christ, this morning, command you to search for that burglar to give him also the hundred dollars which was hidden under your mattress?

Whether we attempt to live only the spirit of his life, or whether we try to make our lives accord with the literal interpretation of his teachings, we must

173

discover an ideal which we *can* follow—for if we profess an ideal which we know we cannot follow, we are spiritually dishonest. We are rich in ideals of Christ. We have many of them: Ideals of what Christ *is* to us, of what he *taught*, of what he *did*, and of how he taught others to *live*. Christ *is* our Redeemer, our Saviour, Lamb of God, Prince of Peace. Yet, we cannot "follow in his footsteps" to become the Redeemer of the world; nor its Saviour; nor the Lamb of God; nor yet the Prince of Peace!

We have ideals of what Christ *taught*, and yet as devout Christians we are confounded when a non-Christian asks, "If a gangster shoots you in the left leg, does your Christ teach that you should turn the right one so that the gangster may put a bullet in that leg also?" We have ideals of what Christ *did*— healed the blind, made water into wine, walked on the water—and yet we go to the oculist, prohibit the making of wine, and drown unless we swim. We have many ideals of the way Christ taught men *to live*, yet if you were ready this morning to start for mission work in distant Samoa, would you decline all support offered by our missionary societies, provide no money or tickets for your journey, and take with you not even an extra shirt or a clean collar?

Have not conditions changed so that Christ would not expect us to take off our shoes before entering the home of the friend who invites us to dinner this Sunday afternoon? Have conditions changed so much that Christ no longer expects us to follow *all* his teachings? And, if so, where shall we draw the line—what to follow, and what not to follow? We seem lost—for, after two thousand years of Christianity, we are confronted with the astounding fact that we have *no* ideal of Christ which can surely guide us in the changed conditions today.

There is a reason: We have studied *what* Christ did and what he taught, but we have never dared to answer the question, *"why* did Christ do what he did, and *why* did he teach what he taught?" In the pulpit, we avoid answering it, by saying that man is so stupid he should never attempt to comprehend the ways of God. Alone with it at night, we try to throttle it, or sneak around it in the dark. Never having met it courageously, we have failed to recognize the divine purpose which determined all Christ's acts and teachings—the purpose which would determine his way of life if he were here today, the purpose which should determine our lives now.

Although we seem so lost that we cannot decide whether or not it is possible today to live as Christ taught us to live, yet we know that Christ *does* expect us to follow in his footsteps! "I am the way . . . no man cometh unto the Father, but by me," is without qualification; "Greater works than these shall ye do," does not permit us to do less than he did; and "I am with you always" includes today as well as yesterday. Christ has commanded us, and our part is to discover *the* ideal which determined his way of life, and then so to live that our lives shall accord with that ideal!

Can we find the ideal we need in the thought of

today? The Fundamentalists assert that we can follow in Christ's footsteps by accepting him as our Saviour and by holding fast to the orthodox doctrines of the church. Yet, it is not enough to accept Christ as our Redeemer; we need also an ideal which will teach us how to live *after* we have so accepted him. As to orthodoxy, the New Testament reveals that Christ's teachings were opposed to the orthodox doctrines of his church, and that his activities were violations of its orthodox practices. Since Christ opposed orthodoxy, how can we follow in his footsteps by being orthodox?

If we turn to the Modernists for our ideal, they tell us that "following in the footsteps of Christ" is *a matter of diet*—a diet of new ideas. What they give us is sweet to the taste, soft to the palate, and easy to swallow. But they give us a diet of ideas only—for they fail to do the works of Christ. So, when we reach their pastures on the mountainside, they fail to provide the thousands of loaves and fishes, and give us only five thin sugar wafers and two tiny sardines.

And if we turn to the "truth scientists," for the ideal we need, we discover that they have reduced the living Christ to a diluted Idea (and man to a reflected idea), so that there is nothing for us to do but to *ideate!* This is not the Christ way of life! Christ working at carpenter work, or Christ comforting Mary and Martha, or Christ driving money lenders from the Temple, or Christ on the cross redeeming all mankind, is more than an idea!

The Christ Men Can Follow

If it seems impossible to find the ideal you need to help you follow in Christ's footsteps, *study the way Christ lived his life, in the light of the truth that our human types and our problems are similar to those of Christ's time!* Then, you will understand why Christ did what he did, and then you will know how he would live today, and how you should live.

Cease thinking that Samaritans, publicans, high priests, and Pharisees existed only in the long ago. A church member, who never misses a religious service and has never smoked a cigarette in his life, is a *Pharisee!* A protected grafter, who turns over a fixed sum to his district boss and keeps all that he collects above that sum, is a *publican.* And we would have a *high priest* of Christ's time, if we could combine a Supreme-Court-Justice and a Dean-of-Theology—born to position as a royal prince is born the son of a king. The *"cornfields"* of Christ's time can be likened to the apple orchards of our farmers, from which bad boys sometimes steal apples; *public houses,* similar to our restaurant-saloons before prohibition; and *"speaking in public places,"* the same as talking from a soap box at a street corner.

Recognizing that basic human problems are similar in all ages, and understanding the *terms* of Christ's time, we can interpret his life in terms of our life today, and comprehend what Christ did in the light of *why* he did it. This gives us a new ideal of the Christ, the ideal which I bring to you this morning. It is neither greater nor less than those ideals which we have cherished in the past, but it is the ideal which

177

we now need to guide us—the ideal which we *can* follow.

Christ is the Great Adjuster! This discovers the divine purpose which determined Christ's every act and all his teaching—for there was a purpose in all he did. His every act broke down some restrictive form of law, to reveal its spiritual intent. His every act *readjusted* the observance of some old law, so that it would meet the new needs of his time! There is no exception!

Religious worship is necessary to hold man's mind to the consciousness of God; and in Moses' time, when the tribes were wandering from one place to another, it was essential that some men should be responsible for the carrying of the Tabernacle from place to place, and should be prepared to conduct the services. Because of the conditions of his time, Moses appointed one family to consecrate its members to perform such service, and commanded all others to support this family.

Then two thousand years passed, and Christ came. Conditions had changed. Yet, priests were still chosen only from those who were "born of the blood," and no other human being was deemed fit to enter the service of helping others spiritually. Although this had led to arrogant and tyrannical rule from within the Temple, yet the idea of a "sacred family of priests" had become so fixed in the minds of the Jews, that they believed the priests when the priests told them that no act of life could be pleasing to God unless in accord with the regulations of the church.

178

The Christ Men Can Follow

So Christ threw aside the precedents of centuries. He adjusted the ideas of the Jews to a new ideal of spiritual leadership. Strolling by the seashore one day, he saw two fishermen. Crude men they were— and swearing perhaps, as our longshoremen swear— yet he chose them to become spiritual leaders. And again, passing the office of a grafter and extortioner —a cruel man—Christ turned to him, and said, "Follow me." And thus he chose another member of his group of twelve priests to carry his message to the world. In choosing his followers from fishermen, net-menders, and despised tax collectors, Christ led man's mind back to the truth that God made *all* men in his own image, not merely the family of sacred priests.

It was tremendous! It readjusted for all time the policy and practice of choosing spiritual leaders. It has changed the world—for it was this adjustment which opened the way for millions in all ages to accept Christ as their spiritual leader, although he was not a member of the priestly family! It doomed religious autocracy, and initiated spiritual democracy. Yet in making the adjustment, Christ did not break the spiritual law—for all men are made in the likeness of God. He violated only the church's orthodox observance of the law. He violated an observance of law to fulfill the spirit of the law—to lead man to know that every man born of God is fit to be consecrated to spiritual service.

There was a purpose in everything Christ did. Whether we study those acts of Christ which may

179

seem to us the more important, or those which may seem only incidental, we find that his every act was determined by the ideal of *adjusting* ideas and observances of laws of the past, so that their spiritual intent should be restored to meet the needs of men of his day. He threw aside the sacred traditions and orthodox practices which had come down through the years because they no longer met the needs of his time.

As Sunday is our rest day, so the Sabbath was the *rest day* of the week in Christ's time. Then as now good church members stayed quietly in their homes on the Sabbath studying the Scriptures, although Christ sometimes tramped the countryside. On one of his Sunday walks—accompanied by a number of friends, a hundred at least—he cut across a farmer's cornfield. Being hungry, his friends "helped themselves" to ears of corn, and began to eat.

Some church members, who were watching—watching, perhaps as the farmer watches for bad boys who help themselves to his apples—saw Christ's followers taking the corn. The church members were astounded, for the Sunday Blue Laws of Christ's time forbade the picking and eating of corn on Sunday! Since it was an "unlawful" act, they came out to question Christ about it. By his attitude and answer, the Great Adjuster cast aside their restrictive practices of keeping the Sabbath holy. He *adjusted* the ideas of observing the Sabbath, so that life on Sunday should accord with the spiritual intent of the law—reëstablishing the old spiritual Truth that the

The Christ Men Can Follow

Sabbath was made for man, not man for the Sabbath.

In the early days the ancient law was, "Keep the Sabbath day to *sanctify* it . . . Six days shalt thou labor and do all thy work; but the seventh day is the Sabbath of the Lord, thy God; in it thou shalt *not do any work*." To understand this Commandment, we must be spiritually honest. We must admit that we have no right to twist the meaning of the Hebrew word *qadesh*—the word which is translated to "sanctify" and to "keep holy"—so that its meaning shall accord with *our* ideas of today. *Qadesh* is translated *defiled, sodomite,* and *unclean* in other verses of the Bible. The word means *set apart.* That which was defiled was set apart from clean things; that which was holy was set apart from common things; the day of rest was set apart from the days of work. To "keep holy" the Sabbath day means to set it apart from the days of work.

In times of wandering tribes only a few men were patriarchal masters; all others were bond-men or slaves. God wanted his race to be free. For the masters, he decreed that they should free each other from debt every seven years; and that, if they had purchased slaves of Hebrew blood, those slaves were to be set free during the seventh year of service. For the bond-men, God ordained the Sabbath and set it apart from the days of work so that the workers should not be forced to slave for their masters seven days each week. *It was set apart to free man from the restrictions of masters.* It belonged not to the masters, but to God! It belonged to God, but was

181

set apart for the good of *man*—for God said, "Keep the Sabbath therefore; for it is holy *unto you.*"

By Christ's time, the spiritual purpose of the law had been lost. During the ages the church had built up so many rules of what man must do and must not do on the Sabbath, that the day had become a day of restrictive observances. Man was no longer free on the Sabbath. The church had so changed the day, that it seemed that man had been made to fit into the restrictions of the Sabbath, instead of the Sabbath being set apart to free man from restrictions.

So, Christ, the Great Adjuster, reëstablished the truth of the old law to meet the needs of man in his age. He restored the spiritual concept of the Sabbath as a day set apart, *not to bind man by many observances, but to free man from restrictions!* In doing this, he did not destroy the law, but *readjusted* man's ideas of observance, and fulfilled the law by revealing its spiritual intent. It was a church-rocking readjustment! It restored the truth that the "son of man is Lord (master) even of the Sabbath day."

If, tomorrow, you remember but one thought of this sermon, remember that Christ did not teach a life of restriction. He taught a life of joy! "These things have I spoken unto you, that my joy might remain in you, and that your joy might be full." While church members "disfigured their faces that they might appear unto men to fast," Christ feasted joyously. When asked, why his followers feasted at times when good church members solemnly endured

182

fasts, he replied in effect, "How *can* they fast and be sad, when *I* am with them?"

As in the past, so today Christ would teach joy. He might suggest that you study his New Testament. He might teach you as though you were little children, just as he taught others long ago—asking you to study some Greek words—*euthumeo* and *hilaros,* for instance. And, since it is the Greek word *hilaros* which is translated "cheerful" in the verse, "the Lord loveth a cheerful giver," he might ask you to be *hilariously happy* this morning as you drop your dollar bills in the collection plate!

Oh, he would shock us! He would probably shock us most by his teachings of a merry religious life and of joyful church services. He might come to this church to expound the Scripture—to explain that God *commands* us to worship him with happy songs and joyous dancing; he might cite the example of David, chosen of God, who joyously sang and danced in worship before the most sacred object of the ages, the Ark of the Holy of Holies. Yet, even if we listened with our ears and smiled approval with our lips, our hair would rise in horror, if one of our ushers should accept Christ's teaching of God's word, and joyously dance down the aisle with his collection plate!

Oh, how would Christ feel, if he were compelled to sit in one of these pews today, surrounded by your punctiliously solemn faces, and forced to listen to your pitifully pinched voices, singing hymns as though they were wails from within prison walls—as indeed,

I think they are—wails of your souls imprisoned in sinful solemnity! Would not Christ tell us that we need a *readjustment* of our concepts of God's love and joy, as much as the good churchmen of his time needed a readjustment of their ideas of religious life?

And, would not Christ readjust our ideas of wealth? We either worship it as the Golden Calf, or curse it as the root of evil. As to Christ's attitude toward our twenty hundred millionaires, we need not remain in doubt—for he painted a word picture for us, which tells us *why* he said, "Go sell all that thou hast and give to the poor."

The rich young man who came to Christ for advice, wanted a complimentary ticket to eternal life. He felt that he deserved such a ticket because he had never committed murder or adultery, had not stolen or borne false witness, and had not dishonored his parents or hated his neighbors.

Such a man needed a *readjustment* of his ideas of values, so Christ said, "Sell all that thou hast, and give to the poor . . . come and follow me." But the young man preferred to keep his possessions. He went away. He was sorrowful. Christ had led the rich young man to realize that he prized the wealth of his lands more than he treasured the wealth of his soul. To the Rockefellers, the Cleveland Dodges, and the Helen Goulds—and to all the other rich givers of great gifts for the advancement of world welfare and the support of religious work, Christ would *not* say, "Go sell all that you have and give to the poor." It would not be consistent with his life.

The Christ Men Can Follow

He himself had many wealthy friends among his followers.

Christ did not condemn possession of wealth. And those who attempt to interpret Christ's teaching by that of the apostle who wrote, "The love of money is the root of all evil," should frankly explain that the word which is translated "love" in that particular verse is *never* translated "love" in any other verse of the New Testament. It does not mean "love"; it means "lust"—it is the *lust* of money which is the root of evil; and Christ condemned the lust of keeping wealth without using it for the good of others, and the attitude which prefers the wealth of things to treasures in heaven. To such he would say today, as he then said, "A rich man shall hardly enter into the kingdom."

Christ taught that those who are first in matcrial wealth or wordly position may be last in spiritual worth; and that those who possess the least gold may possess the most spiritual treasure. He taught that things are not of primal importance. He did not teach his disciples that they should inherit eternal life because they had forsaken all things, but that they should be first, because they had forsaken all things *to follow him!*

Christ *readjusted* ideas of values—placing spiritual values first, saying, "Many that are first shall be last; and the last shall be first." And at another time, "Seek ye first the Kingdom of God, and his righteousness; and all these things shall be added unto you!" Christ was not the destroyer of values, nor of laws. He was the Great Adjuster. His one purpose was to *readjust* the religious ideas and practices of his day, so that man should again realize the primacy of spiritual values.

Of course, in the old days—when members of his race were sheep and goat herders, and when guests came from sheep and cattle paths—then, it was a *kindness* to take off one's shoes before one entered a home. But, with our swept streets, our concrete sidewalks, and our carpeted limousines, Christ would not insist that people today take off their shoes before entering a house. When there were no railroads, no fast steamships, no automobiles; when there were no chains of hotels; when each home on the road from one village to another was a haven of hospitality, at which each stranger was bathed, given fresh linen, and fed, *before* his name was asked—then, it was not necessary to provide oneself with raiment for a journey, or with money, or with script.

Since conditions have changed, and since every act of Christ's life and all teachings were strung on the divine thread of spiritual adjustment—since he cast aside the observances which were no longer needed in his day although they had been valuable in the ages preceding him—so today he would readjust our ideas of religious life. Christ is the Great Adjuster! This ideal we *can* follow. This ideal we *shall* follow. It is neither the ideal of the Fundamentalist, nor that of the Modernist—for the one asks us to do the impossible, and does not expect us to do it; while the other asks us to do little or nothing, and to do as we please about it.

Our new ideal is based on the fundamentalism of Christ. It has little to do with details—washing of hands, or praying of prayers, or brushing of teeth, or saying grace—but it embodies the purpose which *determined* Christ's way of life. The Fundamentalist insists that we must accept Christ's teaching literally word for word, although he knows that neither we nor he will attempt to follow such an interpretation. Our ideal differs: We can accept it, honestly intending to follow it; and it is an ideal which we *can* follow.

Moreover, our ideal differs from that of the Modernist, who asks us to destroy our old ideals, and then almost hints that—since one man's idea of what is right and wrong is as good as another's—we may live about as we please. The Modernist's ideal makes it easy for us to laugh while we slide through life, but it fails to inspire us manfully to march in Christ's footsteps.

Our ideal demands spiritual consecration. It is based on the modernism of Christ. It leads us to cast aside forms and observances when they obscure the spirit of the law, but to discard them only to uncover the spiritual truth which has been obscured. It does not destroy the old ideal, but—by discarding its form to reveal its glory—it inspires us. We can accept Christ's teaching literally; we can live not only in accord with its spirit, but live actually as he taught men to live—adjusting our present ideas to the old ideal, and living so that our lives today accord with that ideal.

We can adjust our *attitude toward wealth*—neither cursing the rich because they are rich, nor fawning and smirking like unmanned slaves before the rich because they possess great power. We can recognize spiritual value. We can value the man for the man's self—whether he is rich or poor, schooled or untutored, high caste or low caste. We can be joyously happy, whether seen with a greasy-handed mechanic in overalls, or with a society snob in spats.

We can readjust our ideals of *individual values:* We can stop valuing a person as a clothes peg—determining social acceptance by the number of suits or gowns he or she can afford to hang on such a peg in the course of a season. We can realize that the grandeur of an Eiffel Tower cannot compare with the majestic daring of the soul of a workman, three hundred feet up in the air, putting steel girders in place.

We can readjust our ideas of *service for others;* we can help the sick, instead of inquiring about their health; we can comfort a negro, as Christ comforted a Samaritan, knowing that we render thus a greater service than we do when we preach "do unto others, as ye would that they should do unto you." We can readjust our *public welfare efforts:* We can cease enacting laws to be applied on the outside to remedy the man within; we can trust the soul to manifest its own goodness, instead of blistering it with ethical plasters and poultices to "draw out its badness," or binding it with legal splints so that it cannot move!

The Christ Men Can Follow

We can follow the life of Christ *in our business world:* We can readjust our concept of man's values, as Carnegie did when he looked deep into the soul of Schwab when Schwab was an unschooled boy, carrying drinking water for working men. When Carnegie saw the spirit that was in Schwab, he did not hesitate because the boy lacked a technical label or the brand of a certified university. As Christ chose his followers because of the spirit within them, so Carnegie chose Schwab because of the spirit in Schwab. In this, Carnegie followed in Christ's footsteps.

We can cease being stupid *professional and intellectual snobs,* so that we shall never again refuse an instructor's position to a great Tyndall, or to a Huxley, merely because he had not at that time been tagged with a university degree. We can recognize that the mind of a Burbank knows more of biology than is known by a hundred professors of biology; and we can learn to listen prayerfully to a member of the plumbers' union, so that in time and with spiritual growth, we shall prefer the teachings of The Carpenter to those of the Divinity School Dean!

We can follow in Christ's footsteps, *multiplying our joys* a thousand times, by recognizing the divinity within the soul of every man. We can be rid of our unhappiness—for unhappiness is the result of the mistakes we make when we try to "select" associates, friends, and mate, on the basis of our assumed superiority. In itself, such a false assumption leads us to miss the joy that was Christ's—the joy which a consciousness of divine equality brings! Though

189

we have chummed with a few dukes and princes, chatted with a king or two, known intimately some of our great thinkers, and talked far into the night with a President or a Lord Chief Justice, yet we may find more originality of thought and more gladness of happy companionship in the soul of a milkman or the chumship of a chauffeur.

What a sad life Christ would have led if he had carefully "selected" his associates from among the university high priests, the rich elders, and the praying Pharisees! But, what joy to live with tumultuous Peter and lovable John! Happiness is a result— the result of recognizing divinity in the soul of every man, and barring yourself from none. As Christ redeemed the spirit of the law, to readjust the saddened life of his day to a life of joy, so we can readjust our ideal to accord with that of the Supreme Adjuster. We can follow in his footsteps—hour by hour, to fit joyously into the plan divine.

We have an ideal which we can follow—*"I send my messenger before thy face, which shall prepare the way before thee."* It is the ideal of the Divine Adjuster—*"I am the way . . . no man cometh unto the Father, but by me!"* Its glory shall lead us— *"And his face did shine as the sun!"* And we shall attain the goal—*"And they shall see his face!"*

THE VOICE OF SAINT FRANCIS

Dr. Hough here shows us St. Francis in the scenery and setting of his age, surrounded by the great personalities of his period: Abelard with his penetrating intelligence and magnetic temperament; St. Thomas with his genius for architecture in theology; Innocent III, who sought to make politics the instrument of the Kingdom of God; Dante, "the voice of thirteen silent centuries." Few men of the American pulpit could have given us so admirable an interpretation; few have such a sense of history.

In the first book of *Best Sermons, 1924,* a sketch of Dr. Hough appeared, with one slight error, I regret to say, making him a graduate of Union College, which should have been Scio College—later united with Union. Since 1924 Dr. Hough has given us several books, two especially rich, *Synthetic Christianity* and *Evangelical Humanism,* the last being the Fernley Lecture in London, 1925. One remembers with delight his castigation of Menckenism for its corrosive blasphemy, its advocacy of liberty as license without shame and without inhibitions, and its apotheosis of disease. The whole book is a joy, both for its thought and its art, which even Dr. Hough will not easily surpass.

If in his interpretation of St. Francis, the glamour of a saint of the order of poets has blinded him, somewhat, to the high, hard way which even a poet must walk to sainthood, it is a forgivable fault, so bewitching is the personality of Francis, so like what we fain would be, disinfected of the things that make us hateful to ourselves and others. One is grateful for such a sermon, in celebration of the year of the Poor Little Man of Assisi.

THE VOICE OF SAINT FRANCIS

LYNN HAROLD HOUGH, D.D.

CENTRAL METHODIST CHURCH, DETROIT

He being dead yet speaketh. Hebrews 11: 4.

The men of the present cannot be wise without remembering. They cannot be creative without hoping. They cannot be efficient without acting. And the art of remembering so that memory drips with the honey of a gracious wisdom is one of the rarest arts of a highly disciplined mind.

There were many mighty voices speaking in the Middle Ages. And often with a sudden sense of surprise we come to understand how deeply human and how permanently significant was their quality. There was the voice of Abelard, the author of *"Sic et Non,"* that curious compilation in which the opposite pronouncements of great church fathers are set clearly and unhesitatingly over against each other. It was a restless and penetrating mind which Abelard brought to the tasks of thought, and a warm and magnetic temperament which he brought to all human relations and experiences. Perhaps he deserves the tribute so often paid to Petrarch of being called the first modern man. There was the voice of Saint Thomas in whom erudition and mental power

193

and saintly character were happily and productively combined. The patient and thorough dialectic of the *Summa* will reveal how profound and how skillful was the mind of the Middle Ages when the garnered riches of the past were gathered into it.

There was the voice of Innocent III, that high and imperial Pope who bent monarchs to his will and whose earnestness of character was equaled only by his determination to make the Church the supreme moral and spiritual power among men, a power which would make politics themselves the instruments of the Kingdom of God. There was the voice of Dante. That dark and haggard face, those deep and piercing eyes belonged to a personality which at last became fully articulate in the *Divine Comedy*. The whole human experience of a thousand years was subjected to a moral and spiritual analysis of the most searching kind, and the tale was told with a passionate beauty in which the Middle Ages found their supreme literary expression. And when the rose of love and fire bloomed at the climax of the Paradiso one of the great insights of the human spirit had been expressed with complete felicity and power. It may seem less than fitting to speak of the voice of Gothic architecture. But it must be said that to the ear of the mind, which is far behind the eye, Gothic architecture has spoken with a voice which cannot be forgotten when once it has been heard.

Classic art had a kind of finality well symbolized by the circle. And classic architecture has the same restrained and exquisite completeness. There is a

perfect harmony, but there is no expectation. It is
like the period at the end of a sentence. Byzantine
architecture is well symbolized by the dome. It has
an imperial majesty. It is proud and strong and rests
heavily, very heavily, upon its foundations. It is the
spirit of a great empire, made visible in stone. But
in Gothic architecture building becomes Christian.
The pointed arch, and the flying buttress, the cathedral poised as if it has come down from above instead
of being built up from below, all the glory of aspir-
ing distances tell the tale of a building which expresses the very genius of expectation. The pointed
arch itself tells of perpetual aspiration always more
completely fulfilled and never perfectly satisfied.
That is the very genius of Christianity.

So arresting are the messages which come to us
from the Middle Ages. So haunting are its voices.
And among them all the most memorable, the one
whose clear, lovely quality carries farthest, the one
which carries in itself most surely the promise of its
own immortality, is the voice of Saint Francis. The
year 1182 saw his entrance into the world in the little
Italian hill city of Assisi. His father, a wealthy merchant, was away from his home when Francis was
born, and on his return insisted that the name Francis
should be given to his son. There was a gentle and
gracious mother who knew how to be silent and to
wait. And there was in the lad himself something
of the shrewd sagacity of his father, some sense of
the lyric music of life which may have come from his
mother, and a spirit all alive with the exhaustless

vitality which sometimes makes youth so splendid
and so hauntingly beautiful. The young nobles of
the city felt the charm of Francis as he grew up and,
more because of his gay distinction of spirit and his
bubbling happiness than because of the free hand
with which he spent the money his father gave him,
they became his constant companions. Francis
wanted all there was of the joy of life. He loved
France. He loved French songs full of grace and
beauty and hot impetuous passion. And he tasted
of the sweetness of every experience he could make
his own. One can scarcely claim for him the white
flower of a blameless life. But one can claim that he
came to the taste of ashes which indulgence leaves
with an honest sense of just what it really means.
He wanted to be a great soldier. He lay for months
a prisoner after one of the little wars of his period.
He wanted to be a great knight. He got no farther
than a brilliant equipment. Something was "gnaw-
ing at his heart half-hungrily, half-awake." Illness
came to him. Long, long thoughts took hold of him.
Was he in love? asked chaffing companions when his
mind quite left them in the midst of their revels.
Yes, he was thinking of a lady more wonderful than
any they knew. But how should he tell them of the
grace and loveliness of that lady Poverty who was
beginning to haunt his dreams?

One day, before the crucifix, the figure of the great
sufferer itself seemed to become articulate, and the
gay young wastrel, troubled by such deep strange
thoughts, suddenly felt that the Son of God himself

commanded him to build his church. He took it quite literally at first in the terms of stones and mortar. Francis was never of that company who escape from immediate responsibility by subtle figures of speech. His father was the complacent sire of a bright young knight of extravagance with whom the careless élite of the city kept company. But he was angry, indeed, to see the keen young business man with a touch of dissipation upon his face becoming a dreaming lover of piety, who turned his dreams into hours of labor for ruined churches. The struggle of wills was intense. For all the distinguished gentleness of his manners Francis could be very firm. With a dramatic Latin gesture he gave his very clothes back to the man who looked at him with such hard, cold eyes. Henceforth he would say, "Our heavenly Father." He found himself confronting the fastidious coward in his heart as he met a repulsive leper. He crushed the feeling and followed the leper, a loving friend. He sought lepers out and made every gracious quality of his a gift of vital friendliness to their bitter lives. And so he tasted that personal self-sacrifice which from the outside often seems so bitter and from within is often so full of the sweetness of gracious spiritual joy.

A gifted friend who carries about with him a subtle quality of spiritual understanding and sympathy once wrote to me, "Francis said somewhere that we praise the Saints, and justly so, but we do not realize the cost of sainthood. That is particularly so of Francis himself. His personality is so wildly fascinating because he was a saint of the order of poets, and the glamour of his genius hides from us the fact that he walked the same high, hard path that the humblest saint must walk in order to win his victory." Much of the tale of this inner discipline, of this battle in hours when the vision waned and only a stern steadfast loyalty held the lonely battler to his warfare, is of course hidden away in the heart of Francis himself. But through the singing wonder of his pilgrimage we do now and again hear the breaking voice from that austere and terrible struggle in which Saints are made, and we do catch glimpses of a prayer which repeats the very experience of Gethsemane. There are lovely vines with exquisite flowers and luscious fruit hanging upon the walls of that cathedral of the spirit which Francis built. But the walls themselves are of stone which has been quarried in hours of that agony of spirit when the strength of the soul is born.

Francis was all the while being watched by keen and critical eyes. He bore reproach and scorn with a kind of lyrical happiness. And as men watched him they felt something strange and deep tugging at their hearts. A capable and successful merchant surrendered to the subtle moral and spiritual appeal, sold his possessions for the poor and entered into fellowship with the strange and joyous young knight of Poverty and of Christ. The fellowship grew and by and by Francis, who desired above all things to live a life perfectly conformed to that of Jesus, found that he too had twelve disciples. The glory in his eyes,

the telltale splendor of his voice and the bright aston-
ishment of his life captured the mind and conscience
of a young Italian girl, and, as the event proved, some
central sources of character and power were released
when she and those who followed her accepted the
way of Francis. Always a loyal son of the Church he
sought the approval of the Pope, and that great per-
sonage, Innocent III, gave his favor to what soon
became a new order. All about Italy the new happy
singing spirit of poverty and service spread and soon
the whole continent of Europe felt new winds from
heaven blowing in its face. There was nothing too
difficult for Francis. He actually made his way into
the presence of the Mohammedan ruler against whom
a crusade was being conducted. He would have won
by love where others would win by war. And he did
succeed in winning the astonished interest and respect of the Islamic ruler and was allowed to come
away safely leaving strange thoughts of a beautifully
loving face and shining eager eyes and a voice full of
the tenderness of a great expectation behind him.

The joyous simplicity of the earlier years of the
order is a thing which leaves a perfume delicate and
lovely in the mind of every reader who understands
the tale. But what was a joyous and creative spirit
was gradually changed into a powerful, almost military, organization. Perhaps in a measure the change
was inevitable. But it fairly broke the heart of
Francis. He accepted the decision of his ecclesiastical superiors. But the light of the fellowship of
the Little Brothers in their first rapturous days was

the brightness for which his own heart ever yearned. At least he himself could be loyal to the dream of a brotherhood of utter simplicity and poverty which left even learning for one face which gave life its every standard, its every hope and its every joy. To him the supreme gladness lay in supreme endurance for the grace of Christ. And when, dying at Assisi, he ordered his poor worn-out body to be placed upon the ground, that sacramental touch of the friendly earth gave the last seal to a life which met every experience in utter simplicity with a naked directness which left no room for the protecting sophistries by which we make easier our lives. Even birds had gladly gathered about him. If they did not understand his words, they did understand his love. And it was more than a symbol when they sang rapturously above the spot where his spirit took flight. He left behind in the Church a powerful organization. He left in the human heart an imperishable dream.

In a new and different world we dwell. And strange new voices are those to which it has heeded. The voice of nationality has spoken in a fashion which Francis did not know. For in his days the Tudors had not witnessed the birth of the lusty consciousness of a kingly young giant in England, and Louis XIV had not given imperial grace and splendor to the national consciousness of France. Cavour had not planned and wrought out with the great leaders who stood at his side the unification of Italy, and Bismarck had not achieved the building into unity of Germany. The voice of machinery is a sound which would have been difficult and alien to Francis. And all the wheels and belts of the industrial revolution tell the tale of the making of a different world. The voices of highly organized production and transportation and salesmanship tell a story of the capacity and the power of the human spirit which even Innocent III could not have foreseen, though he, more than Francis, might have understood and sympathized with the quality of mind which made it possible. The voices of science telling their vast stories of the uniformities of the physical world and all the astonishing processes of the biological realms would have been simply beyond the mind of the Little Brother of Assisi. The masterful and rugged voice of labor he would have understood, for he knew the ways of privation and of lowly demanding toil. But a labor whose own gesture becomes imperial would have caused in his mind deep and anxious thoughts.

"He being dead yet speaketh." It may seem that Francis can have no message for this modern world. It may seem that he can have no power to capture its imagination and to haunt its dreams. But these strident modern voices are not quite so sure of themselves as once they were. Nationality has commanded glorious allegiances, and yet overwrought national self-consciousness almost tore hope out of the heart of the world in the tragedies of the Great War. The machines we have made have all too often made slaves of us. The spirit of the living creature has not been able to dominate the wheels. And sometimes we fear that altogether machines have become our foes and not our friends. The new knowledge has taught us how to be so preoccupied with forces and things that we forget the glory of self-sacrifice and the wonder of love. It has taught us how to produce chemicals which would destroy a great city in a few hours; it has not taught us how to live together in friendship and mutual understanding. Labor never forgets its rights—and God knows they must be made secure. But does it sometimes forget its moral and spiritual responsibilities? Can an imperial régime of Labor, based upon the doctrines of economic determination alone, bring peace or good or beauty to the world?

All these so tragic matters, which the experience of the years immediately behind us has made so unescapable, do make it abundantly clear that the modern voices leave us wistful and lonely. The golden word has not been spoken by any of these glittering figures which have made and broken the modern world. So we turn again to Francis, who knew the wonder of appreciation without exclusive possession, who knew the poison which so often lurks at the heart of the word "mine." We turn to the divine and joyous self-forgetfulness which heard the song of life like the sound of many waters in the midst of every experience of tragedy and pain. We turn to Francis, to whom the way of Christ was not like a distant sunlit mountain one could love but one might never climb, but rather an immediate and perpetual opportunity satisfying and glorious.

We are awed and humble as we stand before the

The Voice of Saint Francis

Little Brother who wedded Poverty. We have not, like him, completely made the great adventure. We have not, like him, traveled the road of Christ without hesitation, the whole of the way. Yet we cannot forget him. With a voice perpetually young and perpetually powerful he speaks to our spirits, and finds his way—a searching presence—into our minds and hearts. And as he comes we seem to see beyond him another figure, infinitely loving and compassionate and strong. Come into our world again, Little Brother of long ago. We need—ah! how sorely and deeply—to hear your voice. And we need, beyond the power of telling, to meet the Master who will walk with you when you come.

THE VISION SPLENDID

Rabbi Silver is one of the most picturesque and brilliant preachers of the Jewish Church in America. Born in 1893, educated in the public schools of New York, in the University of Cincinnati, and in Hebrew Union College, he was ordained rabbi in 1915. His first charge was with the Congregation L'Shem Shamayim, Wheeling, W. Va., whence he was called in 1917 to the rabbinate of The Temple of Cleveland, perhaps the largest synagogue in the United States; where, by his initiative, a magnificent new Temple and Religious School has been built.

During the World War, Rabbi Silver served abroad on a mission for the governments of the United States and France; and was decorated by the French government for conspicuous service. He is a member of the Executive Board of the Central Conference of American Rabbis, of the Board of Governors of Hebrew Union College, and of the Jewish Publication Society. He is also vice president of the Zionist organization of America, as well as a member of various boards of charity and public service in his own city.

In the following sermon an ancient ethical idealism—serene, luminous, authentic—flings its white light across the tide of our days and years, to consecrate and to command. It expounds the two profoundest desires of man, which together make the paradox of life: "May thine end be in Life Eternal, and thy hopes, may they endure throughout all generations." The glow of its vision and the glitter of its exposition are alike enchanting.

THE VISION SPLENDID

ABBA HILLEL SILVER, D.D.
RABBI, THE TEMPLE, CLEVELAND

Choose you this day whom you will serve. Joshua 24: 15.

We are told in sacred lore, that when their hours of study were over, and the wise men left the halls of the Academy, they departed from one another with the following quaint and beautiful blessing: "Mayest thou behold thy world during thy lifetime, but may thine end be in Life Eternal, and thy hopes, may they endure throughout all generations." On New Year's Day, we too take leave, not from one another, but from the old year, and from all that it held for us of good and evil, of gain and loss; and I know of no more seemly benediction which we can bestow upon one another at this hour, than this self-same prayer of the Rabbis.

If I were to bless you this day, between the dark and the dawn of the New Year, with the choicest gift in the treasure-house of God, I could think of none more rare and precious than this. It is three-fold benison, each part segment of a perfect whole: "Mayest thou behold thy world during thy lifetime." Is there anything more complete than this? To see our whole world while we live! The world of our

207

desires and the world of our hopes! To win every goal, to taste every fruit, to slake every thirst at the fountain of success. What a generous benediction this is! Surely this is what we pray for on this, our Holy Day. "Grant us life, long life; grant us health, happiness, prosperity, peace. Let us not die ere the last mile of our journey is covered and the last beautiful scene glimpsed. Permit us to see our whole world while we live."

And how thoroughly human a prayer it is! What man is there who would wish to close the fascinating book of life before the last chapter is read and the last page is turned and the story is fully told! Unless he be of those who have suffered much, whose eyes have been darkened by unutterable sorrow, and from whose hearts anguish has drained all love of life. We all wish to live, to see all, to know all, to taste all, to have all. The world is so resplendent with the works of God and the works of man, with the beauty that dwells in the earth and in the habitations of the children of earth. Our souls are hungry for this earth beauty and this life beauty, for all the wonder and grace which are in existence. How very human then is this prayer, and how truly it voices our deep-most longings. And yet, somehow, the wise men of old, who uttered this valediction, keenly felt its incompleteness, for they hastened to supplement it: "But may thine end be in Life Eternal, and thy hopes, may they endure throughout all generations." On the face of it, a paradox! If one could see his whole world in his lifetime, why should his end be in life

eternal? If one could realize all his cherished hopes
here and now, why should they be extended throughout all subsequent generations?

But the Rabbis, who saw life steadily, felt this
wish to be inadequate, because unattainable. They
knew that no man can see his whole world in his
lifetime, nor realize his high hopes in his generation.
But they also knew of a world which every man could
realize in his lifetime, and of a hope which every
man could see fulfilled. In the eyes of the Rabbis
there were two worlds; the world of our wishes and
desires, and the world which these same wishes and
desires create for us and in us. The world of our
dreams and hopes, and the world which these dreams
and hopes surround us with. In a sense every man
builds his own world. Every man constructs his own
world, his universe of wish and desire, the far-flung
constellation of passionate cravings and longings,
whose fiery center is self. The worlds of no two men
are alike. Some build their world of clay, of carnal
wishes and coarse desires. It is narrow, never extend-
ing beyond the reach of the senses. Others fashion
their dream-empires of finer stuff, of the needs of the
mind and soul as well as of the body. Theirs is a
larger estate, reaching out through spiritual roads
into distant worlds. Still others, who are caught up
by some vision and touched by some inspiration,
shape their worlds out of ineffable beauties, transcendent and measureless to man.

And each builder would like to see his dream-
world come true in his lifetime. But God, the

Abba Hillel Silver, D.D.

Master Builder, who has his own plan and his own architectural design, has so ordered his Universe, that none shall see his world fully realized in his lifetime, and that the finer and subtler the stuff the dream-world is made of, the more difficult shall it be of attainment. Even the clay-world is hard to attain. Low desires and earthly cupidity, even when satisfied, leave ashes in the mouth. Each fulfilled desire incites to others, stronger and more impetuous. "The sea hath bounds, but deep desire hath none." Passion means suffering. Until our hankerings are appeased, we suffer, and after they are appeased we soon weary of them. When we are in want, we strive for the necessities of life; when we have the necessities of life, we crave for comforts; when we have comforts, we crave for luxury. When we have luxury, we cry for the moon—a mounting fever of discontent, an endless cycle of futility. The Greeks called it "The Torments of Tantulus."

Difficult as the clay-world is of attainment, even more difficult is the dream-world which some men wish to see fulfilled in their lifetime—the world which is not circumscribed by the ordinary wants of life, the world fashioned out of the silver sheen of ideals and the gold of aspiration, the world patterned after the similitude of God's own perfection. The man who, conscious of his high estate, fashions such a world, and who, by his dreams, would lengthen the road between himself and the beast, and shorten the road between himself and God, the man who projects a wish-world of justice and peace, an empire of knowledge and love, of truth and beauty, that man will never see his world fulfilled in his lifetime. Such wish-worlds are eternities in the making. No single hand can effect them, no single generation can encompass them. Such dreams lead the dreamer, not to the goal of consummation, but to the pit and the dungeon, the rack and the cross, and all the miserable artifices of a world afraid of his dreams. Such dreams lead the dreamer along the dolorous road of frustration and loneliness, to death.

Many illustrations come to our mind when we think of this. Let us but choose two—an ancient and a modern one. Moses, a leader of men, built for himself a dream-world of heroic design—to liberate a people from the yoke of bondage—to give it a law and a land—to fashion it into a priest-people and to send it forth a messenger of a new revelation and a new covenant. Did he see his world come true? On the top of Mount Nebo, he died a lonely and a world-wearied man, his tired eyes straining to catch a glimpse of the land of his unfulfilled promise. He freed the people. He broke the chains of their body. He could not break the chains of their soul. He gave them freedom, they enslaved themselves. He gave them a law, they flouted it. He gave them a hope, they destroyed it. Where was his world?

And what became of the dream-world of that modern dreamer—Woodrow Wilson? Somewhere in the Capital of our land, there lived for two years a broken old man, alone with his memories, ruminating among the ruins of his shattered dream-world. He had visioned mankind healed and redeemed, made one in peace and freedom. He failed. During the early years of the great world struggle he sought to maintain neutrality. He failed. He gave his life blood to establish a covenant of peoples to enforce peace. He failed. He hoped for peace without victory, and failed. He hoped for peace with victory, and failed. He hoped that justice and comity would follow the Pentecost of calamity, and behold, violence and hatred everywhere. Did he see his world in his lifetime? He died even as his dreams died.

Our ancient sages knew the sorry plight of such world builders. They therefore added to their benediction this phrase: "But may thine end be in Life Eternal, and thy hopes, may they endure throughout all generations." The end is not here—cannot, should not, be here. A world which a man can achieve in his lifetime is unworthy of him—unworthy of the reach of his imagination, the chivalry of his spirit, the hardihood of his faith. Only such tasks and ambitions are worthy of us as lay bare the finitude of our bodies and the infinitude of our souls, the impotence of flesh and the omnipotence of spirit, the brevity of our days and the eternity of our dreams. Blessed is the man whose dream outlives him! Blessed is the man who is strong enough to see himself grow old and powerless while his ideal remains young and green. For then, old age assumes a dignity which compensates for our infirmities. The flame of life may burn low, but the holy incense of our visions will rise inextinguishable from the undefiled altars of our ageless souls.

In his picture of *Dorian Gray*, Oscar Wilde tells us of a young man, radiant and beautiful as a god, whom a great artist painted in the full splendor of his youth. When the man beheld the finished masterpiece, he burst into tears. "How sad it is," he cried, "that I must grow old. My face shall become wrinkled and wizened, my eyes shall grow dim and colorless, but this picture shall remain always young. Oh, if it were only the other way! If the picture could change and I could remain always what I am now!" His wish was granted. Throughout the succeeding years his picture—his dream-world—changed with the changes that came over him, while he remained unalterably the same. Through successive stages of degradation and shame, through sin and cruelty and vice, he remained the same, young and beautiful—but his picture—the mirror and reflex of his soul—took on all the ugliness, all the viciousness, and all the spiritual disfigurement which were his. At last the horror of the picture, the ghastly deformity of his dream-world, drove him to madness and to self-destruction.

This is the tragedy of one who wishes to outlive his dream, whose life-picture is tied up with that which is physical and transitory. When such a man grows old, he will have memories which will embitter his days; for all his glory will be of yesterday, and all his hopes as if they had never been. In the midst of life he is in death. Israel Zangwill, in his *Italian*

213

Abba Hillel Silver, D.D.

Fantasies, brilliantly sums up this truth. "He that dies in the full tilt of his ambitions is buried alive, and he that survives his hopes and fears is dead, unburied." And the ancestors of this brilliant writer, in their equally incisive way, declared: "The righteous are alive in death, the wicked are dead in life."

The world, then, of dreams and ideals which man creates for himself, cannot be, should not be, achieved in his lifetime. But the Rabbis knew of another world which they believed every man *could* and *should* achieve in his lifetime. It is the world created for man by his own ideals. It is built up of mental and spiritual reactions to those ideals, out of enthusiasms and exaltations which these very ideals and loyalties create within him. For the ideals of man give to his life a definite content and a definite scope which are his real world. This, then, was the meaning of the Rabbis: "May your life be blessed with the vision of a world so beautiful that it will crowd your life with beauty, even though the vision cannot be fulfilled in your lifetime. Life may deny you the world of achievement, it cannot deny you the world of poetry and romance and the rich savor of living which the very presence of the vision within you will create for you." Therein does the spiritual differ from the physical. The physical must be owned or consumed to be enjoyed, but we need not own or consume or realize our ideals in order to enjoy them. We enjoy them in the quest, and struggle for them, in our devotion to them.

An ethical book written by a Jewish mystic of the

eighteenth century tells a naïve and charming folk-
tale. There lived somewhere a lonely and pious Jew,
poor and forgotten of men, whose entire possession
in life was one single tract of the Talmud. He had
no other books. The pious man spent all his days
reading and re-reading this one sacred tract. It filled
his entire life, it became his world. He guarded it,
he loved it, he treasured it. When he died, so runs
the tale, this precious tome of sacred lore was trans-
formed into a radiant maiden of surpassing loveliness, who led this faithful devotee to the Gates of
Paradise. Quaint, is it not? But how profoundly
true! In similarwise did Beatrice lead Dante along
the terraces of heaven. For every high devotion,
for every transfiguring wish, or hope, or prayer, an
angel is born unto us to be our ministrant and
guardian.

Such is the potency of ideals. They give us a
whole realm of celestial beauty in which to live, even
while these ideals are passing through the tragic
stages of denial and frustration which lead to their
ultimate transfiguration. And such ideals are within
the reach of all men. One need not to be learned, or
highborn, or opulent, to have them. They are more
precious than gold—and yet the pauper may have
them for the asking. Some men have vast estates,
but they are lost in waste and weeds. Others have
a few square feet in front of their little homes, but
love plants a flower-bed there and a tree, and behold,
there is beauty and the dream of perfection.

The cobbler at his lathe may have an ideal of high

artisanship. He will see the charm of his work during his lifetime. The day-laborer who is conscious of the indispensable character of his work, the merchant who is faithful to his standards of service, the employer who finds in his office a challenge to unselfishness, the professional man who regards his calling as a consecration, all of them have a dream-world which will outlive them, but one which will abundantly bless them throughout their lifetime.

These ideals are near at hand. You need not ascend mountains to find them. They have no habitation. They are everywhere. They are not only near, they are seeking us. Halevi, the mystic poet of the Middle Ages, exclaimed: "I have sought thy nearness, with my whole heart have I called upon thee, but when I went forth to find thee, I found that thou hadst been seeking me." Our ideal is seeking us. Open your eyes, it is here, in your home, in the multitudinous acts of mutual love and sacrifice, in the exalted experience of friendship, in shop, store and office, in your community, in social work, in civic work, in religious work, in the humblest and highest task it is there.

"Behold, I have set before thee this day, Life and the Good, Death and the Evil. Choose thou Life!" Amen.

TWENTY-FIVE YEARS

Gentle, gracious, tender, modest in spirit and exquisite in style; rich in reminiscence—in pictures of faces now fallen into dust, but vivid in memory; ripe in mystical fellowship with God and in ministry to men; fragrant with wisdom learned by living and the chastened hope born of experience: it is difficult to describe this noble and beautiful address, in which a great Christian leader shares, as friend would share with friend, in intimate and sympathetic mood, the thoughts, memories and musings awakened in his heart on the occasion of the double anniversary of his ordination and his consecration.

Some of its sentences read like the record of our own inner experience: "My gravest difficulty is to believe that God is love"; "thinking things through leads you away from credulity into doubt before it brings you to belief"; "our knowledge of God at its best leaves vast unexplored regions of his being untouched." Yet the words, "a something mystic in me," tell us how by a deep inward way we may pass from belief to faith, and why "when your belief comes, it comes to stay," bringing inward sustaining for the obligations and vicissitudes of the years: "The Incarnation does not answer my questions but it abates my questioning."

If I had read this address as a young man it would have set me on fire with a passion for the Christian life, its challenge, its daring, and its great adventure; at this date and distance, by the mercy of God, it stirs me like great music, with a sense of the wonder of Christian faith and the joy of Christian service. For such leaders as Bishop Brent we praise God and give thanks; they belong to the Church Universal.

TWENTY-FIVE YEARS

CHARLES HENRY BRENT, D.D.

EPISCOPAL BISHOP, WESTERN NEW YORK

I remember the days of old; I meditate on all thy doings;
I muse on the work of thy hands. Psalm 142: 5.

You, my dear friends, have gathered from this diocese and beyond to celebrate with me the twenty-fifth anniversary of my consecration as bishop. As it happens, it is also the fortieth anniversary of my ordination to the ministry. I am confident that it would be unseemly—certainly it would be distasteful to me—to presume to preach a sermon to you. At such a moment, the past rises vividly before me and I have an instinctive desire to share with you such of its features as friend would share with friend in intimate and sympathetic fellowship.

I cannot plunge immediately into the days of my ministry as though it were a thing detached. So closely woven a fabric is the whole of life that it is impossible to divide it into sections that do not overlap or run into one another. My ministry is the natural outcome of my boyhood. For three things I am deeply thankful—that I am Canadian born and bred, that I had a mother who for character and spiritual culture was the peer of the best, and that a country rectory, where my father served for forty-two years, sheltered my young days. From my Canadian breeding I got that fine, just discipline which held within bounds a nature that could easily have gone on the rocks; to my mother's wise and loving influence I owe all the good that is in me; and it was my father's long rectorate in the little village where I was born that burned into my soul the high value of stability. Love of my country home has never abated and has kept burning a steady flame of sympathy for country folk and country problems.

I do not recall an instant of my life when I aspired to any vocation excepting that of the ministry but on one brief occasion when I faced the possibility of becoming a musician. As a boy at school, the ministry seemed to me the one vocation worth considering. My most recent reflections confirm my earliest. I know nothing that is worthy of comparison with the ministry. Were I again on the threshold of life, I would choose as I have chosen. As a youth, other walks of life, excepting music alone, held no attraction for me. It was taken as a matter of course by my parents that I would proceed to ordination, which I did after teaching a year and a half at my old school, Trinity College, Port Hope. Having graduated at Trinity University, Toronto, in 1884, I was ordained deacon in 1886 by the Bishop of Toronto, Dr. Sweatman, who also ordained me priest in 1887. Fifteen years later, he assisted at my consecration as Bishop of the Philippine Islands. Bishop Sweatman was a typical Anglican of his day. He had a warm heart but a stiff manner. The effect he always had on me was to rouse self-consciousness and a desire to run away from so great dignity.

As the bishop could not offer me a title in his diocese, I sought one elsewhere. At the suggestion of my classmate, the Rev., afterwards Bishop, Charles Scadding, I came to St. John's, Buffalo, as organist and curate. I had not the least intention of staying permanently in the United States and rather looked forward to returning to a Canadian country rectory. The biased English history which I had read had seriously warped my mind so that it took ten years to wipe out my prejudices and fit me into the American nation.

Two events combined to take me away from Buffalo. After a short period at St. John's, I accepted a position as curate of St. Paul's in charge of St. Andrew's Mission, then on Spruce Street, which I revived. In those days it was a risky move to place candles on the altar. I ran the risk. The bishop summoned me and bade me remove them. I did not set such store by the candles as I did by my rights as a priest. I asked the bishop to allow me the same freedom as he allowed others of his clergy. He refused and I left.

The previous summer I had attended my first retreat. It was conducted by the Rev. Fr., now Bishop, A. C. A. Hall of the Society of St. John the Evangelist. It awakened my spiritual life as it had never been awakened before, and I was strongly drawn to him by his powerful, spiritual character. His offer of a place at St. Augustine's colored mission in Boston

came at the moment of my trouble with Bishop Coxe.
I accepted it and entered on a period of training
which was so sound and inspiring that I would covet
it for every young priest. I was as ignorant and
heady as any young fellow could be. But under the
gentle, wise guidance of the men about me—Frs.
Hall, Osborne (afterwards Bishop of Springfield)
and Torbert—I was gradually trained to recognize
my ignorance and shortcomings.

During the three and a half years of my life at the
Mission House of the Society of St. John the Evangelist, I learned invaluable lessons, chief of which was
that of the ordered life. Daily meditation was a
severe and joyous task. Ability to concentrate the
attention for a long period on a given thought can be
taught by no other means. The practice of the
Presence of God is the foundation not only of piety
but also of intellectual character. The love of Jesus
Christ, the application to modern life of the principles by which he lived, and the overwhelming importance of the unseen, were instilled into my being
in a manner and to a degree from which there is,
thirty-five years later, no escape. The daily round
of services—the Eucharist, the daily offices, the observance of the hours—was free from formalism and
always a privilege rather than a duty.

I was favored by the associations to which I was
admitted. Fr. Hall became my dearest friend. Although I call him brother, I think of him as father.
His fearlessness, his noble integrity of character, and
his indefatigable industry, shot through and through

by common sense, thoroughness and accuracy, mark him out as one of the most spiritually influential pastors of our times. My thoughts turn affectionately to his Vermont home, where, held by the limitations of age, I know his thoughts are with us today as ours are with him. Fr. Osborne was of another type. He was filled with restless energy, a busy pastor rather than a student. During the past year he entered into rest at an advanced age. Shortly before sunset, as he sat with his nurse during the long evenings, he would preach sermons to imaginary congregations, and at the close, in faltering tones, ask his nurse: "Do you think I have helped any one today?"

With Fr. Torbert I had the privilege of long association. Upon Fr. Hall's recall to England by his superior in 1891, Bishop Brooks, just consecrated, placed Torbert and myself in an abandoned church in the South End which was revived under the name of St. Stephen's. There we worked, side by side, as brothers, though Torbert was the priest in charge, until God took him ten years later. A more gentle, understanding soul never breathed. I would much rather accept his instinctive conclusions than the reasoned findings of most men. He came more nearly to having a right judgment in all things than any man I have ever known. He did much to cure me of snap judgments and quick temper. When an irritating occurrence happened, he always approached it with prayer and a sane and quiet mind. His considerateness of me, his junior in years and subordi-

nate in office, was a model for all rectors. He shared
everything, preaching, services, visiting, on absolutely equal terms. When death broke our partner-
ship, I could look back on nearly fifteen years of
loving companionship without misunderstanding or
shadow. A more loyal and united congregation never
existed than that to which we jointly ministered. It
was the pastoral work which held it together. There
is no room for doubt that in house-to-house visiting
lies the strength of the Church. The rector who fails
to come to know his people in their homes, who, if
he calls at all, does so perfunctorily, or on the occasion of a marriage or funeral only, is not a pastor.
He may be a signboard, but he is not a reservoir of
spiritual influence, let his pulpit eloquence be that of
angels, and his organizing gift that of a Napoleon.
We usually think of Phillips Brooks as a preacher.
He was first a pastor and then, because of it, a
preacher. He is quoted in Bishop Lawrence's
Memoirs as saying:

"I wish I could devote every hour of the day to
calling on my people. I know of no happier or more
helpful work that a pastor can do, and I call as much
as I can. How is it possible for one to preach to his
people if he does not know them, their doubts, sorrows, and ambitions?"

It would be difficult to discover the secret of the
spell that Bishop Brooks' preaching had on people.
It lies hidden in that subtle thing, personality. He
had at times such an influence on me that I was af-
fected physically. I felt as if I might be the string

of a harp on which a master hand was playing. I vibrated to his touch. But of this I am convinced, that much of the secret of his power lay in his experimental knowledge of human life, worked out in his pastoral relationships. There is no need of setting preaching and pastoral visiting one against the other. The good pastor is always worth listening to in the pulpit.

My last memory of Bishop Brooks is a couple of weeks before he died. St. Stephen's Church was situated in a neighborhood known and loved by him. He once said to me as we walked through the squalid streets, that he yearned to come and live among the people resident there. It was originally known as the Boston "Neck." When we built our parish house, after delving a bit, we struck the beams of a wharf and after that, the deep blue sea. As I was sitting in the Diocesan House, the bishop thrust his head in the door. Seeing me, he sang out: "Hello, Brent! How are things down on the 'Neck'? Stiff?" and vanished, leaving behind the echo of a deep-throated laugh. Two weeks later, his mortal remains were carried shoulder high by a corps of students out of the church of his love to their last resting place in Mount Auburn.

Life in the South End moved on without an uninteresting or dull day. The South End House with its great head, Robert Woods, Denison House under Helena Dudley, Hale House, Lincoln House, latterly under the care of my brother, sprang up about us and turned their social cohorts loose on the problems

225

which beset us. Our own Rescue Mission played its part through well-nigh twenty years. As I walked through the district, as likely as not I would meet Edward Everett Hale prowling around his "beloved South End." The close of my ministry there came abruptly. On the Festival of St. Michael and All Angels, 1901, Torbert died. The tears were hardly wiped from my eyes before I got a wire from San Francisco advising me that I had been elected Bishop of the Philippine Islands. We were seated at dinner—Russell Talbot, Thatcher Kimball and I. Immediately we sought an atlas to discover where the Philippines actually were. Although the Spanish-American War had taught me a little distant geography, I should have hated to stand an examination on the subject!

From the first I felt that it was my duty to go. My loving parishioners made it easy for me, and though I greatly doubted the wisdom of the Church in selecting a bishop without making adequate provision for the work, I trusted myself to the good faith of the Church, and, as dear Bishop Greer counseled me, never looked back but "lived in the top story of my decision."

This is the only change of place in my whole career which I have made with a quiet mind. Even when I left Buffalo, it was with such keen regret that but little persuasion would have anchored me there with the intention of fighting out what seemed to me a just battle. I have never felt a moment of doubt after declining the various positions to which I have

226

been elected. I attribute this to the silent influence of my father's long pastorate. Stability looms large in the pastoral life. I recall once visiting Kenilworth where I met an old dame who had been selling strawberries at the entrance to the castle through sixty-two years. Upon my return to Westminster where I was staying, I said to Canon, now Bishop, Gore: "I admire the stability of the English people," quoting the old lady as an illustration. He replied: "She is a vegetable and not a person." It was probably true. Mere settling down in a position, devoid of the spirit of adventure, is not stability. Stability is ever using all of the numerous opportunities in a given place to the full. Sometimes the best thing a man can do is to move. But the place where he is always has the superior claim. It is for the place that is beckoning him to prove that his duty is elsewhere rather than where he is. I recognize now what I failed to recognize then, that I had not exhausted all the possibilities of Florence Street. There remained enough to consume the vitality of a lifetime. I closed the first chapter of my life in the ministry after being a rector for two months out of my fifteen years of service, years rich in opportunity and rare fellowship.

On December 19, 1901, I was consecrated Bishop of the Philippine Islands in Emmanuel Church, Boston. The only survivors of those who took official part in the service are Bishops Hall and Lawrence. Bishop Hall was the preacher and the sermon he then preached has colored my subsequent

227

career—that it is to a ministry of reconciliation to which we bishops are called. The beautiful service lingers in my memory. At its close, as we were removing our vestments, Bishop Porter approached me and said: "Bishop, I have a piece of advice to give you." Now, thought I, I shall receive some wise counsel from this great man. "When you go to the Philippines," he continued, "take a bed with you, for those Philippine beds find out every bone in your body." I was somewhat shocked at his levity but later learned the wisdom of his counsel.

I cannot turn from that great moment of my life without offering a love tribute to Bishops Doane and Satterlee, both of whom, though much senior to me, true brothers and friends until death closed their eyes.

I did not sail for the Philippines until the summer when I joined the party of Governor Taft via Suez. Never was a more callow and unprepared bishop flung into a difficult situation. I knew nothing of Spanish, I had a violent distaste for working in a Roman Catholic country, and I was singularly innocent of many important things germane to the situation. However, certain duties shone out plainly and today I would make no change in their order. I felt that our first responsibility was for the American and English population. The ease with which the white man deteriorates east of Suez cannot be exaggerated. Then I knew that among the considerable pagan and Mohammedan peoples of the Islands, there was ample room for evangelizing efforts, which proved to be so, beyond my expectations. About work among the Roman Catholic element in the Islands I was doubtful. Certainly there was humanitarian service to be rendered but beyond that I could not say. Institutional enterprises loomed large at the time. Since then I have modified my views. Hospitals and schools are invaluable where the community is not sufficiently advanced to supply them. But as public spirit and scientific knowledge progress, it would appear to me an undesirable thing to continue them—certainly not, unless we can equip them, and carry them on, on as high a level scientifically as, or higher than, the publicly supported institutions. Among the Mohammedans of the Southern Islands, school and hospital work is simply indispensable. It is the one means of exhibiting the Christian spirit among the followers of Islam whose only knowledge of Christian nations is that they make better weapons and fight better and exploit their neighbors more successfully than Moslems. It is for this reason that I still hold tenaciously to the Moro School in Jolo which has been operative now for ten years, though the difficulties of securing support are increasingly great. It is for the same reason that I advocate friendly relations of the institutional life of the American Churches established there and the patient evangelistic missions of the French. The Turks have been cruel and ruthless, it is true. However, what can you expect? It is Christianized peoples who have provided weapons and taught the Turk how to use them. We Christians slay and kill under a

229

more restricted system than the Mohammedans but, as the late war testified, we do it on a large and unparalleled scale; and thoroughly well, when the die is cast.

J. R. Green once said: "I fancy that just as I got a new way of looking at Northern matters from my stay in Italy, I may get a new way of looking at all Christian and European matters by sojourning on African ground a few months. A 'niggerview' of history would be a novelty." It is just the "niggerview," as Green terms it, that is needed above all other views today. We must look at the Turk through Turkish eyes, at the Frenchman through French eyes, at the Russian through Russian eyes, with a knowledge of the history of each written by himself, if we are to escape the blighting curse of little nationalism ànd deal out justice to the nations.

It was among the pagan peoples that I learned that equality before God of all men, which I count to be the chief treasure which I have honestly made my own in a lifetime. We assume without much thought that our race and our nation is the superior one on earth. Or is it that with a common humanity we have developed ourselves under superior conditions to others? Given the proper environment most men rise to a high plane, whether the negro or the yellow or the white man. A temperate climate has much to do with it, backed by the heritage of the ages. Consequently, we may never glory in our national exploits and advancement as if they were our own unaided accomplishment. Mere national-

ism has become abhorrent to me, as making for strife
and dissension. The rule of service must be extended
from the individual to the nation so that the most
highly developed nation must be the servant of all.
There is no other gospel for national life.

The problems of the race are the problems of mankind. The opium problem stands as a clear illustration of the fact. I proposed an international conference to solve it in 1906 in a day when such
conferences were few. Since that time we have
entered into an age of world-wide gatherings for the
solution of world problems. The value of the League
of Nations largely consists in its opportunity for
working out differences and frictions in consultation
around a common table. In 1910 our experience in
the missionary conference in Edinburgh led me to
propose a like gathering for all the churches, which
took the form of the World Conference on Faith and
Order. This is the most ambitious attempt of all and
the most essential. The unity of Christendom is not
a luxury but a necessity, and the world will go limp-
ing until Christ's prayer that all may be one is answered.

But world-wide movements in themselves are un-
availing; neither do they exempt Christians from
local effort. Local effort with world-wide intent fills
out the picture and together they produce results.

Sixteen years passed with rapidity in the Philippines. During that period most of the American
Army had several terms of service in the Islands, so
that I knew the majority of its personnel. I num-

bered among my more intimate friends Generals Pershing, Wood and Harbord, as well as junior officers and enlisted men. So that when the war came and General Pershing asked me to come to France, though at first I had to refuse, later it was the natural course for me to take. My service in the Army was built on the coöperative principle. I first secured Chaplains Paul Moody and Francis B. Doherty, representing respectively the Congregational and the Roman Catholic Churches, and founded an office. Remembering my life with Torbert, we ordained that there should be no secrets, but that the correspondence of one should be the correspondence of all, that we would talk out our problems together. These principles were carried out to the letter. If my own diocesan life proves as rich and empty of shadows as the Chaplains' fellowship in the A. E. F., I shall be a happy man. Much that was attributed to me was due to Moody, Doherty, Allen and Ronan, whose loyalty and affection I shall ever treasure.

In 1917 I had twice been urged to consider allowing my name to stand for Bishop of Western New York but declined. When a third request came, I was moved to agree to it. The torture of the days following my election I shall never be separated from. My reason urged in one direction; a mystic something in me, in another. To this day I am uncertain whether I should not have been of more service to the Church loyal to the end in the Philippines, rather than alive in America. No other dioceses of the Church have tempted me. Western New York, where I began my ministry, across the river from my ancestral home, presenting as it does a large rural problem where my chief interest lies, alone could have won me. My life here, as I close my ninth year as your bishop, has proved a blessed experience. With a united diocese responding to my leadership, a loving fellowship among the clergy, and steady spiritual development marking the years, I can look forward to the balance of my days with buoyancy and hope. My dear coadjutor is loved from end to end of the diocese and is to me a thoughtful, generous-hearted brother. Never has there been a break or a harsh word between us, and there never will be. I can say with a full heart and happy lips: "My lot is cast in a fair ground; yea, I have a goodly heritage."

But I must not stop with these pleasant reminiscences. Although the years roll on, I find life more in the future today than when I was twenty. The way to keep young, as I find, is to look ahead and to consort with young people. I am inclined to think that the world appears worse than it formerly did partially because there are no longer any secrets and society lies before us as an open book. We know more about the whole world today at any given moment than we knew about our own country when I was a boy.

I am no *laissez-faire* optimist, however. The world does not progress by chance. Human development is not a necessity. It comes through the choice and labor of individuals or groups of individuals. The

233

work of the Church has its roots deep in the unseen world, and as long as it keeps them there, well watered by faith, she will have vitality to grapple with the most serious social problems of the day. It is her place to spiritualize the methods and findings of science. My gravest difficulty is to believe that God is love. The ruthless, inexorable ways of nature are staggering. Early in my career I was brought under the influence of that master mind, Huxley. He and Darwin taught me more about the ethics of thinking than all my other preceptors combined. "Think things through and you'll think things true," has been a sort of motto of my life. Thinking of this sort leads you away from credulity into doubt before it brings you to belief. But when your belief comes, it comes to stay.

I wish I could believe that reconciliation between the Christian religion and science had been reached. I cannot find it to be the case. Religion of a sort and science can walk hand in hand, but not so the Christian religion and science. There is a better understanding between the two than formerly, but there is a long road to travel before they can be called friends. It is into the Incarnation that I plunge headlong and find in it my sole salvation. It does not answer my questions but it abates my questioning. If the "Word made Flesh" always addressed God as Father and always lived as his Son, if with almost his last words he rent the heavens with an unanswered question, then I can afford to follow in his steps. After all, we know nothing except the way things behave. Our knowledge of God at its best leaves vast unexplored regions of his being untouched. I often think that what we do not know of God inspires us with that fear which is the beginning of wisdom, and what we do know of him as revealed in Jesus Christ, inspires that love which can be so rich as to be all consuming.

When I was younger I firmly believed I would live to see the phalanxes of Jesus Christ united in one Church. Though my belief that this is bound to be a fact some day still abides unshaken, now I look with the eyes of Balaam:

> I see him but not now,
> I behold him but not nigh.

Labor for unity must lay its claim on every Christian soul. It will come, when it does come, not with observation, but through the slow processes of the mills of God. I cannot understand people who are indifferent to or idle in the case. It stands as the great background of all Christian thought and life.

Then the second thing of vital importance is to link up faith and works so that each is lost in the other. The Christian way of life is essential to the Church. The truths and principles by which Jesus Christ lived, and having wrought them taught, have supreme claim on our loyalty. It may be difficult and painful, it may cause persecution and misunderstandings to obey, but it is in such obedience and dependence that we achieve the glorious liberty of the children of God. There is no aspect or department of life which can escape the Christian demand; the domestic circle, citizenship, business, politics— all must be put to the Christian test. The Church must discover and teach Christ's mind on marriage and divorce; on war and peace; on buying and selling; on legislation and government. It is a slow and painful process, but it is worth the trouble. It is for this that the Church exists and only this.

When I went to the Philippines, it was with the conviction that the missionary enterprise was the greatest undertaking of the Church. I believe this now with increased and immovable conviction. It makes so little difference where a man serves that I am surprised that more young men and women of the finest culture and character do not make the venture. I suppose their failure is due to a superiority complex—they are afraid their labor will go for nothing, that it will not receive public attention, that opportunity will not be given to use all their ability. Of course, I believe that opportunity's home is within a man and does not depend on external facilities. It thrills me to think of Bishop Roots in China, of Schweitzer in darkest Africa, or Father Allen in Liberia, and our own Deaconess Shaw in Bontoc. Were I young again and furnished with all the knowledge I now have, I should not stay in this country a moment. It will always remain as a doubt in my soul whether, in returning to America, I may not have chosen the lower rather than the higher, however strong my missionary motive. The way that parents oppose objection to their children making the glo-

rious missionary venture is discouraging. They did
not hesitate to give their sons for the country's sake,
in time of war, why not for the Church's sake in time
of peace?

It is true, I suppose, that our day has "struck a disturbed patch of history, and we know it in our
bones." At any rate, suppressed disorder has burst
through the surface of things. The responsibility
for the eruption rests squarely on the shoulders of all
the people, the rich, the privileged, the highly educated being the most culpable. All the ninepins of
life have been knocked over by our own bowling.
We are now engaged in the effort to set them up,
though with no certainty that some one will not send
another ball hurtling down the alley of time and mess
up the human situation again. Be that as it may,
we have no cause for complaint or dismay.

Christians are constructionists. We must endeavor
to reconstruct, and to reconstruct on spiritual foundations as substantially as can be. But I have been
driven to the conclusion that Christianity is too essentially eternal and belongs too much to Christ to
waste energy on trying to build a permanent structure out of impermanent material. Its main business is with the within, for the things that are seen
are the children of time, and pass away leaving not
a wrack behind; and the things that are not seen
alone abide forever. Our great task as Christians is
first with our own inner selves. Given that a man is
morally solvent and honestly loves God as his Father,
he cannot go far wrong in what he does with him-

self in the social fabric. Life will resolve itself for such an one into a steady purpose to shape self and others into building stones, living and human, who will fit into the walls of the City of God and enhance the strength, purity and beauty of that enduring fabric, which rears its stately walls in time, though they are not of time.

In other words, it is the spiritual that really counts —and by the spiritual I mean the good, the beautiful and the true which stand the searching test of Jesus Christ. Loyalty to this trinity, no item of which may be omitted without disaster, gives the zest of a game to human experience and activity. After all, we are as children, furnished with many and multiform blocks, who build for the practice of building. The exercise develops latent power. Human life is just that—an exercise in the environs of space and time for the development of our real self. The structures we raise, governments, industries, institutions, are all doomed to eventual decay in the rolling ages, but that intangible something created by the activity which erected them is conserved without loss and carried within us into the enduring City, of which the Church is the agent and symbol, as immortal building material.

A youth catches a vision. In it he is apt to see a panacea for all ills. Whereas it is only a tiny fragment of the truth, though he cannot recognize it for what it is. His little church, his little scheme of reform, his puny plans, he thinks to be the whole and sets out to transfigure the world with them. Happy

is he who does not lose the zest and joy of living
when he awakes to the magnificence of his task and
the pettiness of the means which he would employ.

As we grow older, we see more clearly. If we cease
to be world reformers—and most of us start out with
that intent—we must lose our desire for world
reformation and conversion. The edict goes out ultimately to all who survive:

> It is time to be old,
> So take in sail;
> The God of bounds
> Who sets to seas a shore
> Came to me in his fatal round,
> And said: "No more!
> No farther shoot
> Thy broad ambitious branches, and thy root.
> Fancy departs; no more invent;
> Contract thy firmament to compass of a tent,
> There's not enough for this and that.
> Make thy option which of two;
> Economize the failing river,
> Not the less revere the Giver,
> Leave the many and hold the few.
> Timely wise accept the terms,
> Soften the fall with wary foot;
> A little while
> Still plan and smile,
> And—fault of novel germs—
> Mature the unfallen fruit."
> Lowly faithful, banish fear,
> Right onward drive unharmed;
> The port, well worth the cruise, is near,
> And every wave is charmed.

Charles Henry Brent, D.D.

The greatest lesson of life has been learned when one has accepted the fact that, whatever his other activities, he can best aid the coming of the Kingdom of God by loyalty to the near duties which once seemed small but which somehow loom large with advancing years—the maintenance of a fearless soul in the maze of common life, the steady cultivation of a living faith in a loving God who holds and controls the destiny of man, and the jealous safeguarding of inner peace which is the just heritage of a quiet conscience.

A New Yorker, born in 1870, Dr. Knubel was educated at Pennsylvania College, Gettysburg, and at Gettysburg Theological Seminary, with later studies at the University of Leipzig, entering the ministry of the Evangelical Lutheran Church in 1896. He was the founder, in 1896, of the Church of the Atonement, New York City, of which he remained pastor until 1923; and since 1918 he has been President of the United Lutheran Church of America.

The sermon following is particularly timely in a day when, as a keen observer has remarked, men have lost their grip on things which they held firmly when they knew them less and believed in them more. In a universe so bewilderingly vast it becomes increasingly difficult to ascribe purpose to the movement and development of things, and yet without purpose the process is unintelligible, and in the end actually terrifying.

By the same token, to ascribe purposefulness to God implies that he cannot obtain his ends all at once, and is in so far limited; hence the dilemma which Dr. Knubel faces, showing that God is in that respect limited, and that we are called to be his co-workers. God, the Old Struggler, as Dr. Johnson would say, invites us to fight with him for the establishment of righteousness; and it is thus that our little lives attain epic worth and eternal meaning.

PROOF OF DIVINE PURPOSE

FREDERICK H. KNUBEL, D.D.

PRESIDENT, UNITED LUTHERAN CHURCH IN AMERICA,
NEW YORK CITY

Who gave himself for us that he might redeem us from all iniquity and purify unto himself a peculiar people, zealous of good works. Titus 2:14.

Just beneath the surface of this text three common truths are reiterated. Each is attractive in itself. Our special and final aim, however, will be to behold an unusual combination of the three, whereby our interest in them ought to be thrilled. First of all, we are reminded once more that there is such a thing as divine purpose behind human events. The writer emphasizes God's great deed, "He gave himself for us." This act is so stated by him, however, as to impress the design thereof for humanity. All the impulses for good in men's lives were caused, according to the text, by that deed. We were thereby redeemed, purified, made zealous for good. The man who was writing to Titus had evidently gripped the idea of God's purposefulness.

A mighty thought has laid hold upon any man when he becomes convinced that God has a purpose in him, in his nation, in mankind. Many have aimed

243

to give expression to the conviction. No one is quoted oftener than Tennyson in this respect: "And I doubt not through the ages one increasing purpose runs." Furthermore a suggestive word has kept on running over the lips of America's leaders, revealing their confidence in a purpose of God for our national life. Daniel Webster gave it terse currency by his emphasis upon "one country, one constitution, one destiny." The word is destiny. It was freely used by Washington, Lincoln, McKinley, Whittier, Lowell, Longfellow. These all were persuaded of a divine design in our existence as a nation. Even our coins continuously carry, "In God we trust." Turning to individual lives, who of us has not in sober moments asked himself, "Why am I here?"—wondering over the problem of purpose. What man fails to recognize that no greater inspiration could be his than the consciousness of a distinct divine plan which is to be accomplished through his life? Nothing else can give equal zest, endurance, confidence to our days. In any event, this is the first suggestion from our text.

We are next reminded that even God must struggle to gain his ends. That simple statement, "He gave himself for us," covers of course the simple story of Jesus. Discerning eyes always recognize, however, beneath that tragic story, effort, power, struggle, agony. It was with mighty sacrifice that he gave himself. The prophet's bold imagination pictured that struggle effectively, "The Lord hath made bare his holy arm in the eyes of all the nations." God has his sleeves rolled up, while the world in wonder beholds. There is something strikingly suggestive in the thought that even God cannot with ease accomplish what he wishes. We may in this connection readily let our minds run back to heathen mythologies and their narrations of the struggles of the gods. It is enough to remind ourselves of the twelve labors of Hercules. They are all gross, material fancies, however, as compared with God's exalted struggle for righteousness. Men are very busy nowadays with their hopes and plans to outlaw war. As long, we may be sure, as this world lasts, God's bloody war against sin will not cease.

Yes, God must struggle to gain his ends. We are all conscious of an element of rebellion against God in our lives. We have been impressed by the persistent contrariness of the world. Psychologists do not care to admit what is plain to us all, that it is always easier to do wrong than it is to do right, to form bad habits than good habits, to establish evil character than noble character. We stand with Paul against the psychologists, "The good that I would, I do not; but the evil which I would not, that I do." It is all the resistance of men against God. This resistance he must overcome. Even God must struggle to accomplish his purpose.

A third and most beautiful truth underlies the text. It becomes more wonderful the longer one contemplates it. The idea is that God in his struggle takes men as co-workers with him and thus creates with them a compact struggle in this world of ours for the end he has in view. Note the expression thereof in the text. He purifies "unto himself a peculiar people, zealous of good works." This reads in the Revised Version, "that he might gain for himself a people for his own possession, zealous of good works." He compacts them as a people, causes them to be possessed with his own thoughts, sets them on fire and makes them burn with zeal for his righteous purposes.

Let us recall the romantic, thrilling story of the Crusades. For two centuries the whole of western Europe was set on fire with the conception of a purpose of God that demanded struggle. It gathered men, women, and even children to march in armies against the Turks in Asia and to regain the sacred places in the Holy Land. The cry of Peter the Hermit as he preached the crusade was, "It is the will of God." Thousands and hundreds of thousands marched for months. Crusade after crusade, wave after wave, was formed, only to break in horrible exhaustion and death. Looking back now a thousand years upon those scenes we feel quite unable to understand what was taking place, excepting that we recognize the compact readiness of men in self-denial to do hard things in the name of Christ. We know it was all a misguided effort, but it provides for us a vivid picture of the right idea we are aiming to see —God and his true ends, his summons to men and women and children to mass themselves for the doing of his will, his inspiration of them to struggle with him that his purposes be fulfilled.

That right idea is a reality. Through the ages

men upon men have caught the vision of the divine will. Without excitement and flags and trumpets they have come strongly, increasingly, to enter together into the purpose of God and to take part in his struggle. Seeing how Christ gave himself they have given themselves freely. This is the formation of the "peculiar people," "the people for his own possession, zealous of good works." In other words this is the formation of the Church of the centuries, the militant Church, the struggling Church, which would do "good works," which would accomplish God's will, which would see his purposes attained.

We find therefore that our text asserts at least these three facts. There is divine purpose behind human events. God himself must struggle to accomplish his aims. He takes men into his purposes and forms with them a compact struggle to gain his ends. Our fancy may picture a simile to these facts. The world is a bedlam of noise, of countless sounds and voices. They are just as confused and discordant as the countless events of human lives. May we not conceive however that a great Spirit of Music exists, whose constant purpose is to work harmony out of these clashing cries. What patient effort, what ceaseless struggle that Spirit undergoes in overcoming the persistence of discord! We can scarcely hear the songs of the world because of the clashing noises everywhere. That Spirit persists however and gathers to himself those whose souls love the "concord of sweet sounds." They come to him, the world's masters of music, great composers, sweet singers. With him they carry on the struggle that harmony may reign over discord.

Returning now to our three facts, we have recognized no doubt that they are not unrelated to one another, but form parts of a complete process. That relationship is a more intimate one than we would suppose.

Is that first idea of a divine purpose behind human events true? Is it not just a beautiful fancy like the simile concerning the Spirit of Music? There is a controversy quite as old as the thinking of man concerning our ability to show design even in nature. Once more in recent days a prominent physician and neurologist declared it non-existent and disprovable. We know however that his is not the last word upon that topic. The same question arises concerning history. We look back through the story of the centuries and the nations. We see only the working of natural forces, the movements of races, the philosophies that come and go, the schemes and the counter plans of men. Sometimes we are arrested by a world convulsion, like the war of our generation. No orderly, consistent trend is apparent in history. We wonder, nevertheless, if there must not be some intelligent, controlling influence which holds it all under rein and drives it to a determined goal. Would not the earth otherwise seem a useless existence? How many of us, however, are ready to repeat with conviction Tennyson's faith, "I doubt not through the ages one increasing purpose runs"? Our question becomes an even more difficult one when we meet those who have personally experienced repeated and bitter adversity in life, until the iron has entered into their souls. It is the same when we listen to those whose contacts have been with the misery of men, with inhuman degradation and oppression and martyrdom. How often these say to us, "There is no God."

The alarming doubts which thus enter our minds gain more pointed intensity when we seek evidence of purpose in our own lives. Does the path we have traveled reveal any guiding control over its whole direction? Has there been something beyond haphazard chance in what befell us along the way? Was it our own strength of resolution alone which ultimately determined the meaning and the movement of our days? Sometimes no doubt all of us think we trace footprints of another who has walked with us and, apart from any decision of ours, set the pace and the path. It is to be hoped also that each of us can recall at least one distinct event of so special a character that no other explanation will satisfy excepting to say, "God did that." These, we all admit, are not sufficient for us. We are not content with a faith which sees God only as intervening occasionally for our welfare. If we want the Lord at all we want him all the time. The heart of the Christian longs for assurance of a steady guidance. Even more, he desires evidence that an all-wise purpose for him is back of that guidance. Are there any proofs of divine purpose in individual life? To be made sure of it would fill life's cup full.

Frederick H. Knubel, D.D.

It is here that the wonderful relationship of the three facts in our text enters in. The first, concerning divine purpose, is proved by the second and the third. My persuasion as to God's fine, sure guidance of my life may be based upon the resistance to him of which I am conscious. It may be founded also upon the realization that he has brought men and women into my life who, entering into his purpose for me, gave themselves for me; the fact that they are in my life is evidence that he is there. We may well listen to these witnesses.

As to the former of these, we have all been puzzled at times over the rebelliousness of our natures against the good. He is a strange man and must be essentially a weak man who has never seen with horror some gross wickedness as possibly done by him. Even though the actual temptation to do it may never have come, he knows he could be susceptible to its influence. How frequently also we find that our worst inclinations become prominent at the times when noble possibilities are before us. Low thoughts steal as intruders upon our holiest moments. Then, too, what a long, long trail our favorite sins travel down the years we have come. He who thinks he has solved the mystery of iniquity needs to consider only his ignorance of himself.

We ought thus come to appreciate fundamentally that evil is not merely the absence of the good. It is not merely the weakening remainder of some grossness in the long past. Lack of culture does not cause it. There is nothing negative to it. It is positive and powerful, strong with all the strength of the life it inhabits. Virulency, struggle, rebellion, are its characteristics, however insinuating and ingratiating it appear at times. Furthermore, like all positive forces, its resistance is most manifest when antagonized. The wild beast rages because his captor is hemming him in. The fire hisses because the quenching water is falling upon it. Here then is the important consideration for us. The raging of wickedness in my life, the very rebellion against God which my soul manifests is the evidence of his activity towards me. It is just and only because he has a purpose with me and is moving for its control over me, that the evil in me resists him. The necessity of God's struggle with me is proof of his purpose for me. Let him alone be alarmed whose soul is at ease, whose conscience is quiet. Let him on the other hand rejoice in the assurance of divine purpose in his life who finds that God has no easy task with him.

The other evidence is an even better one. There is proof of God's purpose for me through the presence in my life of the many who for his sake have given themselves for me. He took them into his struggle with me. We have seen that the mystery of iniquity in our lives is great. Even greater is the mystery of the loves in our lives. Pascal wrote somewhere of our utter unworthiness of any love bestowed upon us. It is true. There is absolutely nothing in any man which merits a genuine love from another, which can satisfy that other. There is no reason why that other should love him. Love is unreasonable; it is

251

always a pure gift of self. There is no explanation of love. It is a mystery, unless it be traced to an original, personal Source. Its existence, then, is proof of that source, proof of God and of his loving purpose.

Our lives possess such loves. Some men touch us and contaminate us, hurt us. How many others, however, have brought the purpose of God for us and have been expended in blessing upon us. Above all how steadily they have come. There has never been a year of life without them, never a time when some life containing the purpose of God for us was not touching our lives. What evidence they furnish, therefore, of the steadiness of his purpose. How lavish, too, he has been with them. It is said that to produce one American Beauty rose one hundred others must be sacrificed, and that their strength gives beauty to the one. A similar sacrifice of many lives has been made that whatever is beautiful in our lives may be made to develop. These all gave themselves for us. How simply therefore we are brought back to the opening words of the text, "Who gave himself for us," and to the story of Christ's sacrifice for us. Men will ever linger over it as a supreme revelation of love and a supreme evidence of divine purpose in our lives.

The proofs we need have now been placed before us. A manifest responsibility rests upon the man who has been persuaded that God has an intention for him. Let him meet it rightly as have others who gained the same conviction. Under such circumstances Samuel said, "Speak, Lord, Thy servant heareth." Isaiah: "Here am I, Lord, send me." Mary: "Be it unto me according to thy word." Paul: "Lord, what wilt thou have me to do?" What do we say?

TILL DEATH US DO PART

No moral and social issue now before us is more intricate, or more urgent, than the preservation of the institution of marriage, against which so much of our literature is a conspiracy of realistic cynicism or downright salacity. Since the World War the dogma that the extra-marital relations of men and women are not the business of society, if no children are involved, has rapidly gained ground. Judge Lindsey and others actually propose a companionate, or trial, marriage, in the effort to solve the problem; a mistaken effort, since what they suggest is not marriage at all in any meaning of the word.

In such a situation it was fitting that a great spiritual leader should make so vital a matter the theme of his address to the Convocation of his Diocese. An appreciation of Bishop Slattery appeared in *Best Sermons, 1925;* since then, by the retirement of Bishop Lawrence, he has become Bishop of Massachusetts. Much as we are indebted to a busy and fruitful pen, seldom has Bishop Slattery written anything more to our need than this sermon, in which spiritual insight joins with practical sagacity. Instead of dealing with divorce laws, and such like matters, he tells us plainly what the Church can do and how it can do it.

Here is wise counsel, born of wide parochial experience and observation, and it behooves us to heed it. The Church can and must do something; it can help the home in vital ways, often aiding parents in delicate situations. Above all, it can show forth not only with its lips, but also in the lives of its members, how much it cares for the family and its integrity.

TILL DEATH US DO PART

CHARLES LEWIS SLATTERY, D.D.
EPISCOPAL BISHOP, MASSACHUSETTS

What God hath joined together, let not man put asunder.
Matthew 19: 6.

The rapid increase of divorce threatens the best
life of the Nation. In 1924, the last year for which
we have complete figures, when in Great Britain
there was one divorce for every ninety-six marriages,
and when in Canada the ratio was one divorce to
one hundred and sixty-one marriages, our country
presented the appalling contrast of one divorce for a
little less than seven marriages.

I might plead for a uniform divorce law which
should at least maintain in the whole nation the
highest ideals of individual States; but this question
is now receiving the vigorous attention of the American Bar Association, which is peculiarly equipped to
deal with it. I might plead for the disowning by our
Government of the divorces granted with shameful
facility in Paris. But today I must ask you to think
of only one detail of the problem, and that is, What
can the Church do about it? The Church has a grave
responsibility towards the integrity of the home, and

257

therefore must be alert to see in what ways it may help in meeting the alarming situation.

I

Obviously the first duty of the Church is to do everything in its power to see that the marriage of its youth is entered into with full knowledge of one another and with genuine seriousness. In sermons, in confirmation classes, and privately, the clergy should speak of marriage quite plainly. They should urge parents to lay aside all prudishness and timidity, and give to the young the information which they ought to have. If parents feel themselves incompetent, they should be urged to seek the help of the beloved family physician; if he also hesitates, the rector must himself take up the task. To these guides of youth there is not only the right but the solemn responsibility to speak out clearly, so that the sacred truth shall be taught by a recognized authority, and not learned incidentally in the glaring and vulgar publicity of a casual conversation with other young people. I believe that in homes where parents do their full duty, boys and girls will have no temptation to make cheap what belongs to the confidence of those whom they love best; and the boy's standard of morality will be the same spotless standard which he expects of his sister. Among young people themselves there is no need to return to the excessive shamefacedness of the nineteenth century; but, in getting rid of one extreme, our children have gone too far towards the

258

other extreme. We must ask them to check the swing of the pendulum. Over-intimacy is playing with fire, and ignorance should be warned of its peril. I believe in the young people of our day and their essential goodness. I learn that in some places the youth themselves are opening the revolt against their own indiscriminate conversation and acts. The Church, with boldness and assurance, must aid them in their return to dignity and chivalry.

In the next place, the Church must warn parents that they must earn the wish of their children to share their counsels, so that it would be unthinkable that a daughter should be married without her parents' knowledge as well as consent. Many marriages are failures because they have been the result of a sudden emotion: there has been no real knowledge of one another; there has been no sane planning of the home which they must enter. Too late each discovers the other's hot temper; to like the same things one has to sink to the other's third choices; and both discover that the marriage is a failure. All the reflections which should have preceded marriage follow it with threatening tragedy. What are the parents doing in this critical period before the marriage? Sometimes they are busy over the world; more often they are too timid to ask questions, afraid of intrusion on their children's pleasure; they are criminally negligent when a loving word of warning or of encouragement might protect their children's virtue and lasting happiness.

Here let me say a word directly to the clergy. A

good many of you are approached by young people who, coming without witnesses, ask you to marry them. Your first duty is to ask if the parents of both are entirely willing that they should be married, and know of their intention to be married then and there. Often they will say no. They may confess that one or more of the parents are not willing; or they may say that they wish to give their parents a surprise when they return home. The man with any sense of responsibility will stop instantly. He will refuse to solemnize the marriage unless the parents' consent is secured. Sometimes the door will be slammed in the parson's face, and the foolish people will seek a more indulgent minister. At other times the good advice will be taken, and several days later a group of people will come back with the happy couple, and a marriage which might have been careless and flippant becomes sacred and full of deep joy.

There is more to be weighed. Some parents are quite daft in their worldly ambitions for their children. Money or social position may blind them to the genuine qualities of character and ability, on which alone true married happiness can be founded. Sometimes the children are wiser than their parents, but yield to parental persuasion that it would be a blessing to have a great house or a great place in the eyes of men, even if all is not thoroughly congenial. Some of the best stories in literature are built upon this theme. You would suppose it impossible for mature people who must have read these tales to be so absurdly contemptuous of their child's future happiness. The bauble may be an earldom or only a prosperous butcher-shop: the principle is the same in every walk of life, and the broad road to disaster is equally plain.

The surest way to lessen the evils of divorce is to take all due precautions to see that the original marriage promises success before it is solemnized. I remember one distinguished clergyman who obliged every bride and bridegroom before the wedding to sign a paper solemnly pledging themselves never to break the marriage tie. Of course they made the pledge a moment later by word of mouth: he simply wished to impress upon them that the words meant what they said. A more important safeguard would be to urge the pastor to tell his charges in the weeks before the marriage what all the joys and difficulties are; to warn them that to be selfish and to insist on one's individual rights means speedy calamity; that love is not self-indulgence, but mutual sacrifice; and so to make sure that these people whom he loves as his own children shall be true to their marriage pledge. All this implies the thorough pastoral relationship, which enters into friendship for every member of the families of the parish; whereby young and old feel the right of the good shepherd of their souls to say all that is in his mind and heart for their perpetual welfare.

II

So much for the start. Afterwards there may come the time when friction arises. The beginnings of in-

compatibilities and quarrels are often ludicrously in-
significant. The wife may like one kind of food, the
husband another. The husband may like company,
the wife may prefer a quiet evening of reading. The
wife may like the children to be dressed in gray;
the husband may prefer brown. Why is there no one
sufficiently interested—a mother, a father, a friend,
a rector perhaps—who can lessen the tension with
a flash of humor, or with a good-natured scolding,
which can bring both husband and wife to a normal
view of the case! I am more and more aghast at the
trivial grounds on which men and women allow their
homes to be shattered. There are quite enough of
the homes which break apart because of some fla-
grant cruelty, some hideous sin, some unbearable
crime—but even these may begin with a little thing
which goes rolling up its villainy till the molehill has
become a mountain.

The Church, as a loving friend, may well be alert
to give its strong and affectionate help. Here is the
opportunity for the Doctor Lavendars of the Church
who have won the right to enter the door and become
angels of mercy and reconciliation. Often a clergyman discovers that a divorce is sought by husband
or wife because one or the other has fallen in love
with another man or woman, and wishes to be set
free to enter a new marriage. There ought to be such
stern teaching of the Church that no one married by
the Church service could ever think such a course
possible. Any one who suspects that an attachment
is beginning to form should shut his eyes, put his

hands over his ears, and run for his life. That temptation cannot be played with. Before the youth enters the first marriage, the friendly rector should warn his beloved parishioner, man or woman, that this and similar temptations may come, and that these temptations must be instantly rejected in the name of honor and of love.

III

At length we meet the member of the Church who describes to us the sorrow which seems to make a continuance of marriage impossible. We may be convinced that the separation in some form is inevitable and necessary. Here is no mere incompatability of temper, but downright sin and shame which, having been forgiven again and again, seem to be permanent, and destroy all hope of a righteous marriage.

The Episcopal Church permits under certain circumstances the remarriage of the innocent victim of a marriage broken by the one cause recognized in the First Gospel as a sufficient cause, if we accept the ordinary text. This cause not only must be the real cause, but must be definitely stated in the decree of the court granting the divorce. The State permits divorce for lesser reasons. There are then for the innocent partner three ways of meeting the question of the future which follows the wreck of marriage. One is to marry again, if one wills, whatever the cause of the divorce. Another is to marry again, if one wills, only if the cause is the one cause recognized by the Church. Still another is the heroic way of remaining absolutely true to the marriage vow—"till death us do part." I have known both men and women who have been true to that high ideal. In a world accustomed to quick divorces for almost every reason, and quick remarriages, these fine people stand out as bright and shining examples of self-sacrifice and of complete loyalty.

I can see little good accomplished by philippics against the grievous increase of divorce in America. The Church must do something. The only thing the Church can do is to show forth by the life of its members how much it cares for the family and its integrity. Let us give high praise to the leaders of the Church who really lead, who do more than the law requires of them, and who tell, by concrete instances, what marriage is to the Church. I remember the morning many years ago when a young wife came to tell me of her misery. For her children's sake she had tried to continue the unbroken home. And now, also for her children's sake, she found that she must yield to what she believed the inevitable break. I warned her that as a Christian woman with the highest ideals, she must, whatever happen, consider herself a married woman still, and carry herself with the same dignity as in the past. She tried to get on with a legal separation, but she was forced later to secure an absolute divorce. But through all the years since no one has ever been allowed to think that remarriage was ever possible for her. The State does not require so much, neither does the Canon of the Church. Quite unconscious of her influence, she stands before her group of intimates as an example of the integrity and sacredness of the Christian home.

The Church, therefore, has a genuine contribution to make in this tragic problem. It may guard the youth at the time of marriage and make them quite sure that they know so thoroughly the people whom they intend to marry that they can make with confidence the lifelong vow. The flippant, casual marriage will cease within the walls of our churches. Then divorce, if it comes, will be the end of marriage till death breaks the bond. When men and women in the Church are ready to make this sacrifice, if it is a sacrifice, then the world will listen to the Church. It will believe that the Church has such influence over its members that, just as Telamachus in the early time jumped into the arena and by his horrible death ended the gladiatorial combats, so great-hearted husbands and wives will lead the way to the ending of the evils of divorce. Men will think and pray, and enter into marriages which will be unions of lifelong mutual respect, of lifelong mutual love.

Beyond all warning or appeal, is the example of a happy, united home. Children so fortunate as to be brought up in a truly Christian home, where love reigns supreme, will themselves have slight danger of contributing to the breaking of the marriage tie. They will desire above all else to give to their children the priceless gift of such a home as their parents have given them. They will say reverently before

265

God and man, "Till death us do part"; and they cannot dream that their vow shall ever be broken.

So we come to see that the only genuine solution of the problem is Christ. When men and women give themselves in complete surrender to him, it becomes impossible to talk of the selfish rights of husband or wife. His spirit of love and self-sacrifice takes possession of both, and for the sake of each other, for the sake of their children, and, above all, for his sake, the home becomes sacred, and no taint of disloyalty, no shade of self-interest, no suspicion or misunderstanding, can invade it. Christ lives in that home, and its love and its joy speak of heaven. When all the members of the Church give themselves completely to him, the unbroken loving family will be the universal rule within the Church.

The Church must provide the leaders; then it shall have such influence as shall make it surpass its strongest and happiest days. So shall it give effective emphasis to the sanctity of the marriage tie and the responsibility of those who enter it to the Nation, to humanity, and to God.

THE RELIGION OF BROTHERHOOD

A New Hampshire man, born sixty-one years ago, Dr. Marshall was educated at Tufts College, and ordained to the ministry of the Universalist Church in 1891. After brief pastorates at Beverly and Swampscott, he spent fourteen happy years with the First Church in Melrose, Mass., where he still has his home. Since 1917 he has been manager of the Universalist Publishing House, Boston and Chicago; and manager of much else besides, by virtue of his faith in fellowship and his knack of negotiation—"spiritual politics," a friend described it; serving as a kind of *liaison* officer in promoting contact and conference between widely separated individuals and groups, both in the Church and in industry. In short, he has lived the religion of brotherhood, of which he here speaks.

Such a sermon, brief but big with meaning, as crisp and epigrammatic in style as it is crystalline in insight, is not simply an inspiration; it is an event—summing up swiftly the practical mysticism and daring spiritual radicalism now brooding in many hearts, but expressed by few. It is electrifying in its challenge, showing that brotherhood is not a mere poetic metaphor in the Gospel of Jesus, but its basis and very essence; and that the religion of brotherhood must begin with the brotherhood of religion. A sermon at once more thrilling and searching it is difficult to imagine, with its glow-point of mystical vision at the end, showing that the way of the brotherly life leads to a realization of God and the Life Eternal.

THE RELIGION OF BROTHERHOOD

HAROLD MARSHALL, D.D.

UNIVERSALIST PUBLISHING HOUSE, BOSTON

I am the way. John 14: 6.

The great discovery of our age is not the universe within the atom but the universe within the soul. This has enabled us to rediscover the religion of Jesus, and we find that it was neither a church nor a creed but a way of life by which we possess ourselves. The first and most dazzling result of this discovery has been to give us back our long-lost spiritual freedom.

Paul and Augustine and Calvin are the trinity of misfortune that overbore Jesus' exultant, "Ye shall know the truth and the truth shall make you free," and reduced it to a despairing cry, "O wretched man that I am, who shall deliver me from the body of this death?" They have laid upon lesser men The Great Fear. In terror whole generations have crawled away from God and hidden under little creeds. Jesus was unafraid of God. He did not prostrate himself before him; he laughed up into his face.

It is quite obvious that in the first flush of this rediscovered freedom liberty has run to license. Slavery

269

does produce manners, if it cannot develop morals. It molds behavior into a counterfeit of character. It is obvious that some men and women, particularly young men and women, no longer afraid of the tabus of yesterday, are riotous if not wanton. The modern Sanhedrist, honestly believing that the only way to God is through his temple, raises anew the cry, "These young men and women eat with sinners. Away with them."

The priests and the Levites are right in realizing that between their religions about Jesus and this religion of Jesus it is a duel to the death. Christianity as the way of life is another Samson loosed among the pillars on which ecclesiasticism and dogmatism rest. It is this rediscovery of Christianity as the way of life that makes sectarianism a spent force, morally impotent and spiritually sterile.

But discovery that stops with discovery is useless. Columbus might as well have found a cloud as a continent at the end of his voyage if adventure and agriculture and industry had not followed him. As we begin to explore this rediscovered religion of Jesus, we find it to be a religion of brotherhood; that Christianity as the way of life means the way of brotherhood for all men, with all men. Love your enemy not because he is your enemy but because beneath his enmity is the eternal fact of brotherhood. Because there is one God and Father of us all, no child of God can be outside the pale of human brotherhood.

Our present problems, however, are not created by

270

The Religion of Brotherhood

those who deny this but by those who seek to ignore it. When Jesus' disciples began to practice his religion of brotherhood, a good churchman of the day wrote that "they who have turned the world upside down are come hither." The menace to much of our present way of life does not come from Socialism or Bolshevism or any other ism, but from the religion of Jesus. The old paganisms of class and caste and sect, and race and color, are making their final stand against the religion of brotherhood. Even we who have been so largely occupied in preaching brotherhood are girding ourselves for the far more difficult task of practicing it.

Now what does the practice of brotherhood mean? You are invited to a beautiful home upon which generations have lavished wealth and taste. The possessor shows you its treasures and then takes you out into its great park. Presently, behind a screen of trees, you see some rotting hovels, and squalid men and women and filthy children. "My brothers and sisters," explains your host. "You see, I was grown up when father died and they were only children, so I took all his property." An explanation in terms of religion about Jesus, but not an answer in terms of the religion of Jesus. Nor would he see any difference in the situation if the children did not have the same earthly father, or if they lived in the next town or the next continent, or if their skins were black or yellow. "Have ye not all one Father and are ye not brethren one of another?"

But this does not imply anything so easy and futile
271

as a division of the common heritage. "Henceforth I call you not servants but brethren," is a Magna Charta of the dispossessed, but it does not relieve possessors of responsibility. Brotherhood does not deal with ownership. That is as Cæsar decrees—so long as men are childish enough to need a Cæsar or foolish enough to endure one. Brotherhood deals with the deeper question of use, which alone gives meaning to possession. The practice of brotherhood means that we all have a right to find in the abundance of the Father's house satisfaction for our needs, but not indulgence of our greeds.

Whether the title of a farm or a factory rests in an individual, a corporation, or a coöperation, is no more important than whether the farm shall raise potatoes or wheat, or the factory make shoes or hats. Whether the farm raises wheat for bread or poppies for opium, whether the factory makes plows or machine guns, is a matter of life or death. If the title to the Dupont plants passed to Marxian Socialists or Russian Communists, it would make no real difference if they still made gunpowder.

Furthermore, an employer honestly and intelligently trying to live the brotherly life may find in that purpose a barrier to immediate relief from the burden of ownership. He will remember the story of the prodigal son and the disaster that followed a foolish father's yielding to a foolish boy. He will see in the father's suffering, while the boy was debauching himself, merited punishment for his evasion of responsibility, and he will understand that no small

272

part of the joy over the prodigal's return was because it made it possible for the father to forgive himself. He will see that the practice of brotherhood may mean bearing a cross of economic responsibility until through his strength his weaker brethren shall be made strong.

And the practice of brotherhood means the ordering of the world. Biology has long since confirmed Paul's discovery that God has made of one blood all the nations of the earth. Every civilization built on less than that has crashed or crumbled to ruin, and submarine and aeroplane are no more enduring than phalanx and legion. Ten years ago we proved that we could blast any civilization we can build into blazing and bloody ruin. Unless we can learn to practice brotherhood, our children's children must go back to the cave, perhaps to cannibalism. Brotherhood does not concern itself overmuch with squabbles between "patriots" and "pacifists." It does not tell us whether we must fight the German or kill the Japanese. But it does tell us that any government that bids us hate any man or race is pagan and any church that sanctions an appeal to hate blasphemes the God who is Father of us all and betrays the spirit of Jesus as Judas betrayed his body.

The other day a great dirigible floated over our city, so beautiful in the sunlight that we forgot it was built to drop bombs and not bouquets. Suppose Jesus had been in command of it and released its burden of death upon the men and women and little children below? Would the heavens have opened and a Voice declared, "This is my beloved Son in whom I am well pleased"? And is there reason to suppose the Father would be better pleased if the bombs were dropped by any of his other sons? And would it make any difference to him whether they fell on New York or Boston or Berlin or Tokyo or Peking?

Whether those who have discovered Christianity to be this way of the brotherly life can win the world to brotherhood depends on how far they themselves are ready to practice it. Across the centuries, with the emphasis of his cross upon it, comes Jesus' prayer "that they may be one." Yet he is still crucified wherever, in the name of Calvin or Luther, of Wesley or Murray, men build churchly walls against their brothers. For men and women to come together in churches and conventions and talk about Christianizing the world, without making a serious attempt to achieve a common fellowship of service for the need of the world, is merely to say, "Lord, Lord." The time has come when the churches must decide between Apollos and Christ. In conflicting and competitive sectarianism is the apostasy of our time.

Twelve men were together in one place. Humble and unlettered men, hated where they were not despised. Twelve men were together in one place—separate bodies, different minds, differing types. Twelve men were together in one place. Had that been all, they themselves would have outlived the memory of it. Twelve men were together in one place, in one spirit. So through walls of stone and walls of hate he who had made them one came in and abode with them. Other men having eyes to see saw him in their faces, having ears to hear heard his voice in their voices, and each understood in his own soul.

For nineteen hundred years his other disciples have missed days like that by calling the first one a miracle. Yet the memory of that day of fellowship with him and with each other has outlived the centuries, not because men would remember, but because they could not forget. Here and there those who have lived greatly and loved much have been filled with it as it filled the house in the long ago. Then they have gone in and out among their fellows revealing in their lives that which neither kings nor things can give—or take away. Here and there some group has had enough of his prayer fulfilled to realize what it might mean to be one with the Father, with him and with each other.

Can we repeat the Day of Pentecost today and every day? Yes, if we honestly seek it with all our hearts. Upon that depends our future. God was long before the churches. Will he be even longer after them? Yes! if we go on trying to evade or ignore the religion of Jesus as the way of life. No! if we set ourselves to walk in that way.

It will help us to do that if we realize that it is the way of Life, not merely a way of living. Living is one of the deceits of time from which Jesus could not wholly free himself—hence Gethsemane. But when he made himself a metaphor of life, he lifted himself out of time into the eternal, and saw that a spring morning for a violet, a century for a crystal, and an eon for men are alike in the processes of God.

To know this will help us to pass the final barrier, and from living enter into Life. It is by that way we go out and God comes in, until each of us can say, "I and my Father are one."

FAITH VERSUS SUCCESS

Dr. Imes was born in Memphis in 1889, the son of an Oberlin graduate working as a home missionary of the Congregational Church in the South. He was educated at Fisk University, Nashville, and at Union Theological Seminary, New York City, taking special courses in the social sciences in the graduate school of Columbia University, receiving degrees from both institutions. His first pastorate was at Plainfield, New Jersey; his second in Lombard Street Presbyterian Church in Philadelphia, where he spent six years.

At present Dr. Imes is pastor of the St. James Presbyterian Church of New York City, the largest congregation of colored people of that denomination in America. He is a member of the Association for the Study of Negro Life and History, and contributed a monograph to its journal, entitled *The Legal Status of Free Negroes and Slaves in Tennessee.* St. James Church is located in West 137th Street, in the largest colored community in the world; and its minister is a type of the finely trained prophetic leadership which his people now enjoy—a matter for deep gratitude among men of good will of all creeds and colors.

The following sermon is an honor to the American pulpit, noble in spirit, striking alike in insight and art, practical and pungent in appeal; the word of a Christian teacher working heroically to change an environment now hostile, now apathetic, without bitterness and retaliation, and in the spirit of Christ—at once a challenge to Christian understanding and an invitation to fraternal coöperation.

FAITH VERSUS SUCCESS

WILLIAM LLOYD IMES, D.D.

ST. JAMES PRESBYTERIAN CHURCH, NEW YORK CITY

Thy faith hath saved thee. Luke 7: 50.

We have in the scene before us three unforgettable
people: a Street Preacher, a self-satisfied host at
whose home the Street Preacher was a dinner guest,
and a woman of the street who became a heroine of
faith.

There need be no apology for thinking of the
Saviour of Men as a Street Preacher, for he would
have been glad to bear the title. He was known as
the "Friend of sinners," and indeed his enemies
hurled it in derision, although he accepted it as a
mark of honor. It is in this episode of his remarkable
career that we find two extremes of human life
brought together; a successful, aristocratic, religious
churchman on the one hand, and a derelict, common-
type, unchurched outcast on the other. And, for all
that, the verdict of the Master, this Street Preacher,
was that not the former, despite his religiosity, but
the latter, by reason of her faith, was acceptable to
God.

Here we see the Master dining out. He is guest of

279

a rich and influential citizen of Jerusalem. The host is the very apotheosis of success, that human standard of happiness. Simon is his name, and he is very probably a landed proprietor, with city and country estates, and a power in Jerusalem's commercial life. He is successful therefore in his material welfare, eminently so. Further, he is successful in his social life, for he is an aristocrat to the finger-tips. He prides himself upon his good birth and breeding. His invitation of this Street Preacher was only a matter of curiosity, for Jesus was plainly a man of the common people, with no desire for social preferment or honor above any other. Therefore Simon, with half-veiled contempt of his Guest, is plainly an aristocrat of social standing as well as of wealth. Finally, Simon is assuredly a successful man in religion, and here we touch the most subtle of all temptations that enter into a man's life who strives for success. To be successful in religion, to be sure of one's self, of one's creed, and of one's moral and spiritual affairs, is not this considered, without debate, the best of all success? If so, Simon was here, above all other things, a saved and happy man. Proud Pharisee, even Saul of Tarsus could not have been more sure of his "zeal toward God" than Simon. And this is the picture of the host of Jesus, on a day long ago in ancient Jerusalem.

But turn to the other part of the picture. Here is the Master, the Street Preacher, a man of the lowly people, and with honest preference for the simple and beautiful things of life. He has come to reveal true inwardness of life to the world, and through his life to provide the redemptive plan of God for mankind. He had accepted the invitation of this self-righteous, satisfied man of fashion, this religious aristocrat, because it is just such lives that need a Saviour most, although they rarely confess their need. Jesus had accepted, too, the scant and contemptuous courtesy afforded in Simon's magnificent home at the hands of the haughty servants whose studied neglect of Oriental civility had betokened their employer's true attitude. Jesus, without greeting or anointing, without refreshment for sandaled feet, had been given a couch at the end of the banquet-table, far removed from the honorable place at the side of the host. But he cares not for all this, for wherever Christ sits, that place becomes thereby the head of the table. One might come into this banquet-hall of Simon's by chance, and, if only the Lord of Men be there, his place is alone the greatest. Would that you and I at each family table could thus discern The Lord as Head!

While the banquet was at its height, the servants flitting here and there to satisfy the wants of the guests, the musicians playing and the dancers reveling, there came into the luxurious hall a figure strangely in contrast to the occasion. A woman, evidently having the garb of the underworld, with wild eyes and flowing hair, clasped a small jar of costly ointment to her bosom as she entered. She looked in amazement and dismay on either side of Simon, as if the object of her search ought to be there. Finally, with a little cry of recognition, seeing Jesus reclining in a corner of the hall, she ran toward him, and gaining the side of his couch, fell at his feet, broke the perfumed box, and sobbed as if her heart would break.

To any one save Jesus this would have been a most unwelcome embarrassment, and a scandalous happening. But the Master was in nowise disturbed, and, because he knew the heart of his self-satisfied host, who was even now whispering with his nearest neighbors at the table in suspicion of Jesus, began one of his inimitable parables:

"A man had two debtors, the one owing him five hundred pence, and the other fifty. And when they had nothing to pay, he called them to him, and frankly forgave each one all that he owed." "Tell me," he suddenly thrust at Simon, "which one of them will love him most?" And Simon, sleek opportunist that he was, said glibly, "I suppose he to whom he forgave the most." To which Jesus rejoined, "Thou hast rightly judged." Then with piercing keenness Jesus unmasked the hypocrisy of his host, and pointing to the woman of the street, who was still at his feet crying like a child, he compared her to one who had been forgiven most, and who loved much.

The lesson went home and struck deeply. Simon had never had any one to talk to him about religion like that. *Now* he knew that the sham of his own successful life had been exposed, and here was an erstwhile woman of the street, and a notorious sinner,

who was not only better than he, with all his religion,
but was, by the Master's own estimate, a heroine of
faith. "Thy faith hath saved thee," he said to the
sobbing woman; "go in peace." Back somewhere in
a half-forgotten chapter of her stormy and shameful
life, perhaps when she was running with painted
cheeks through the byways of Jerusalem plying her
unholy trade, Christ had been the only one who had
ever given her a vision and a desire for a better life.
In him she had seen what life really could be, and
the wholesome and wistful longing had come into her
heart that she, too, might be like him.

What was this idea of *faith* that the Master put
forth? Our day has need for examination into so
great a matter. Faith saved this woman of the
street? Then it must have supremely great power!
Faith saves us today? Then it must have for all the
world immense meaning! What is this faith, and
what are its distinguishing marks?

Undoubtedly, faith must be, by its very first action,
a *leveling power*. Travelers in mountainous countries are struck by the miracle of nature which shows
them from a distance the great difference in height
between certain peaks, and upon their near approach
to the base of the mountains, the relative sameness
in their apparent height. So, in infinitely greater
measure, our lives are in the sight of God as they
come near to him. We are very like one another,
after all. The best and the worst of us are pretty
much the same sort of folks. The greatest heresy
of all is that which tries to make us believe that any

of us by nature may be different from each other. Not by nature, but by grace alone, may we be different. There is even in the realm of grace a principle of democracy, so that in all God's world this fact of our oneness as children of Our Father is inescapable. This force of faith in its leveling power was most aptly shown in the remark of a poor London woman in the slums, says Thomas Nightingale, when she was asked by a fellow citizen whether she was not proud to live in an "empire on which the sun never sets." With fire and spirit she replied:

"What's the use of living in an empire on which the sun never sets, if one has to live in an alley on which the sun never rises?"

And you and I cannot help paraphrasing her apt reply by saying: "Dear British sister, you are right, for in our American life we, too, are asking from behind the veil of color-prejudice, 'What's the use of living in the "land of the free and the home of the brave" when one has to live in an alley of rankest race-hatred?'"

In this same America of ours there are those of us who feel that its greatest help to mankind will be the measure of its insistence upon this leveling power of faith. Let me state, with all joy in personal testimony, what my college did for me that above all things else seems to me significant. My Alma Mater taught me, first, absolute fearlessness and wholesome freedom in my devotion to the truth; second, to live in an environment which might be hostile to my equal participation in all rightful human fellowship, and yet not to compromise with that environment, but rather to work heroically to change that environment, without bitterness and retaliation, and in the spirit of Christ.

To have a faith of less than this plain and straightforward outlook upon life seems to me to be preposterous, criminal, and absolutely anti-Christian. I cannot imagine my college abandoning such ideals any more than the Christian Church would abandon them. I cannot imagine that leaders in education, religion, politics, business or any human endeavor would be so dense ever as to suppose that true progress could come save by these ideals of freedom and truth. To cling to Christ through such loyalty and love surely must mean the leveling power of faith.

Then faith has a *contagious power*. Like the wonder of the induced current which the student beholds in the laboratory, so is the influence of life upon life in the sphere of faith and character. Your faith, my friend, is of little consequence in itself until it has learned to expand and spread with a sort of holy contagion. Others want to be loyal and true because they see in you the value of truth and loyalty. "We help one another," said a wise teacher of mine, years ago, "just by being here." We may safely challenge ourselves to live in the region of a vital faith, and not know its contagious power. No less than any other part of God's natural and moral order, this realm of faith is governed by a wonderfully strong and beneficent law. When that memorable all-day debate took place between two great Abolitionists, Frederick

William Lloyd Imes, D.D.

Douglass and John Brown, in an old rock-quarry near Chambersburg, Pa., there was only one human comrade to hear the argument, and he was an ex-slave from South Carolina. He had known the rigors of slavery and its hideous cruelties in far greater measure than most other slaves, but after he heard the plea of Brown to Douglass for recruits to go with him on the ever-to-be-remembered exploit at Harper's Ferry, and Douglass asked him what he would do, Shields Green made this admirable decision of faith, "I think I'll go with the old man!" And he did go, flinging his life away in a glorious martyrdom for you and me, that ex-slave from South Carolina, for he felt the contagious power of a great faith.

Yet, ever more wonderful than either the leveling or contagious power is the *expulsive power* of faith. Thomas Chalmers phrased it in his "expulsive power of a new and greater affection." And while we are all aware that the protagonists of the new psychology have warned us of overworking this point, yet there is abundant evidence for believing that the best method of overcoming the evil of life is that method which substitutes the good and the true for the evil which we would fain destroy. The greatest apostle of Christ's gospel said to his fellow-Christians of the Church in Rome, "Overcome evil with good." It is not all ancient wisdom. Penetratingly is this truth felt in our educational life today, for here teachers who are wisest deal with positive methods of increasing both intellect and character. So Christ is not interested in our bad past half as much as he is ready

286

to point us to a good present which we may possess if we will only receive it by faith.

Simon could never see any good in Mary because he knew she had been a woman of the underworld; he never had stopped to reason that it was probably because of the extortion of landed proprietors like himself that women like Mary had to make traffic of their bodies and souls. People do not want our moral lectures, anyway. They do not even care to have preachers berate them about their shortcomings, and this is natural. That man who is wrong knows it better than you do, Mr. Moralist. He does not need you to tell him of his sin. He knows its ghastliness already a thousandfold better than you know it. He does want you to point him to a way of help to a better life; this you may do if you can assure him that the power of faith in Christ is supremely an expulsive power. Oscar Wilde says in the introduction to that fascinating little autobiography of his, *De Profundis,* that there were two great turning points in his life, the first, when his father sent him to college, and the second, when society sent him to prison. It was in the latter place that the gracious experience of faith's expulsive power took place within his soul. He was given only one thing in his lonely cell beside his cot, tin cup and place for water and bread. This was his New Testament. It was in the original Greek, and Wilde, who was an excellent classical scholar, read it understandingly and explored its vast domain of spiritual experience with Christ. There for the first time he realized the beauty and power of a life of faith. Christ became to him more than merely a human name, and in this power of a new-found faith he felt the old life of sordid evil and disgusting folly forever expelled.

My comrades of this new day, I have no higher desire for our faith than this. Somehow, we must come to know that spiritual ideals of truth and freedom as Christ taught and lived them are also possible for us through him, and that, indeed, no other ideals will satisfy. These aspects of faith are ways in which the Kingdom of God is being brought in, replacing the old order of selfishness, blind creedal submission, smug satisfaction with things as they are, and all other hurtful and evil things. It is faith that saves! "Thy faith hath saved thee!"

Dr. Speight is a Britisher by birth, educated at the University of Aberdeen, with further study at Exeter College, Oxford; he entered the Unitarian ministry in 1912—after serving a year as assistant professor of logic and metaphysics at Aberdeen. After pastorates at Victoria, British Columbia, and in the First Church, Berkeley, California, he came to King's Chapel, Boston, in 1921; having served as Chaplain in the American Army overseas during the World War, 1918-19.

In 1922 Dr. Speight was a member of the Commission investigating religious minorities in Transylvania; the following year he founded the Student Federation of Religious Liberals. His ministry at King's Chapel has been singularly happy and influential, alike for his power as a preacher and his catholicity of spirit; a notable feature being the week-day service to which he brought leading preachers of every communion, a volume of whose addresses he edited, entitled *Week Day Sermons in King's Chapel.*

To the great regret of his fellow-workers, Dr. Speight recently resigned King's Chapel to take the chair of philosophy in Dartmouth College; and while he will be missed from the "firing line," he will keep in touch with us as literary editor of the *Christian Leader.* The following sermon is a persuasive appeal to those who live negatively, and by their apathy and neutrality are "murderers of the enthusiasms of the Church."

THE POSITIVE LIFE

HAROLD E. SPEIGHT, D.D.

KING'S CHAPEL, BOSTON

Peter, seeing the disciple whom Jesus loved following, saith to Jesus, Lord, what shall this man do? Jesus saith unto him, What is that to thee? follow thou me! John 21: 20.

In the ascending scale of life various stages of development are often marked by differences of structure and function that can be explained only in the technical language of the biologist. But there is one very simple distinction between lower and higher types of living creatures. It is the distinction between those creatures which are rooted, almost like plants, to a very limited location, depending for nourishment upon what floats by in the water or the air, and those creatures which seek their food in active wandering from place to place. Some of the latter, as we know, have a wide range of movement— migratory birds, for example, going thousands of miles when the seasons change. Even for mankind, mobility is a very important factor. By organization and invention we have found ways of bringing the products of distant parts of the world to the quietest New England village, and settled community—life is thus made possible by transportation of goods, but

291

this is only an extension of that power of movement which makes life so much richer and fuller for some species than for others.

In human life actual bodily movement from place to place becomes less important. Only a few tribes of little-civilized people now migrate with the seasons in search of pastures for their flocks. But the ability to profit by the widening range of movement and communication is becoming more and more important. One can indeed make a valid distinction between human beings—those who passively rest where they happen to be placed by circumstances and are content to accept whatever a kindly Providence sends their way, and those who actively increase the range of their interests, preferring one thing to another and going where the preferred thing can be found. The mental and spiritual life of two individuals often differs as much as the existence of a sea-anemone, clinging to a rock washed by the tides, differs from that of those extraordinary eels which, spawned on the weeds in the Sargasso Sea in mid-Atlantic, find their way to a habitat in the fresh-water rivers of America and Europe.

The difference is that between what we may call the positive and negative types of people. We see it in the intellectual life. So many are dependent on what comes before their eyes; the more glaring the headlines or the more conspicuous the wayside billboard, the greater their response and attention. Others, but not so many, know what they want and seek it out; in a few cases, as with scientists engaged in the study of very definite fields, a lifetime is devoted to the search.

The difference is seen also, and is just as important, in the moral and spiritual realm. How many think of the good life in merely negative terms! There is the man who, impressed by the dangers which lurk in a life of action, wraps up his talent and hides it where no harm can reach it. His dominant instinct is that of protection. One opportunity after another for investing his talent goes by, and he is rather pleased with himself because, clever fellow that he is, he has avoided the pitfalls of investment by putting his talent well out of reach. The fact that he has it safely put away gives him quite a feeling of satisfaction: he, at any rate, is no pauper. He is a man of property, virtuously cautious. By "playing safe" he feels he is rendering a distinct service in helping to preserve the stability of interest nowadays exposed to danger. He is amazed to find that his caution, instead of being commended, is rebuked. His has been only a negative virtue; and, because he has been more concerned in protecting what he has than in enlarging it, the doom is pronounced upon him—"Take therefore the talent from him and give it unto him that hath ten talents . . . from him that hath not shall be taken away even that which he hath." "From him that hath not"—he supposed all the time that he really had his talent because it was wrapped up where only he could find it: he had the only key to the lock-box. But the judgment revealed the fact that it was not really his at all—"From him that hath not."

A good many people think the good life can be achieved by inaction. An issue arises which involves a choice, either for themselves or for the community to which they belong. They know perfectly well that if they take one side or the other they will run the risk of making a mistake, of hurting some one's feelings, of speaking without full knowledge, perhaps even of turning out to be wrong. It is safer to do nothing and get in no one's way, to stand on the sidelines and watch the game or the contest. Then whatever mistakes are made or accidents occur they have no responsibility for the damage done—and there's a world of comfort in that thought. Let others, if they must, organize committees and leagues for and against; they will wait on higher ground and perhaps in time the dust will clear and it will be seen who was right. There is a kind of safety in such negative virtue; but it is a temporary safety.

I am not a particularly good climber, not having a good head for height, but I have occasionally undertaken to scale a slope that required special effort and care. Once I found myself engaged in a climb that proved to be rather beyond my skill and I faced the question, "Shall I go on or turn back?" It was not at all an easy question, for it was hard to say which was the more difficult course: sometimes it is harder to climb down than to climb up. I found safety in staying where I was, keeping my eyes on the vegetation close to my face and avoiding the sight alike of the valley below and of the cliff above. In a little while I found it quite a comfortable position: the avoidance of decision was almost as pleasurable as a solution of the difficulty ever could be. But at last I realized that I could not stay there forever. Inaction was not itself a solution: it was only a temporary escape.

It is not a comforting thought, but I think it is true, that the progress of mankind to higher levels of life, the success of efforts to spread enlightenment, and the development of a religious faith adequate to meet the complex needs of our modern life, are hindered more by the apathy of the Looker-on than by the definite opposition of men of evil purpose; more by the people who wrap up perfectly good talent than by robbers who menace the talents that are in circulation. Good-natured people who sympathize with and approve of idealistic enterprises but decline to do any of the spade-work, the "apathetic fringe," as it has been called, on the edge of any movement that calls out human loyalties, not only withhold the positive help they might give, but become an actual hindrance for the simple reason that they discourage those who are at work.

"To the Church of Laodicea," said the Spirit to John on Patmos, "write . . . I know thy works, that thou art neither cold nor hot: I would thou wert cold or hot." The Census of 1916 showed 41,926,854 Church members in the United States. Later reports have brought the total now to approximately 48 million. Forty-eight million Christians in earnest, what might not that mean! But to how many is the Spirit still addressing the reproach of the Laodiceans —"thou art neither hot nor cold"? They are not hot enough to be positively concerned with definite objectives in personal and social life, nor cold enough to withdraw; they are looking on with the kind of sympathy that the really active worker sometimes finds harder to bear than opposition. "He that is not with me is against me," said Jesus. The people who are registered in Church and Census records as Christians, but who do not feel that this implies any positive responsibility, who are too busy, or too wrapped up in private concerns, to make their Christian allegiance count, are, all unwittingly, hampering the efforts of those who take their Christian loyalty seriously. They are, to use the striking word of a Canadian preacher, "murderers of the enthusiasms of the Church, which is a very fearful charge to be laid against any man. For an enthusiasm is a breath from God, which comes to possess a man unto his stirring to do something and to dare something in the brave venture of faith. When a man is caught into an eagerness of this sort, he is caught into greatness for a moment. And all who are inadvertently creating a public opinion in which enthusiasms are difficult to retain, are, by their sins of omission, doing their best to annihilate the driving force by which the world grows from flesh to spirit." George Meredith said of the man who defends his inaction on the ground that he is but one and that therefore what he does or leaves undone will be of little account, that in him we can see a nation dying.

In one of the stories of the appearance of Jesus to his disciples after death there is a very human touch. Jesus has been repeating to Peter the injunction, "Feed my sheep." Each time Peter protests his love for Jesus, in the hope that his ardent words will erase the stain of his earlier disloyalty in the judgment hall, Jesus gives Peter a task, as if to say, "If you mean what you say, prove it by what you do." "Then Peter turning about," we read, "seeth the disciple whom Jesus loved following" . . . and . . . "saith to Jesus, Lord, what shall this man do?" Peter did not see why he should accept the obligations Jesus had laid on him unless others, including John, were going to do their share. Have you never heard a man raise just such a question as Peter raised, and (putting his comment into modern words) say something like this: "Yes, I grant you that is the ideal, but until we all feel that way and accept that view, how can any one of us do anything about it? When every one will come in, you can count on me." What did Jesus say to Peter? "What is that to thee? Follow thou me." The sheep were waiting to be fed, the work was waiting to be done, the world was waiting for the gospel, and Peter's duty had nothing to do with the question whether John was to be given the same or any other task.

No! Inaction on your part and mine, on the ground that the hundred or the thousand others who might act have not yet done their share, is inconsistent with professed devotion to the ideal. When you do your part, that may prove to be the signal to others, may prove to be the kindling spark which will spread the fire; your action may have consequences far exceeding your own personal achievement. Anyhow, "What is that to thee, follow thou me." The religion pictured in the Bible—at any rate that religion which found expression in the prophetic leaders of Israel and in the Christian beginnings—is concerned with positive action. "Go ye, serve the Lord." "Go tell this people"—thus the word of the Lord through men of prophetic insight. "Go and preach the Kingdom of God," "Go out into the highways and byways," "Go thou and do likewise"—thus Jesus. "Work out your own salvation," "Be not overcome of evil, but overcome evil with good"—thus Paul. And an unknown apostle adds his challenge . . . "We look for new heavens and a new earth wherein dwelleth righteousness. Wherefore, seeing that ye look for these things . . . give diligence . . . looking for and hastening the day of God."

It is as easy in public concerns as in personal interests to mistake inaction for safety. It is tragic to see how very well-meaning persons busy themselves in the effort to prevent any new thought upon the new problems of our time. The great gift of human reason they would prefer to see wrapped up and protected, forgetting that reason, like any other true wealth, is conserved only in its wise use. And so, wherever new interpretations are being offered and discussed they see only danger; they fly to any and every means to suppress the exercise of reason unless they can be assured in advance that their own conclusions or prejudices will be sustained. But there is no safety—there is dire peril—in a policy of such inaction, for those who live, as we do, in a rapidly changing world. "The dogmas of the quiet past," wrote Lincoln in 1862, "are inadequate to the stormy present. The occasion is piled high with difficulties and we must rise to the occasion. As our case is new, so must we think anew and act anew."

Be positive! Don't be content to stand for something if there's any danger that while you are standing for it others have to do the running about for it! Be positive in conviction! St. Paul confessed that he knew in part only, but he knew: "I know in whom I have believed." The world is not really interested in what you don't believe, nor is it helped one whit by your denial of what another man believes unless in the very act of denying another's error you affirm something that it is more worth while to believe.

Be positive in your response to the Spirit of God! If you discern in any of your experiences, or in the utterance or action of any other man, a challenge to your better self, make a definite response. Be either cold or hot: do something which commits you. Do not deceive yourself or others by any of those words of faint praise which have murdered so many enthusiasms. Beware of an emotional response which absorbs energy that is needed for an active response.

Be positive in your outlook! Believe with the old

Harold E. Speight, D.D.

Pilgrim pastor that "the Lord hath more light and truth to break forth out of his holy word." That light and truth will be ours in proportion to our active preparation to receive it, and in proportion to our expectant desire for it. Our limited experience is fixed only by our limited active desire, even as the air all about us is at this moment full of vibrations or impulses which we can translate into music or human speech only if we go through the labor and discipline of preparing and tuning a sensitive receiver.

The early Christians were looking for and hastening the coming of the Day of God. Can any one claim the name of Christian today who is merely watching and waiting and taking what comes and leaving it to others actively to look for the new earth and the new heavens wherein dwelleth righteousness? No! The Christian, if he is anything at all, is a commissioned man, accepting a task—and still better a cause—from One who swept aside every last excuse of the cowardly or contented disciple, "What is that to thee, Follow thou me."

THE RHYTHM OF REACTION

Born in Wisconsin in 1890, educated at the Universities of Minnesota and California, and at Drew Theological Seminary, Dr. Stafford entered the Congregational ministry in 1914. After three years as assistant to Dr. Cadman, in Central Church, Brooklyn, he went to the Open Door Church, in Minneapolis; serving as Chaplain in the American Army in France in 1918; returning to the First Church in Minneapolis at the end of the War, where he remained for four years.

In 1923 Dr. Stafford went to the Pilgrim Church in St. Louis—the great mother-church of the Congregational order in the Middle West—where his gifts as preacher and leader have won for him a place of influence and command; in the same year appeared his striking book, *Finding God*. As this sketch is written the news tells of his call to the pastorate of the Old South Church in Boston, in succession to Dr. Gordon.

The following sermon reveals a preacher who sees the pageant of history and its reactions against a long background, seeking to fortify us against setbacks, both in national and individual experience, by interpreting them as challenges to our courage and our faith. It is a most helpful sermon and one much needed, finely conceived and carefully wrought out, teaching us that setbacks need not be failures unless we let them be so.

Born in Wisconsin in 1890, educated at the Universities of Minnesota and California, and at Drew Theological Seminary, Dr. Stafford entered the Congregational ministry in 1914. After three years as assistant to Dr. Cadman, in Central Church, Brooklyn, he went to the Open Door Church, in Minneapolis; serving as Chaplain in the American Army in France in 1918; returning to the First Church in Minneapolis at the end of the War, where he remained for four years.

In 1923 Dr. Stafford went to the Pilgrim Church in St. Louis—the great mother-church of the Congregational order in the Middle West—where his gifts as preacher and leader have won for him a place of influence and command; in the same year appeared his striking book, *Finding God*. As this sketch is written the news tells of his call to the pastorate of the Old South Church in Boston, in succession to Dr. Gordon.

The following sermon reveals a preacher who sees the pageant of history and its reactions against a long background, seeking to fortify us against setbacks, both in national and individual experience, by interpreting them as challenges to our courage and our faith. It is a most helpful sermon and one much needed, finely conceived and carefully wrought out, teaching us that setbacks need not be failures unless we let them be so.

THE RHYTHM OF REACTION

THE RHYTHM OF REACTION

RUSSELL HENRY STAFFORD, D.D.

PILGRIM CONGREGATIONAL CHURCH, ST. LOUIS

He that endureth to the end, the same shall be saved.
Mark 13: 13.

If you and I had the ordering of the world, no
doubt we would try to run it on a different plan from
that now in operation. We would see to it that
matters were so arranged as to produce a steady upward grade along all lines of legitimate human endeavor. We would tolerate no lapses, no reverses,
no stops, not so much as a slowing down of the
ameliorative processes of human development.
The question suggests itself whether, if we were
in a position to accomplish this reorganization of experience, we should not thereby be omitting, along
with the hazards and troubles thus prevented, also
the zest and adventure of living. But that question
can only arise in the abstract. For actually, as sometimes we feel that we know only too well, we live in
a world where things do not move forward and upward smoothly. If one were to chart the curve of
progress in any department of our interest, personal
or social, one would find that it proceeds through a
series of starts and stops, with sudden drops of level

303

and not infrequent writhings backward and forward, as the incalculable element of free will in our fellows plays havoc from time to time with our plans, and as the equally surprising and apparently capricious behavior of nature, ill correlated with human intentions, produces also sometimes catastrophes shattering our ambitions, or at least forcing us to revise them radically. At every point, in life as we know it, setbacks are likely to occur, through circumstances which, arising beyond the region of our control, obtrude upon the area we seek to govern. And sometimes these setbacks become, so far as we personally are concerned in the present chapter of our experience, actual failures.

But a setback can only become a failure on condition that we yield to the discouragement it invites, and relax or relinquish our efforts to carry on the projects in which we are concerned. It is fair to say that a far more dangerous enemy of advance than any hostile force irrupting into our fields of operation is this discouragement. For when a man yields to the temptation to be downhearted because things are not going his way, then he resigns hope; his vigor spends itself thenceforth in vain regrets, rather than upon constructive efforts; and thus he stands self-condemned to calamity and defeat.

But discouragement carried to this degree—discouragement to which a man succumbs instead of resisting and rising above it—is a token of impatience, born of short-sightedness, due in turn to lack of confidence in the continuous and effective purpose for righteousness which indwells the universe. Looking at the little segment of our lives which lies within the present range of our memory, knowledge and anticipation, as though that were all the life we were to have, we demand feverishly of fate (in which, in this mood, we believe, rather than in God) the immediate gratification of such desires as we choose to embrace: "we want what we want when we want it." But we cannot always have it when we want it; nor would we make so little allowance for possible delays upon our way, if we but saw further into the reaches of the Infinite, and took a longer view of the course which we pursue.

The only way in which we can gain this longer view is through faith. But to faith in God every intuition of the soul, and every observation we make in the actual world, rightly interpreted, invite us. The best evidence for the reality of things unseen, and of God, the Great Unseen who governs all things, is that belief in a spiritual realm and a supreme spirit is normal to the human mind. He who denies these verities thereby departs from the norm of consciousness and conduct, which is our only ultimate standard of sanity and truth. But he who accepts these verities will not be disheartened by the misadventures which may befall him in the pursuit of his ideals: he will never accept them as final, but, viewing them as mere setbacks upon the path determined by his will in accordance with the infinite purpose for his growth, will cheerfully carry on through and beyond them, guided in this sustained resolution by a long view which assures him that eternity is his, so that there is plenty of time, and he can afford an occasional delay en route.

Now faith in God—in a supreme conscious purpose of righteousness in the universe—reached its highest point in him who was the most normal and consequently the most exemplary of men, even Jesus Christ our Lord. He entertained no delusions—at least toward the end of his ministry, when he had been schooled by trouble to make due allowance for the setbacks of human experience—to the effect that the triumph of his cause and Gospel would come steadily and without break or momentary defeat. So, in the somewhat puzzling apocalyptic passage from which our text is taken, this much at least is clear, that he was warning his disciples, more naïve than he, of all sorts of dangers, difficulties and disasters impending for the world and for the Church; he was warning them not so much, however, of these perils, as against discouragement on their account. The key to the whole passage, however we interpret some of its obscure references, is in these words—inviting his followers to accommodate their hopes and plans to a long view lighted up by assurance of the final victory of God's Providence over all natural and human perversity: "He that endureth to the end, the same shall be saved."

These words, like most other maxims of the Master, are of abiding significance, as applicable in our time as in the first century. Today setbacks still occur; and by yielding to discouragement we shall

turn setbacks into failure; while by overcoming discouragement through faith in the outcome which God
promises to all earnest and sustained right effort, we
can offset our setbacks, and carry the curve of progress upward in spite of them. This truth finds illustration in many regions of current concern. For
a first instance, you will remember that when the
Great War came there were many who felt that it
signalized the moral failure of civilization; that hope
could never more be entertained of human progress,
since such a crime as this could be perpetrated at so
late a date in historic evolution. But civilization sur-
vived the Great War; great virtues of heroism and
coöperation were released by the terrible necessities
of that struggle, within both camps; and we are now
able to see that, whereas the war was necessitated by
certain anachronistic political adjustments in pre-war
Europe, there is no reason at all for supposing that a
new order of international administration may not be
brought to pass, largely under the urgent admonition of this very setback to social welfare, which shall
render repetitions of this catastrophe, if not impossible, at least highly improbable.

Suppose, however, that another Great War really
should come, after all. It is not altogether unlikely
that such a dire result may ensue upon the post-war
frictions of Europe, complicated by America's irritating self-assertiveness. What then? Will it mean,
as many prophets of woe are telling us, the end of
civilization? But civilization cannot end. All that
can end are the external arrangements of society, in-

cidental to civilization itself; the spiritual values which constitute human culture cannot be permanently lost or even obscured. The last time civilization was eclipsed was when Rome was at last overwhelmed by the barbarians in the fifth century. That setback lasted a thousand years. But through that millennium of apparent arrest to all humane forces, the peoples of northern Europe were being civilized. Then at length the cultural resources of Greece and Rome were rediscovered, and, as the dawn of the Renaissance burst in splendor over the western world, an advance was instituted along all lines of classic investigation and achievement, which still continues, and which has far surpassed any accomplishments ever contemplated in the classic period itself. So, even though the present system of society were in another terrible conflict to be dissolved—which God forbid!—yet in the long run of history we may well believe that the outcome would show that dissolution to have been a mere momentary setback for the human race.

Now and again we hear, likewise, from sundry pessimists, that the Church of Christ is doomed; that it is losing its grip upon the popular mind, and can hardly survive beyond another generation or two. I must say that I personally am unable to see any indications to that effect. But what if it were true? The Church, as an institution, or a series of institutions, more or less loosely related and sometimes mutually antagonistic, might disappear; the ministry and the sacraments as now carried on might pass away. But, if, as we hold, religion is an ineradicable interest of the human mind, and in Christ this interest finds its consummate expression and definition, then the Christian religion would certainly once more take on an organic expression to promote the distinctive purposes which this interest subserves, and the Church, though perhaps under another name, would inevitably come to life again.

We have not been wont of late years to consider the possibility of a setback to America's advance as a nation. For we are going through a period of extraordinary prosperity; and prosperous people seldom give much thought to a rainy day. But sometimes I fear that in our luxury and arrogance we Americans are sailing straight for disaster. Certainly something of the sort must occur, if we continue to cultivate a spirit of domineering self-complacency at the expense of the other peoples of the earth. Of course we all hope that no such trouble is coming to our country. But what if it came? So long as there remained in America thoughtful citizens who loved true American ideals—which are universal ideals of liberty and justice—the resurrection of the nation, refined and purified by adversity, might be surely anticipated; and what, to the weaker wills of the generation which suffered it, might well seem the downfall of the nation, would prove to have been only a regrettable but passing phase of its continuous development.

This same principle, that troubles are only setbacks so long as we keep our courage, applies in our personal concerns also. When a man has business troubles, for instance, those troubles may amount to actual failure; but only on condition that he give up trying. The man who, confronted by financial disaster, makes the best and fairest arrangement he can and keeps on trying, turning his hand to new tasks, ever alert for new opportunities, utilizing the very experience which has come to him through hardship as a chart by which to steer clear of similar difficulties in future, may indeed go through what is technically known as a business failure; but beyond the failure he will find renewed success—provided his business is of such a nature as to meet the requirements of his own conscience by rendering some needed service to the public.

In our personal relations, moreover, disappointments frequently come to us. Friends do not measure up to what we expect of them; even our families, it may be, are less loyal or less devoted than we feel they should be. When, in any of the intimate associations of life, one accepts such a disappointment as final, then that association suffers grave damage, if not indeed complete severance. But when, with patience and sympathy, we take a long view of the years ahead in which we may still enjoy this precious contact if now we but show forbearance and maintain a forgiving spirit, then the very intensity of our own loyalty will sooner or later overcome the lack in those whom we love, and a relationship more blessed and more fruitful than ever we enjoyed in

310

the past will succeed this temporary setback to our affections.

Finally, let me speak of setbacks in our moral life. Probably there is not one of us who has not now, or has not had at some time in the past, some hard moral battle to fight. When you are struggling against all the demons of your lower self to do right and keep straight, and the demons get the upper hand, and you do wrong and have reason to be ashamed of yourself, will you accept that defeat as definitive? Will you say to yourself that, having failed once, you must therefore keep on failing, so that there is no further use in trying to do better? Then at and from that point you will be a moral failure. But if you will but look at yourself from God's viewpoint—taking the long view of your spiritual development—you will achieve a patience with your own shortcomings born not of surrender to them, but of resolved and confident determination that, in due season, they shall yet be utterly overcome. Paraphrasing General Grant's saying in the course of one of his great campaigns, you will say to yourself, "I will fight it out along this line if it takes all this lifetime!" With such a bearing toward your temptations, you will be likely to win the final victory long before this lifetime is over; and, in any event, another life is to follow, in which you will achieve the moral goals for which you strenuously strive in the life that now is.

You and I have not the ordering of the world; and in the world as it is setbacks do occur. But let us

311

remember that they are only setbacks, unless we want to make them failures. We are not to let go; we are to hold on, keep at it, and carry through; until the ground lost has been recovered, new advance has been made, and we lay hold upon victory, as companions of our victorious Saviour, who also wrestled with darkness and discouragement, and overcame, and who is with us through the fray:

"He that endureth to the end, the same shall be saved."

A Marylander, born in 1873, Dr. Cramer was educated at Franklin and Marshall College and the Theological Seminary of the Reformed Church, Lancaster; with special studies at Oxford University. Ordained to the ministry of the Reformed Church in 1901, he became associate pastor of the old First Church of Lancaster the same year. Since 1903 he has been pastor of the First Church—his only parish; a Church rich in historic memories where it is a joy to preach, as I can bear witness.

To his labors in a great parish, Dr. Cramer has added an influential ministry in the Church at large, both in his own communion and as a member of the Executive Committee of the Federal Council of Churches, as well as on the Commission on the Relations of Religious Bodies in Europe. He was also a member of the Continuation Commission after the War, and in 1924 dedicated the Memorial Church at Château-Thierry.

God creates by growth, whether it be a universe, a flower, or a soul—such is the message of the following sermon. The preacher reminds us that the seed of immortality—a germ of the Eternal—is a prophecy of the soul, a dim anticipation of personality to be fulfilled by growth, struggle, fruition—like a brown bulb in the springtime which has in it the possibility of the lily. Either it will unfold in great and glowing qualities or wither into secret hardness in the midst of the years.

GROWING A SOUL

W. STUART CRAMER, D.D.

FIRST REFORMED CHURCH, LANCASTER, PA.

Consider the lilies how they grow. Luke 12: 27.

"Grow" is a Spring word. The winter season does not suggest it. In the Spring there is the evidence of growth in our gardens where the pale green shoots tip every branch of shrubbery and perennial. Under the warm sun and April showers they show life. The idea of growth thrusts itself upon us at every turn, in the great out-of-doors. It speaks louder than words. Its lesson is rich in suggestion. It seems to be God's way of reminding us that he is alive. It is the way of life. The idea of growth runs all through his method of promoting the universe. He creates by growing everything he has made. The more secrets modern science reveals about the universe, the more do we realize that this element of growth enters into God's ways of life. Suns and planets, trees and germs, lilies and corn, all grow. There is nothing made in nature that is made by factory methods. It all grows.

Growth, then, is the one thing with which we must reckon in all life; and it is full of mystery. That urge from the unseen pushing the rose into bud and

315

W. Stuart Cramer, D.D.

bloom, that hidden force which liberates the germ of life and breaks the shell that covers it in a grain of corn, expanding and driving it up into the sunshine, bringing forth "first the blade, then the ear, then the full corn in the ear," is the mystery which baffles the microscope; and the scientist and man of faith alike stand before it with uncovered head as if on holy ground. "Consider then the lilies how they grow."

If the lilies grow, then we know that God grows. Sometimes men think of God as if he were full grown, located in some great office, managing the universe. They think of God as a Manager of a great factory which turns out worlds, trees and lilies. But I like to think of God as being immanent in all nature, growing, with such intelligence and love as will eternally perfect all life. What mystery then is wrapped up in the commonest things of life; the grass, the violet, the tree, the ant, the bird; and, most of all, man!

Whatever, then, we think about man must be thought in connection with this inevitable factor called growth. Growth is spontaneous. "Consider the lilies how they grow." They just grow. Here is something that is not man-made. No physician can prescribe for growth. He may tell us many wise things about the care of the body, but growth is beyond his ken. It is God's secret. The psychologist may give us much valuable information about the mind and its functions, but the mind grows out of its very nature. The preacher may suggest much im-

316

portant knowledge applicable to soul growth, but he is impotent to make the soul grow. That is God's business; and it is beyond finding out. We can't fret souls into growth. "Be not anxious for your life; life is more than food." "Which of you by being anxious can add a cubit unto the measure of his life?" "Consider the lilies how they grow."

Growth of the soul, then, is in God's hands. All he asks us to do is to "grow in grace and knowledge of our Lord and Saviour Jesus Christ." This admonition of Peter suggests that we increase our grace and knowledge of Christ. But another interpretation that seems more likely is that he tells us that we who have the grace and knowledge of Christ are expected to grow. Those who have these have the mystic touch of God's Spirit and they will grow. They must grow. God sees to that. He urges us to pray, sacrifice, be earnest and sincere, believe, and the soul will grow. It is its nature to grow. God makes it that way. Because God is in the soul, there is life, and life never stands still. Be sure, then, that if you have God's grace you will grow.

The soul is the seed of untold possibilities; such as eye has not seen nor ear heard. And yet what the eye has seen and the ear heard are marvelous enough. We have seen a Lincoln, a Francis, a John; and they were great souls. How few such souls have been grown! They, however, teach us the marvelous possibilities of the soul. It contains immeasurable energy, aspiration, courage, faith, unselfishness, purity. The aspiration of a Roosevelt, the courage of a Lindbergh, the faith of a Moses, the unselfishness of a Pasteur, the purity of the Virgin Mother of our Lord, all are the immortal inspiration of the human race. They call us to heights that touch the skies. The series of articles on "Growing a Soul" that ran through many editions of *The Christian Century* this year, in which the growth of the soul of Grace Scribner is depicted in her own diary, reveals how souls can grow. She had an active soul. There were many pains of growth in its progress; pains of doubt, discouragement, despair, out of which she emerged to enter again into new doubts; but ever facing forward. When she met the tragedy that took away her life her soul went on into that long eternity, but it went on growing.

Another wonderful thing about growing a soul is that it is possible that it never grows old. The body grows old and weak but the soul need not. It is one of life's tragedies that the soul does get old and decrepit perhaps more often than not. We, however, have known souls that grew more beautiful with age. Being the exception, as perhaps they are, they nevertheless reveal the possibility of it. We hear a great deal about this age's demand of youth in all spheres of life, and the disparagement of age. Is it not because in most souls there comes with age a certain static, stunted, twisted something which is no longer an evidence of life but of death and decay? We know a pastor who for thirty-nine years has served one Church and now at the age of eighty is buoyant, sympathetic and sweet in disposition; and still alert mentally to all phases of knowledge. His people never ceased loving and being truly interested in him. What an achievement when one *grows* old! Too many of us *get* old. When we *grow* old, we never cease to be young.

One of the sad things in the life of Christians is the frequency of soul-stunting. We take our young people through a period of Christian nurture until they are Confirmed. They take their place then in the conventional relationship of the average member of his Church. Growth in the grace and knowledge of Jesus Christ ceases. They settle down to a satisfied membership in the Church. That which they started so auspiciously is crowded out by many other interests in life that have no relationship with the spiritual life of the soul. The soul stops growing and dries up. It is like mind culture which ceases at graduation from High School and College. Thousands of the boys and girls who come out of our educational institutions this Spring will go on into manhood and womanhood without any more knowledge than they absorbed there; and even this will become atrophied.

There is a spring near the city which was once a bubbling, gushing spring, over which the early settler built a stone spring-house. For years now it has been neglected until one of our citizens recently purchased the property and revived it. He dug down into the depths of the earth and rock and found it clogged with débris which he cleaned away. The water was backed into the surrounding earth, but when its natural channel was opened up, it became a running spring. That is what happens to the minds that are gushing, bright, thought-giving and producing when the débris of sense gratifications and senseless pleasures take possession. They clog up the normal flow of the mind and then it ceases to grow. That is what happens to the soul. How many who make a pretense of worshiping God have grown a soul beyond the stature of what it was ten or a score of years ago when in the glow of youth they gave themselves to the Church? How many of you have been growing a soul? You have been growing a bank account, or a business, or a beautiful home in the suburbs, but these are trifles that pass away and are cast off at death. The soul is the only real thing to grow because it is eternal. Emerson said, "The one thing in the world of value is the active soul."

There is a great deal of appearance of soul-growing among the people. We have them in our pews every Sunday morning. We have members in our churches who appear to keep their Christianity alive by attending to all the perfunctory duties required by the church, but whose vital interests are not in growing a soul. They are rather interested in growing self-advancement and realizing self-gratification. Those who are familiar with gardening and trucking know the futility of the strawberry plant that grows suckers out from it in varying directions. Each sucker fastens itself into the ground while at the same time it remains attached to the mother plant. The gardener who permits the suckers to live need

320

never look for beautiful fruit in his strawberry patch. To secure luscious berries he must keep the suckers down. There is growth there, but it is wild growth. Doesn't this remind us of certain Christian people who hold fast to the church, but reach out in many ways and form attachments that sap their life; and while they seem to grow, they really only grow wild? The man who grows as a Christian must realize the grace and knowledge of Jesus Christ with definite purpose and intention, making every part of his life the expression of that loyalty.

We should not be impatient about growing a soul. Many are; and they try to force it. They grow coarse. Coarse growth is apt to be rapid. Fast growing things in nature are not fine. The North Carolina poplar is planted where shade is needed quickly. It is a fast grower but unattractive and undesirable. If you would have beautiful trees you must plant the oak or the linden, which are slow growers. The most valued things in your garden are those that try your patience in their slow growing— the boxwood, spruce and pines. "The warmth of many suns must wait on them; the moisture of many tranquil nights must coax them, before they feel bold enough to expose their inner life to the gaze of sun and stars or the touch of the gentle winds."

"Ay," quoth my Uncle Gloucester,
"Small herbs have grace, great weeds do grow apace";
And since, methinks, I would not grow so fast,
Because sweet flowers are slow and weeds make haste.

321

W. Stuart Cramer, D.D.

The same is true of the social life. The vulgarity that is so popular today is the product of the new rich, who have, by the luck of chance, become the leaders of fashions and customs, setting a pace for our youth that money, without culture, can buy. How different from those who have the traditions of refinement back of them and whose every emotion and act are indicative of that fact!

So it is with the soul. "It groweth after the growth of one that hath all eternity to grow in." Make it grow real, however slow. Our investments in life should be made with the one great object of growing the soul. The returns may be small but that does not matter if they are sure. Growing a soul is the supreme end of life. It, indeed, is the only way the soul can become fit for the companionship of God.

Growing a soul is something about which we must be conscious, but not self-conscious. Carrying a Bible on the street to let people know one is growing a soul is an evidence that the soul is not growing. And yet one should know in his own secret consciousness that his soul is growing. He knows this because in his self-analysis he sees what he has outgrown. He has outgrown fear as the motivating force of his right conduct and learned the joy of love. He has outgrown bigotry in his attitude toward those who differ from his views and has substituted charity and sympathy. He has outgrown pessimism and fatalism and become optimistic about the victory of God in winning the world to his righteousness. He has outgrown his childish ideas of God which made him think of him as a Magic-God, or a Monarch-God, and he has learned to fellowship with him as the Father-God, whose love moves him in all his providences. He has outgrown his selfishness about his own salvation and lives forgetful of self-interests and mindful of others. He has outgrown fear of death and become grateful for it as a stepping-stone to the higher sphere of life. One may be conscious of these evidences as a child is conscious when he has outgrown his garments and steps out with his new suit of clothes that fit him.

Another test of the growing soul is found in the stability of character. The roots of faith, hope and love have gone deep into our life and the temptations that broke us as a reed no longer disturb our moral equilibrium. We feel the security of the oak that weathered the blasts of storm until it is proof against hurricane. Instead of hiding from trouble and temptation we come forth out into the open to face them with undaunted courage, sure that when we are on God's side, there is always mastery.

Finally, there is one test we cannot apply ourselves, but which must be applied by others. It is the test of beauty of character. Of this we must be conscious. The instant, however, that we pride ourselves in it we enter the class of the Pharisee who said, "God, I thank thee, that I am not as the rest of men." Even the Publican who said, "God, be merciful to me, a sinner," was growing his soul. Ruskin said, "I believe the first test of a truly great man is his humility." There is a significant description of Jesus given by John, "Jesus, knowing that the Father had given all things into his hands, and that he was come from God, and went to God; he riseth from supper, and laid aside his garments, and took a towel, and girded himself . . . and began to wash the disciples' feet." Humility was the natural expression of his soul who had outgrown all others in the world.

It has been said significantly: "The surest sign of a great nature is that it can stoop without apologizing for it." The men who entered the mind of Jesus when he pronounced his "blesseds" in the beatitudes were not those who were conscious of their greatness in the things that the world counts great, but those who were "poor in spirit." This virtue of humility, then, is something for which men rise up and call us blessed. It is characteristic of the life that is growing in the grace and knowledge of our Lord and Saviour Jesus Christ.

Dr. Ames was born in Wisconsin in 1870, educated at Drake University and the Yale Divinity School, with graduate studies in philosophy. Since 1900 he has been pastor of the University Church of the Disciples of Christ, Chicago; and since 1918 associate professor of philosophy in the University of Chicago. In *The Psychology of Religious Experience* he did pioneer work in the religious interpretation of group psychology; and as a preacher he is widely known through such books as *The Higher Individualism* and *The New. Orthodoxy*.

A pragmatic Christian philosopher, Dr. Ames is a preacher of persuasive charm and power, simple, direct, stimulating, as witness the following sermon in which he interprets the Gospel for our out-of-door age; albeit reminding us that nature, for all her strange and solemn loveliness and companionableness, does not satisfy the deepest needs of the soul. Jesus was an outdoor Preacher, to whom all nature was an ever-present parable of spiritual truth; but his words tell us what nature can never tell:

"Nature is not always friendly and beautiful; human friendships waver and fail; but the Divine Love flows unwearied and undiminished. The sense of the far horizons of life, and the habit of turning to them for refreshment and strength, belong supremely to the religious way of life. For religion includes the practice of seeing the immediate and the commonplace under the form of eternity. To its anointed insight

'The touch of an eternal presence thrills
The fringes of the sunsets and the hills.'"

THE FAR HORIZON

EDWARD SCRIBNER AMES, D.D.

UNIVERSITY CHURCH OF DISCIPLES, CHICAGO

I will lift up mine eyes unto the hills, from whence cometh my help. Psalm 121: 1.

Some years ago I was presented with a book whose title was *The Far Horizon*, by Lucas Malet. It was given to me after the death of a good friend. Her daughter came one day bringing the book in fulfillment of her mother's request. She said her mother had read it many times during her long and painful illness and had found great comfort in it. My own reading of the book was attended by a double interest, that of the unfolding of the story and that of trying to understand why it had been such a great help and comfort to my friend.

She had been a woman of an active, happy life, devoted to her husband and daughter at home and to a considerable circle of friends. She was of a buoyant nature, loved the out-of-doors, enjoyed the game of golf, and occasionally took a hunting trip into the Rocky Mountains. It was a memorable event when she returned from one of these vacations and proudly showed her friends the skin of a mountain lion which her rifle had brought down. It seemed a strangely

327

ironical fate that a person so athletic, so much given to life in the open, should have been overtaken by tuberculosis of the spine and doomed to years of confinement and suffering, shut away from the vistas of lakes and mountains and sky.

The title of the book she read so much carried the secret of her attachment to it. The "far horizon" suggested the release her soul craved. It is the story of a London bank clerk, retired by his firm after thirty-five years of patient, routine labor. Over fifty years of age, unmarried, he suddenly found himself with empty hands facing an old age of loneliness and freedom. The world around him began to appear in new lights, often intensifying his solitude and his remoteness from its busy life, but at times touching him with illumination and quiet comfort. Thus on the evening of his first day of retirement, through the open window came the voice of the great city herself in answer to his mood—a voice low, multitudinous, raucous, without emphasis, without briefest relief of interval or pause. London revealed herself to him in her solidarity, as a prodigious living creature, awful in her mysterious vigor, ever big with impending birth, merciless with impending death. He had the sense of being changed, of having shrunk to the point of nullity and final ineptitude, while she remained strong, active, relentless as ever. In his bewilderment he found his way to a favorite little open space, one of those breathing spots where the walls and the hard pavements of the city give way grudgingly for a bit of air and light. There in the dusk the twinkling,

evasive lights led down to the river bank and to the
mystery of the edding and flowing tide, the ceaseless
effort seaward of the stream. It was the nearest
bit of nature, unharnessed, irresponsible, and it had
long symbolized for the clerk in hours of depression,
emancipation from monotonous labor and everlasting
brick and mortar. There he could watch the dying
sunset, and the outcoming of the stars, and be tran-
quilized and helped to see life calmly, and to bring
himself in line with fact, to endure and to forgive.

As the story unfolds the bank clerk finds two other
sources of solace and recovery. One is in a human
friendship and the other is in the ministration of religion. Through the friendship an unexpected horizon is opened from which sympathy and understanding flow into his starved soul while it also called forth
from him gallantry and unselfish devotion to one who
had need of his help and rose to greater achievement
through his encouragement. The other far horizon
was that of religion symbolized by the high altar of
his ancestral faith and by its power of absolution
through which his soul at the last could be lifted
through the gates of death into the eternity beyond.
As I read the story for myself I realized that my
friend's fondness for the book sprang from her discovery in it of those far horizons which she herself
had known, and by which she was able to maintain
a sense of the dignity and value of life under the
utmost pain and seeming defeat. It had helped her
to be conscious of the power to lift her imagination
to the far horizons of life's greatest experiences and

to gather strength and inspiration from them.

She learned voluntarily to lift her eyes to the hills, to the hills of nature, to the heights of fine friendship and to far-lying horizons of religious faith and hope. She deliberately sought them out and clung to them when suffering and disappointment might have bade her give up and let the darkness and pain overwhelm her. It was a magnificent battle of the spirit against the principalities, against the powers, against the world rulers of this darkness. She refused to allow her life to be shut in by the four walls of her room. She kept open her soul's great windows of divine surprise and in memory looked out upon the giant forms of the mountains rising above the storms and the mists, with the sunlight playing over their summits. For any one who has ever stood upon one of those peaks and has seen the clouds far below covering the plains and the valleys, there is a lasting memory of exaltation and security. The power to recover that vision is a means of spiritual poise and resilience. There is therefore a kind of moral obligation to have at hand upon our walls or in our books pictures of those hills which on occasion may make it easier for us to lift our eyes from the routine and the narrow spaces of our shops and counters to their distant, light-circled horizons.

My friend knew also how to enjoy friendships. With what eager wistfulness she would listen to the simplest conversations, for they brought into her chamber the outer air of the active, busy world, and enabled her to live more vividly in the interests of other persons. She carried them all in her woman's heart, followed the children to school and to their play, cherished their successes and discounted their mistakes. If people went to see her to give of their strength and courage they came away deeper in her debt, for she was already radiant with a cheerful camaraderie which is given to those who suffer but are not defeated. She could forget herself in the rôle of her friends and thereby help them with their difficulties as if she had none of her own.

And then there were the far horizons of her religion. She was not of the pietistic type. Her own religion had been of the practical, non-mystical kind, but she was responsive to the symbolism of the religion which her favorite book described. That was the Roman Catholic faith. She could feel its appeal to the hero of the story. By its long tradition and its familiar symbols it stretched out a hand from the distant past and touched him with a light from another world. When he came down to the last ebbing sands of life, he turned to the Church for the last rites and gained from them a strange peace and fortitude for the great journey into the hereafter. The Church symbolized the watchful, faithful care of a patient mother who never could forget her child, who had hovered over him at birth with purifying rites and who would stand by him in the hour of death still holding a light above the darkening path. She held the symbols of a greater life than that of nature or of human friendship.

Thus my friend had found three real helps for her

own spirit in the three things which have so often furnished strength and light to the heart of man in the moment of his extremity. Nature, human companionship and religion supplied her with far horizons. All of them lift the soul out of itself and suggest a larger world for contemplation and enjoyment. Man's capacity to respond to these ideal relationships is at once his hope and his despair. Insofar as he is able to see beyond himself and to find release in visions of larger worlds, he lives above his commonplace and routine world. But the three kinds of horizons have different values.

We live in a period which cultivates the enjoyment of nature more widely and more eagerly than any recent time. It may be due to the fact that we so largely live in cities and therefore seek change from the pavements and the brick walls, from the noise and the smoke. It may be because we have studied nature more carefully and with better helps so that we see with larger understanding her landscapes and living forms, her atomic energies and her vast galaxies of stars. Nature's mysteries lead us out of ourselves into immense and incalculable realities. They astound and challenge us. They humble and awe us. They destroy man's conceit of his importance and reduce him to an infinitesimal element, vanishing after a swift, short hour of time. In the infinities of space and time the cares and troubles which beset him seem to fall away like unremembered pulse beats. Such contemplation of nature may remove the strain of self-consciousness and relax nerves tense with anxious thoughts. It is healing and releasing like the vision of all vast, impersonal things—the ocean, the sky and the stars.

It is, however, the exceptional individual who can be long content with the companionship of nature alone. All but the very few crave also the presence of the living mind and heart and the touch of a friendly hand. It is usually a kindness to visit a friend whom accident or sickness has long withdrawn from his ordinary associations. He is glad to get news of his habitual world, to hear of the little incidents of labor and recreation, of neighborhood life and enterprise, of love and work, which make up the story of the passing drama. None of us can know how vital this life of other people is to us until we are withdrawn from it. Only then do we realize how much the accustomed greetings of our neighbors, morning and evening, and the conversations woven into the day's work have come to mean to us. There is no punishment for men so severe as solitary confinement, and there is scarcely a pleasure greater than that of free and hearty converse with old friends.

And this human society is more than a means of recreation. It is essential to sanity and moral health. Men constantly measure themselves by the judgments of their fellows. As children need sympathetic spectators to enjoy their block houses, their songs, their drawings, their creations in the sand or clay, so adults have their friendly auditors, their censors and their impartial witnesses. Our minds are hesitant and tentative about their deepest thoughts

333

until they are made vocal and get confirmed by some competent and understanding souls. Even those rugged prophets who break with their day and generation make their appeal to an inner circle of sympathizing spirits or to a more distant, future jury of their peers. Authors are eager to have their manuscripts read by selected friends before they are given to the public. All copy is edited before printing and in effect censored before publication. Scientific men work in groups and schools, artists have associations, athletes belong to clubs, business men unite in partnerships and corporations, reformers create leagues, all men participate with their fellows to gain objectivity and verification for their thoughts and to furnish stability and guidance for the common will. In such companies of friends every participant shares a larger life. He becomes a member of an order which outruns his personal power and extends beyond his life. There is a mystical quality in such an experience which is generated by the very association of kindred minds in an ideal venture. Where two or three are met together in the name of the divine, there the divine is present in the midst of them.

Man lifts up his eyes unto the hills and finds quiet and strength; but in the horizon which the hills enable him to see he seeks the signs of his human kind. For it is in neighborliness and in the social sympathy of men like himself that he finds the longer ranges of vision and hope. And through the common aspirations of his fellows he rises to the contemplation of the divine. An American traveling in Europe is struck by the spires which ascend so high above the levels of the dwellings, as if the very structure of the towns illustrated the fact that out of the associated life of men there is an outreaching for the divine. The cathedrals and temples are witnesses to the need for something vaster and eternal. They stand above the lower levels of life like sentinels of a heavenly world. Through them man's spirit ascends to its noblest heights and surveys its widest prospect. It is in his religion that man feels himself secure above the tides of time and the storms of fate. At her altars he leaves all the dross, all the littleness of his nature. By her ministration he becomes free of his burden of guilt and fear, feels himself united again with the world's great heart of love, and beholds the far horizon of the spiritual world.

Nature is not always friendly and beautiful; human friendships sometimes waver and fail; but the divine love flows unwearied and undiminished. Nowhere is all this better illustrated than in the life of Christ himself. He loved the hills of his native Galilee. No more touching picture is preserved in the record of his life than in the simple statement that he went into the mountain alone to pray. But he did not remain. Presently he sought again the company of his disciples. He wanted them to watch with him. He craved their comradeship and the sustaining warmth of their faith. But they were not strong enough to bear him up. They fell asleep, they grew hungry and faint, they became confused when

335

danger appeared. One of them at last betrayed him, another denied him with curses, and the rest fled. He alone remained calm and unresisting. But his refuge was in the thought of God. From God would come legions of angels if he summoned them. In God he could see beyond the tumult and the night and behold the far horizon where his triumph was secure.

After all, these horizons of our life are within the natural experience of men. They are within the power of the imagination and this is capable of cultivation. Men working at their desks occasionally turn their eyes to the window and let their thoughts run beyond the walls which shut them in. Or they close their eyes in a moment of reverie and escape into some distant scene of the past or into a gilded hope of the future. And this power of the imagination is not merely a means of escape; it may be made an instrument for setting the day's work in the light of wider relations and deeper meanings. More than ever before men realize the marvelous delicacy and elaborateness of the patterns of life they are weaving. And that realization fills them with a new measure of reverence and of hope. Their souls are tremulous with the knowledge of the share in his creation which God allots them.

This sense of the far horizons of life, and the habit of turning to them for refreshment and strength, belong supremely to the religious way of life. For religion includes this practice of seeing the immediate and the commonplace under the form of eternity.

The Far Horizon

All shapes and sounds have something which is not
Of them; a spirit broods amid the grass;
Vague outlines of the Everlasting Thought
Lie in the melting shadows as they pass;
The touch of an eternal presence thrills
The fringes of the sunsets and the hills.

DIVINE MULTIPLICATION

Dr. Petty has recently come to a throne of spiritual power in the pulpit of the Baptist Temple of Philadelphia; a pulpit made famous and influential, at home and in far places, by the ministry and citizenship of Dr. Conwell, who was not simply a personality but an institution among us. A fellow-worker in a cozy, conservative city bids him hearty welcome and godspeed; bespeaking for him a great and growing ministry, rich in many rewards by the law of Divine Multiplication.

A Californian, now in the fortieth year of his life, Dr. Petty was educated in Occidental College, and in Rochester and Union Theological Seminaries, beginning his service as student secretary of the Y. M. C. A. Ordained to the Baptist ministry in 1917, he became pastor of the Judson Memorial Church, in New York City, where he won distinction, both as a preacher and as an adept in institutional ministry; being a founder of the Judson Health Center.

There is something of the poet in every true preacher, even if he does not write verse; but Dr. Petty has a dainty book of poetry to his credit, entitled *Songs of the Tenements*. One might have surmised as much from the sermon here to be read, with its exquisite handling of a scene from the life of the supreme Poet, who crowded eternity into three swift and gentle years. May the vision grow and abide.

DIVINE MULTIPLICATION

ALONZO RAY PETTY, D.D.
THE BAPTIST TEMPLE, PHILADELPHIA

And Jesus sat over against the treasury and beheld how the people cast money into the treasury. Mark 12: 41.

There is nothing in the recorded life of Jesus that does not have a prophetic significance for the world. This is true because of what he was, and because of what he was in the world to do. That Jesus was human the New Testament teaches us in no uncertain terms. He was a man and lived the life we know. But he was God. This is the fundamental teaching of scripture: God made manifest in the flesh, God caught for a time in the narrow confines of a single personality. To his deity, not only the scriptures but our own experience bear testimony, for never man lived as he lived.

If we accept this surpassing truth then the question at once comes into our hearts, "Why did God in the person of Jesus live as a man among men?" There are two answers. First, that he should make men to know him through the channels of their own experience. A man can understand another man better than he can understand anything else in the world. It is true, of course, that no man ever fully understands another man, for no man at any time

341

fully understands himself. There are mysterious reaches in our own personalities that baffle us. Each of us in moments of high spiritual exaltation finds unplumbed depths in our own souls. This is doubly true when we try to fathom the souls of others. Something there is that eludes us, that stretches beyond the range of our comprehension in every individual that we meet. For in every human life there are imponderable mysteries that cannot be caught by any scale of measurement, nor understood by any canon of judgment.

We cannot understand ourselves fully, nor our fellows even as adequately as we understand ourselves, still we understand human life with its aspirations, its desires, its struggles, its victories, its failures, its smiles, its heartaches, its tears, its loves, better than we understand any other thing in the universe. And so when God would make a supreme revelation of himself to man, he made it in the terms that we could best comprehend.

But God had another purpose; namely, to teach men his way of life. He had taught them through the prophets. He had given partial and fragmentary indications of his program. But the full import of what he wanted men to do, of how he wanted men to live, of what he considered of highest value in life, of what death meant, all of these great questions which ached in the heart of humanity had not been satisfactorily explained so that they were understood. And so God in Jesus was not only revealing himself to men, that they might know and understand and love him, but he was at the same time disclosing his purposes unto men, so that they might learn his will to do it.

Jesus did not have a long human experience. He was killed in his youth. At thirty-three the story of his life was ended in blackness on a skull-shaped hill outside the walls of Jerusalem. Of these thirty-three years only the last three years are recorded, or if some critics are correct, only the last fourteen months. But allowing the three-year ministry the time was short at best, and into this time he must crowd the complete revelation of the eternal God. A task of omnipotence. Its wonderful accomplishment is another proof of his deity. It was impossible for him in so short a period of time to compass the full circle of human experience and to tarry long with any of its details. Of necessity he could only touch quickly the canvas of life and sketch in the outline. It was part of his plan that others should brush in the coloring and complete the picture. This men ever since have been doing. Taking the sketch they have tried to fill in the details.

His teachings were in the form of principles. The application of these principles has always written the story of Christian achievement. In his own experience he was given opportunity to apply these principles with quick deft touches. His ministry was all too short to allow for elaboration, but long enough to make the likeness of God to stand out until men should know him, and his way to appear as a plain path.

Alonzo Ray Petty, D.D.

The great purpose of his life and the shortness of his ministry combine to make everything that Jesus did or said of eternal importance. No word or act of his can be considered as unrelated to his end. Nothing that he marked off for our attention can be neglected. Each happening in his life must be probed to its depth and when understood becomes of divine validity for all who would walk in his way. The reader of a best seller may read rapidly and skip the crowded portions of description if he desires only to know the plot. But it is not so with the story of the life of Jesus. It cannot be scanned. Each word is priceless. Every action is vital. The whole story moves with the thrilling sweep of revelation. We must have it all.

With time so short and with every experience a demonstration of God's purpose there is a profound significance in the fact that once "Jesus sat over against the treasury and beheld how people cast money into the treasury." It brings us face to face with the fact that most of us would forget. God is interested in the way we give. He beholds the returns that we make to him of the blessings we receive at his hands. To some of us this truth comes as a startling revelation. We love to dwell upon the beauty of God's gift to us. We piously and ofttimes carelessly speak of him as the great giver of all good. So he is. But how few are the times when we dwell upon our responsibility toward him. The very attitude of our prayer is the attitude of an extended

Divine Multiplication

palm. The content of our prayer all too often is a plea for larger beneficence at his hands.

We love to think of God as interested in our successes and our failures. But we bring him only our failures. We want that he should turn them into successes. We hold our achievements in miserly fashion for ourselves. We want to creep up close to him in our hours of pain and sorrow. In our hours of joy we forget him. Like Caliban we do not feel the need of him when the sun shines, but reach for his companionship when the storms of life break in blackness and fear upon us. We glory in the fact that our aspirations are matters of concern to him. Unashamed we turn aside from his aspirations for us. We do not like to think that he is as interested in receiving as he is in giving. We strenuously put such thoughts out of our minds. They are uncomfortable. For we are so selfish. And we give back to God so little.

With men we live according to another code. We hesitate to receive gifts that we cannot in some measure repay. We feel that our dignity of personality is lessened if we play always the part of a recipient. We want also to be donors. Our hectic state of mind at Christmas time arises from the fear that some one will remember us whom we have failed to remember. So we make our lists. We check them over and over again. If a gift is received for which a gift has not been returned we are chagrined. In New York City there is a gift shop open on Christmas Day where those who have been caught unawares by the unex-

345

Alonzo Ray Petty, D.D.

pected and unprepared for remembrance of a friend may make suitable return ere the day slips by. We are not so concerned about God. Unabashed we cry for blessing. Content with receiving gifts from him we refrain from returning them in kind. We say with the Psalmist of old, "God will not see."

Jesus taught us that God does see with definite and designed intent. He stands by the treasury watching how men cast in their gifts. And he passes judgment on them as to whether or not they give with their hearts or with their hands only.

Thus we read that as Jesus sat by the treasury many who were rich cast in much. There is something in this verb *cast in* that implies an attitude. There is in the very act a flourish. Something grandiose, pompous, theatrical—a sweeping gesture of display. No meekness is here. Humility is not in the picture. We listen to hear a blare of trumpets. We catch running through the crowd the gasps of surprise at such largess. We see the delighted looks upon the faces of the priests. The admiring adulation of the standers-by feeds fat the conceit of these Pharisees who in the Temple of God use his treasury to enhance their dividends of virtue by a spectacular offering of a size commensurate with their vanity.

What are their motives? Is love the compelling force which brings them here? We cannot believe it. They are giving to be seen of men. They are bartering with God for continued blessing. Enough to bring them praise, enough to pay an obligation, but not enough to touch their own ease of life—thus they

346

give. It is not recorded that they possess that necessary virtue of sacrifice without which there is no adequacy in God's economy.

And Jesus watched them. We cannot miss the illuminating fact that their gifts bring no praise from him. He was penniless. Wealth he had never known. The story of his life was being chiseled with the sharp blade of poverty driven by the hard mallets of deprivation. He had no home. With wistfulness in his voice he had pointed this out on a certain occasion to his disciples when he said, "The foxes have holes and the birds of the air have nests, but the Son of Man hath not where to lay his head." He had no social standing. He was an outcast from the Temple. A street preacher, followed only by the simple of the earth, was Jesus, and with the common people alone hearing him with gladness. He stands unnoticed while the parade of the Pharisees passes by and doles with measured hands only enough to gain their ends. Like Sir Launfal who tossed his bit of gold to the leper, they tossed their gold to God. Enough you say—but the penniless God stands by to behold as without seeing him they cast in their money. He had no word of commendation for them. Which should make us stop and ponder.

They pass by. The treasury chest groans with their gifts. With marked complacency they go their way. Their purpose is achieved. Their desire has been accomplished. They have been seen of men. They do not know that their parade had passed in review before almighty God.

Alonzo Ray Petty, D.D.

As the line passes by to the metallic music of their cast in coin the discord grates upon the ears of Jesus and the harmony of love is drowned by the "sounding brass," for love was not in the gifts and where love is not there is no music for God.

And then suddenly heavenly music. The ringing of two mites thrown by the desperate hands of love upon the altars of God. "Behold there came a certain poor widow and she threw in two mites which make a farthing." Note again the verb. She *threw in*. Here was a motive different from the motive of the many rich who had cast in much. It was quick. It was emphatic. It was final. We do not need to conjecture as to why this widow threw in her two mites. It stands revealed. She had come to the altars of her God answering the call of her heart, but with the voice of her inadequacy calling retreat. Every impulse that had motived the rich to come and cast in much was actively crying out in her heart against her gift. They had given to be seen by men. She dreaded for men to see her paltry offering. The bystanders would jest at its littleness. The cause of God would not be advanced by its giving. Why should she make a display of her poverty? "Remain away from the altar," cried her soul, "God will not miss your mites, men will not know your penury. Your secret is yours now. Make this feeble gift and it will be known to all. You have no place in this line of large givers. Keep to your place. Why should you give to God your all—your living? What has God done for you? See the gleaming pile of

348

gold he has given others. You have been cruelly dealt with. Curse God and die. He deserves no worship from your lips, no gift from your hands. Refrain, refrain." Against the voice of her soul she had battled with all the strength she had. With beating heart, with face ashamed, but with honest desire to give her all she had strained against these barriers that would keep her back. She had broken them. She had slipped to the altar with timid steps of fear and humility. And when she came and saw how small her gift was in comparison with what had been given by the others the temptation was almost irresistible to turn back and to keep her shame of poverty undiscovered to the world.

The impulse to withhold was so strong as to terrify her. But her love was stronger. She could not hold out long against the temptation to flight. Summoning all her spiritual strength she made her gift. Before her heart should fail her, in one supreme act of sacrifice she threw her mites upon the altar. The very intensity of her action tells of the struggle of her soul. She had won her victory. Let them scorn her gift if they would. Let them call it a pittance. It was all she had. It was her living. And she had given it to God.

The penniless God who sat over against the treasury heard suddenly above the jarring, discordant crashing of the gifts of affluence, the grandeur of this music of self-sacrifice. Here was a gift royal and abundant. Here was a gift powerful and sufficient. Here in the tinkle of two mites thrown by the loving hands of poverty was music that blended in accord with the symphonies of his own high purpose. Here was the giving of self, the sacrifice of all. And Jesus, penniless and homeless, but with the eternal song of loving sacrifice singing in his heart, recognized the glory of it all and found in the heart of the widow companionship and in her gift abundance. Yea, abundance such as all others had not given.

He called his disciples quickly to him. With tears of understanding showing in his eyes he pointed out the beauty of that which here had been done. They had not seen her. They had not been looking to see how the people gave. They were looking with the others to see how much. They too had been impressed with the display of the rich. To them also, as with the others, the widow's mites were inconsequential. They were still of the earth, earthy, and the music of life for them as for us was the crash of the heavy gifts of gold.

This was not the first time they had failed to see life truly. Ofttimes before they had missed the true understanding of life's real values. But now as always his patience was infinite. He must make them see. He must make all men for all time see that the *how* was more important than the *how much*. And so he explains, with loving understanding and with a beautiful appreciation of the battle whose victory he had just witnessed, the true inwardness of giving. "Verily I say unto you that this poor widow hath cast more in than all they which have cast into the treasury. For all they did cast in of their abundance, but she of her want did cast in all that she had, even her living."

God measures the quality of our giving with the fine delicacy of love. His balances swing to record the deprivation and sacrifice that place upon his altars our substance. When unselfishness and noble aspiration are recorded with the gift, it is marked in his ledger of understanding as adequate—nay as abundant. Love plus the smallest offering through the processes of divine multiplication makes a contribution the sum of which is of mighty value. Great amounts, with motives other than love and objectives other than service, shrivel into littleness. The gift plus the giver makes both the gift and the giver great in God's sight. But with God always, "the gift without the giver is bare."

How wonderful this discernment of Jesus. How searching for us his disclosure of God's economy. How it transmutes our little into much and opens before us the door to large ministry through the mites of life given to him with the abandon of our hearts. The rich man with his gift of display gives unnoted. How great might have been his praise if with his abundance he had given himself! How much might have been accomplished for the world and how great the blessing it might have brought to him as the giver! But it lay unpraised while Jesus chose the mighty mites of the widow for divine commendation and for the accomplishment of the progress of God's Kingdom.

Love always multiplies our offering, and sacrifice

eternally makes potent to large ends the humblest bringing of our hearts. This will some day be the glory of life for those who give in sublime forgetfulness of self that they shall learn when they shall see, not as through a glass darkly, but face to face, how great the treasure is that they have laid up for themselves in Heaven. For love the golden motive with God is always the determining element. The how much, the measure of gold with man—with him is secondary. Oh, soul, learn thou this lesson and to the treasury of love bring thine all that God may multiply it into greatness and crown thy gift with his eternal acceptance.

WILL CHRIST COME AGAIN?

No man in the American pulpit is more beloved than Dr. Jefferson, and no one is more worthy of homage. For thirty years he has toiled in the ever-changing scene of New York City, building up a "skyscraper Church," as Broadway Tabernacle is called, keeping the light of God aglow amid the garish glitter of the metropolis. His fame has gone from end to end of the land, and beyond the sea, and everywhere his name is a symbol both of practical sagacity and prophetic power.

An Ohio man, born in 1860, Dr. Jefferson was educated at Ohio Wesleyan and Boston Universities, entering the Congregational ministry in 1887. After a brief pastorate at Chelsea, Mass., he came to the Broadway Tabernacle in 1898, where he has had a memorable ministry. To name his books would be to make a long list, among which are *The Building of the Church, The Character of Paul, Nature Sermons, Cardinal Ideas of Isaiah,* besides many stories and essays; in all of which a lucid thought shines through a limpid style—a slumbering lightning mixed with sweetness and light.

The following sermon is typical, seeking to recover the spirit of expectancy which thrilled the Church as it began its morning march in the world; a hope profoundly true and sorely needed, albeit often misinterpreted as to the time and form of its fulfillment—like the messianic hope in the Jewish Church. It asks us to "face tomorrow with beating hearts eager to see some fresh unfolding of the power of God!"

WILL CHRIST COME AGAIN?

CHARLES E. JEFFERSON, D.D.

BROADWAY TABERNACLE, NEW YORK CITY

Maranatha: the Lord is coming. I Corinthians 16: 22.

"Maranatha." That is an Aramaic word. It occurs in our English New Testament untranslated. Paul wrote his Letter to the Corinthians in Greek, but when he came to the Aramaic word "Maranatha," he did not translate it. He let it stand. It is an interesting fact that that word has been allowed to stand in all the translations of the New Testament. When I began this sermon I took down my Latin Testament, and found that while all other words in the Letter were Latin, this word "Maranatha" was untouched. I then took down my German New Testament, and then my French New Testament, and then my Spanish New Testament, and in every one of them the Aramaic word remained. When a company of scholars at the beginning of the seventeenth century gave a new translation of the New Testament into English, under the direction of King James I., they translated every other word in the First Letter to the Corinthians into English, except this word, "Maranatha." They did not lay their hands upon it. In 1582 in the City of Rheims, a company of Roman Catholic scholars had translated the New Testament into English, and while they translated every other word of the Letter, they refused to translate this one. They allowed it to stand "Maranatha." When at the close of the nineteenth century a company of English and American scholars undertook the task of making a new translation of the New Testament into English, they did precisely what the translators of the King James version had done, they left this word "Maranatha" unaltered. The revision committee was made up of two sections, one section composed of British scholars, the other section of American scholars. The American scholars were somewhat more radical than were the British scholars. They were less reluctant to depart from preceding versions, but when the American revision appeared, it was discovered that the American scholars had not ventured to take away the word "Maranatha."

A few years ago Dr. Moffatt, one of the greatest living Greek scholars, gave us a new version of the New Testament into English, and even he did not venture to drop the Aramaic word "Maranatha." This word seems to have a charmed life. Nobody, apparently, is willing to touch it. Through all the Christian generations it has been allowed to stand in every one of the versions. With all this history behind me I should not venture to touch it either. I have no hesitancy, however, in telling you what it means. The Revised Version has done that in the margin, and Dr. Moffatt has done it in a footnote.

Will Christ Come Again?

As some of you already know, the meaning of the word is, "The Lord is coming." Why do you suppose the translators have refused to translate it? Possibly it is because the word is so sacred. It was on the lips of the Apostolic Christians so constantly and so fervently that it seemed sacrilegious to allow the syllables of this word to be lost.

"Maranatha" was a common salutation. When one Christian met another Christian he greeted him with "Maranatha." He lit up the day by the declaration that the Lord was coming. When a Christian wrote a letter to his friends he often wrote at the end of the last page "Maranatha." That was a benediction. He wanted his friends to know that he was still rejoicing in the expectation that the Lord was coming. "Maranatha" was a slogan which the soldiers of Jesus Christ repeated to one another as they went forth to the conquest of the world. They braced their hearts for the great battle by reminding them that the Lord was coming. "Maranatha" was a passing word which Christians in the early times made use of. When they went into their meetings, when they met before day in sequestered places, that was the word which gained them immediate admittance— "Maranatha." It was a word which was used at the celebration of the Lord's Supper. We have a volume entitled *The Teaching of the Twelve* which was written not far from the middle of the second century. In that book, we are told, that it was the custom in the celebration of the Lord's Supper, to offer a prayer of thanksgiving ending with the word "Maranatha."

Charles E. Jefferson, D.D.

And so the celebration of the Lord's Supper came to have a triumphant tone by the repetition of the word "Maranatha." It is not to be wondered at, then, that all the translators have shrunk from tampering with the word. It is the same with this word "Maranatha" as it is with the Hebrew words repeated by our Lord on the cross—"Eloi, Eloi, lama sabachthani!" These words occur in the first two Gospels as they were spoken. There was a sanctity, an awfulness attached to them which made the early Christians reluctant to put them into any other tongue. But whether this conjecture is correct or not, the fact remains that all the translators through nineteen hundred years have refused to blot out the word "Maranatha" and substitute in its place any other word.

What a difference there is between the Apostolic Church and the Church of our day. In externals, of course, they are worlds apart. The people in the New Testament all wore turbans on their heads and sandals on their feet. When they traveled they either walked or they rode on the backs of donkeys and camels. They had none of the comforts and luxuries which we enjoy. They had no telegraphs, no telephones, no railroads, no automobiles, no airships, no radios. Heaven and earth have passed away, all things have become new. Look at the pictures of Tissot and you look upon a world entirely different from the world in which we are living. But the interior world of the Apostolic Church was also entirely different from the mood of the church today. There was a spirit of expectancy in that church which we do not possess. There was a hope then which we have lost. There was a mood of anticipation, to which we are strangers. We do not say to one another, "Maranatha." We seldom think of his coming. That will account in large measure for the difference in spirit between the first century church and our own. Their belief in the early coming of Christ gave an intensity to their life which ours does not possess. We are intense about certain things but not about our religion. There was an other-worldliness in the church of the Apostles which has vanished. The early Christians kept their thoughts upon the other world, the world into which Christ had vanished and from which he was soon to emerge again. We do not think much about the other world. The present world is amazingly attractive and it absorbs all our strength and time. It is a difficult world to manage and we have no time for any other. The Apostolic Church was a radiant church. A distinguished British scholar of Oxford University not long ago wrote a book entitled *The Lost Radiance*. He notes a vivid contrast between the early church and our own. That church was jubilant and ours is not. The face of that church shone. Our face does not shine. One of the reasons why the jubilant tone has vanished is because we have lost the expectancy which the Apostles possessed.

It is surprising that we should have lost the idea of the early coming of Jesus with the open Bible before us. We claim to be Bible Christians. We boast of our devotion to the Holy Scriptures. We are proud of the fact that we get our doctrines from the Bible and from the Bible alone. It is singular that we do not get from the Bible the doctrine of the early coming of Jesus, for that doctrine appears in our New Testament again and again. It is not necessary this morning to go through the Letters of Paul. Let one quotation suffice. To the Philippians he wrote, "The Lord is at hand." He was always saying that. When you open the Epistle of James you find the author saying in the fifth chapter of the Letter, "Be patient for the coming of the Lord draweth nigh." That was his reason for being patient. Every Christian ought to be patient because the Lord is coming. Turn to the Letter to the Hebrews and in the tenth chapter of the Letter you find the writer exhorting his readers to be patient. "Yet a little while," he says, "he that is going to come will come." It had been said by a prophet centuries before this man was writing. He quotes it, pouring into it a fresh meaning. "The Lord is coming." In the last Book of the New Testament you hear a voice saying again and again, "Behold I come quickly. Behold I come quickly. Behold I come quickly." The New Testament closes with an expectant note. On the last page of our Bible there is a radiant face with eyes full of glad anticipation. The man whose face it is has heard a voice saying, "Behold I come quickly," and his exclamation is, "Come, Lord!" How strange it is that with such a Bible open before us we should have discarded the word "Maranatha" altogether.

Will Christ Come Again?

Why have we given up our belief in the coming of Jesus? It is very largely because the Apostles were mistaken about the manner of his coming. They supposed he was coming dramatically, spectacularly, miraculously. They thought he would drop down out of heaven. Not only did one of them think that. They all thought it. Let me read you just two quotations. Luke, about thirty years after our Lord's death, went down into Palestine to get data from which to write his volume of church history. He talked with all the leading Christians he could meet. He got from their lips the important things which they believed. This was one of them: "Ye men of Galilee, why stand ye looking into heaven? This Jesus, who was received up from you into heaven, shall so come in like manner as ye behold him going into heaven." That was what Christians believed throughout Palestine thirty years after the crucifixion. Let us see what Paul believed about the same time. We have his belief recorded in I Thessalonians, fourth chapter, verses 16-18: "For the Lord himself shall descend from heaven with a shout, with the voice of the archangel, and with the trump of God; and the dead in Christ shall rise first; then we that are alive, that are left, shall together with them be caught up in the clouds, to meet the Lord in the air, and so shall we ever be with the Lord." That is very clear and very positive. The Lord is coming out of the sky with a shout. An archangel is going to speak. The trumpet of God is going to blow. All the Christians then alive, and Paul will be among the number,

Charles E. Jefferson, D.D.

will be caught up in the clouds to meet the Lord in the air. That was Paul's joyful belief. Of that he had no doubt. That is the doctrine which he taught his converts. He told them to comfort one another by repeating the words which he had written. But in regard to the manner of the Lord's appearance Paul was mistaken, so were all the Apostles. Every one of them was mistaken. Their mistake is recorded in our New Testament. That mistake cannot be gotten rid of. It was a huge mistake, and it forms a part of the New Testament forever.

At this point let me inject into my sermon an extended parenthesis. Let me explain what has caused the commotion in our generation concerning the Bible. Why do we have so much controversy over the Scriptures? Why are Christians divided into hostile camps when it comes to a conception of the Bible? Many of us already know. Some of you do not yet know. I speak to those who do not know. It is very important that everybody should know just what has caused the controversies which have swept in recent years across the Christian world. We inherited from the seventeenth century a doctrine of inspiration, according to which the Bible is a dictated book. Inspiration, our fathers thought, meant dictation. God dictated his ideas to the Apostles, and they as amanuenses wrote down exactly what he said. The New Testament was a dictated book, and because it had been dictated by the Almighty it could contain no mistakes. Every sentence was true. Every idea was correct. God cannot be mistaken,

362

and therefore in God's Book no mistake can occur. The Almighty cannot be in error, and therefore it is absurd to look for errors in the Word of God. That was the belief of the majority of Protestant Christians fifty years ago, and then the world entered upon a new era. Groups of men began to study the Bible scientifically; that is, they began to search it with scrutinizing eyes. They observed it closely. They compared sentence with sentence. They weighed the sentences. They even pondered the syllables. They studied the New Testament precisely as Herschel studied the stars, and as Charles Darwin studied the plants and the birds. As the result of this scientific study of the Scriptures men saw that the dictated theory of inspiration is not correct. The Bible is not a dictated book for the reason that the Bible has errors in it. Here is one error that nobody can dispute—the opinion that Jesus was going to drop down out of the sky and that Christians were going to meet him in the air, and that this was going to take place in the lifetime of the Apostle Paul.

Paul was the most learned of all the Apostles, the ablest of them all, the mightiest of all, but he was mistaken, and all the other Apostles were mistaken with him. When the fact became known in wider church circles that the New Testament contains errors, there followed a series of explosions. They occurred first in the theological seminaries because there the scientific study of the Scriptures had been carried forward with more thoroughness and boldness. The people outside the seminaries who did not know what was going on began to say that the seminaries were hotbeds of infidelity, that theological professors had been beguiled by the devil, and that all our young men were being led astray. Later on there were explosions in various churches. When a church had a scholar in the pulpit and he announced what scholarship had discovered, there was in many cases a great uproar in the pews. Some people left the church, others felt that the pulpit had been captured by the Evil One. A great many people outside the churches hearing the explosions, and not knowing the cause of them, began to be troubled. The report went abroad that Christianity had been undermined, that the New Testament after all was a book of falsehoods, that the Christian creed was no longer reliable, and that the religion of Jesus was destined to pass away. That, in a few words, is the cause of the explosions which have attracted the attention of our modern world.

When you find that the New Testament is not a dictated book because there are errors in it, what are you going to do? The sensible thing is to modify your theory. You cannot change the New Testament. It remains what it has been, and what it is, and what it always will be. The only sensible thing is to modify your theory. Make your theory wide enough to take in all the facts. Somebody suggests that it is dangerous. I do not think so. Why should it be considered dangerous to acknowledge a fact? The universe must be a poor ramshackle affair if it will tumble down on you when you acknowledge a fact. The Christian religion must be exceedingly flimsy if it will topple over when you acknowledge a fact. Why should anybody be afraid to acknowledge a fact? It is a fact that there is this error in the New Testament. Why not face it and confess it? Why not let the whole world know that you know it is there? It is not at all dangerous to confess a fact. It is dangerous not to confess it. It is dangerous to play fast and loose with truth. It is dangerous to shut your eyes and refuse to stare into the face of an unwelcome fact. The only safe thing to do is to face all the facts without wincing and without running. Somebody suggests that it is very difficult to hold this new theory of inspiration, one wide enough to take in all the facts. That is all very true, but the difficulty is no objection to it. Everything is difficult in a world like this. The corpuscular theory of light is difficult to manage. So is the undulatory theory of light, so is the theory of luminiferous ether, and so is the theory of relativity. The fact is that life itself is difficult to manage. We who have lived it the longest know that the best, but we have to manage difficult theories. The only thing for us to do is to believe that the men who wrote the New Testament were inspired. They certainly got light from heaven. They certainly were assisted by the Spirit of the Eternal. There is no doubt of that. It is equally clear that their inspiration did not preclude all possibility of error in opinion.

Some one may ask, is not the New Testament discredited if you admit that there is an error in it?

Not at all. Some one may ask, is no
if we acknowledge he is mistaken i
portant as the coming of Jesus?
Apostles were mistaken only in regar
and the time of Jesus' coming. Th
was coming, and in that they were rig
in his autobiography entitled *Twent*
that, "Some of us thought that ec
would make itself felt more quickl
break of the war; that it would ra
acute as to bring war to an end.
wrong, but we were wrong only in
the time and the manner in which eo
would make itself felt." Mark his
"only." They were correct in seei
disaster. They were mistaken only
time and the manner of it. These
incidental. The main fact was the
economic disaster, and in seeing tha
mistaken. The disaster was even g
foresaw. "The full extent of the eo
of the war," says Viscount Grey, "is
It is possible we have not seen the wo
Grey did not feel he was disgraced
diplomacy was discredited because
ciates in the British Government fel
cerning the time and the manner
disaster. Nor is Paul disgraced or
ment discredited by an error in reg
manner. Paul did not feel undone
been in error at these points. He w

fact. The Christian religion must be exceedingly
flimsy if it will topple over when you acknowledge a
fact. Why should anybody be afraid to acknowledge
a fact? It is a fact that there is this error in the New
Testament. Why not face it and confess it? Why
not let the whole world know that you know it is
there? It is not at all dangerous to confess a fact.
It is dangerous not to confess it. It is dangerous to
play fast and loose with truth. It is dangerous to
shut your eyes and refuse to stare into the face of an
unwelcome fact. The only safe thing to do is to face
all the facts without wincing and without running.
Somebody suggests that it is very difficult to hold this
new theory of inspiration, one wide enough to take
in all the facts. That is all very true, but the difficulty is no objection to it. Everything is difficult
in a world like this. The corpuscular theory of light
is difficult to manage. So is the undulatory theory
of light, so is the theory of luminiferous ether, and so
is the theory of relativity. The fact is that life itself
is difficult to manage. We who have lived it the
longest know that the best, but we have to manage
difficult theories. The only thing for us to do is to
believe that the men who wrote the New Testament
were inspired. They certainly got light from heaven.
They certainly were assisted by the Spirit of the
Eternal. There is no doubt of that. It is equally
clear that their inspiration did not preclude all possibility of error in opinion.

Some one may ask, is not the New Testament discredited if you admit that there is an error in it?

Charles E. Jefferson, D.D.

Not at all. Some one may ask, is not Paul disgraced if we acknowledge he is mistaken in a point so important as the coming of Jesus? Not at all. The Apostles were mistaken only in regard to the manner and the time of Jesus' coming. They knew that he was coming, and in that they were right. Lord Grey in his autobiography entitled *Twenty-five Years* says that, "Some of us thought that economic disaster would make itself felt more quickly after the outbreak of the war; that it would rapidly become so acute as to bring war to an end. In that we were wrong, but we were wrong only in our estimate of the time and the manner in which economic disaster would make itself felt." Mark his use of the word "only." They were correct in seeing the economic disaster. They were mistaken only in regard to the time and the manner of it. These two things were incidental. The main fact was the fact of colossal economic disaster, and in seeing that they were not mistaken. The disaster was even greater than they foresaw. "The full extent of the economic disaster of the war," says Viscount Grey, "is not yet known. It is possible we have not seen the worst of it." Lord Grey did not feel he was disgraced or that British diplomacy was discredited because he and his associates in the British Government fell into error concerning the time and the manner of the economic disaster. Nor is Paul disgraced or the New Testament discredited by an error in regard to time and manner. Paul did not feel undone because he had been in error at these points. He was sure the Lord

366

know what was going on began to say that the seminaries were hotbeds of infidelity, that theological professors had been beguiled by the devil, and that all
our young men were being led astray. Later on
there were explosions in various churches. When a
church had a scholar in the pulpit and he announced
what scholarship had discovered, there was in many
cases a great uproar in the pews. Some people left
the church, others felt that the pulpit had been captured by the Evil One. A great many people outside
the churches hearing the explosions, and not knowing
the cause of them, began to be troubled. The report
went abroad that Christianity had been undermined,
that the New Testament after all was a book of
falsehoods, that the Christian creed was no longer
reliable, and that the religion of Jesus was destined
to pass away. That, in a few words, is the cause of
the explosions which have attracted the attention of
our modern world.

When you find that the New Testament is not a
dictated book because there are errors in it, what are
you going to do? The sensible thing is to modify
your theory. You cannot change the New Testament. It remains what it has been, and what it is,
and what it always will be. The only sensible thing
is to modify your theory. Make your theory wide
enough to take in all the facts. Somebody suggests
that it is dangerous. I do not think so. Why should
it be considered dangerous to acknowledge a fact?
The universe must be a poor ramshackle affair if it
will tumble down on you when you acknowledge a

and therefore in God's Book no mistake can occur. The Almighty cannot be in error, and therefore it is absurd to look for errors in the Word of God. That was the belief of the majority of Protestant Christians fifty years ago, and then the world entered upon a new era. Groups of men began to study the Bible scientifically; that is, they began to search it with scrutinizing eyes. They observed it closely. They compared sentence with sentence. They weighed the sentences. They even pondered the syllables. They studied the New Testament precisely as Herschel studied the stars, and as Charles Darwin studied the plants and the birds. As the result of this scientific study of the Scriptures men saw that the dictated theory of inspiration is not correct. The Bible is not a dictated book for the reason that the Bible has errors in it. Here is one error that nobody can dispute—the opinion that Jesus was going to drop down out of the sky and that Christians were going to meet him in the air, and that this was going to take place in the lifetime of the Apostle Paul.

Paul was the most learned of all the Apostles, the ablest of them all, the mightiest of all, but he was mistaken, and all the other Apostles were mistaken with him. When the fact became known in wider church circles that the New Testament contains errors, there followed a series of explosions. They occurred first in the theological seminaries because there the scientific study of the Scriptures had been carried forward with more thoroughness and boldness. The people outside the seminaries who did not was coming. All the early Christians were certain of that. In that expectation they were not mistaken. They felt that the Lord must come. Without him they could do nothing. He himself had promised he would come. He must keep his promise. Without his presence they could not convert the world. Without him they could not teach the nations. He must come, but he did not come in the manner which they expected. Paul however was not cast down. Even though he was not caught up in the clouds and did not hear the trumpet of God, he still knew whom he had believed, and he was persuaded that he was able to keep that which he had committed to him against that day. In the last Letter we have from his pen, he says, "I have fought the good fight. I have finished the course. I have kept the faith, and henceforth there is laid up for me the crown." Paul did not consider himself disgraced or his Gospel discredited.

Little by little the early church sloughed off the mistaken conception of the manner of Jesus' coming. They came to see that he was not coming dramatically or spectacularly or miraculously. He was coming in another manner. That manner is described for us in the Fourth Gospel. The Fourth Gospel is the latest of all the Gospels. It gives us the maturest thought of Apostolic Christianity. There is a passage in the fourteenth chapter of the Gospel according to St. John which you ought to read and mark and digest. There our Lord is represented as saying, "I will not leave you desolate. I am coming to you.

367

Charles E. Jefferson, D.D.

In that day you shall know that I am in my Father and you in me and I in you." In other words, the coming of Jesus is to be invisible, spiritual, progressive. He is to come and dwell in the hearts of his followers, and through them is to save the world. Therefore it is a mistake to talk about the second coming of Christ. The proper expression is the "continuous" coming of Christ. He has already come many times. He is coming many times. In the present hour he will come and keep on coming. He is occupying the mind and heart of his people throughout the world. All this language in the New Testament concerning the coming of our Lord is capable of a higher and truer interpretation. When Paul told the Corinthians that the "Lord is at hand," he spoke the truth. He was at hand. He is at hand today. He will always be at hand. When John said, "Behold I come quickly," he expressed words that are true. That is what Christ said, and what he says, and what he will forever say. He is coming quickly. The proper response for us to make is, "Come, Lord!"

There are two serious errors by which the church is handicapped at the present hour. There are groups of zealous men, sincere and conscientious, who are deeply impressed by what the New Testament says concerning the coming of Christ, and they make it the cardinal and crowning doctrine of the Christian Creed. They are literalists and cling to the ancient opinion that the Lord is coming dramatically, spectacularly and miraculously. He is coming out of the sky with the voice of the archangel and the trump of God. He is going to interfere in some mighty and overwhelming way, overturning the world that now is and setting up another. They say he is coming soon. They used to name the date. They missed it so many times they dare not do it any more. Only a fanatic of unusual stature ventures any longer to specify the day on which the Lord will bring the world to an end. They now use ambiguous adverbs. They declare he is coming "soon." Some throw all discretion to the wind and boldly assert he is coming "in the lifetime of men now living." The startling announcement is made sometimes in newspaper advertisements, and sometimes by posters on the billboard, and sometimes by flaming orators on the platform. Men and women of a certain type of mind and of a particular grade of culture are in considerable numbers powerfully impressed and swept away. These advocates of the Second Coming use the Bible with great ability, and hold up the present unhappy condition of the world as evidence that the last days have come. St. Paul told Timothy that in the last days perilous times would come, and that evil men and seducers would wax worse and worse, and such a time, these prophets say, has evidently arrived. It is this combination of Scripture and present day darkness which renders these modern apostles so persuasive and influential. According to their teaching there is no hope for the world through anything which mortals can do. They take no interest in social betterment work, and upon all efforts for community uplift they pour the vials of their scorn.

369

Charles E. Jefferson, D.D.

They denounce all international machinery for the establishment of world peace as devices of the Devil. Arbitration Treaties and World Courts and Leagues of Nations have all been conceived in hell and are tricks to deceive the elect. Some of the more radical of these zealots are too advanced to take any interest in the ballot. They sneer at all efforts to get good men into office. What is the use? Only God Almighty can make the world better. They denounce all movements which aim at better laws. Legislation is of the Evil One. You cannot make Society better by laws. Nothing can be accomplished by statesmen. Only the Lord God Almighty can cope with the evil of the human heart, and we can expect no improvement until he lays bare his strong right arm. Things must grow worse and worse. The more rapidly they get worse the happier we ought to be. It is not till they get as bad as possible that the end will come! What a pity that conscientious and well-meaning men should be so deceived! What a travesty of the Christian religion such teaching is! What a caricature of the Gospel of salvation is a message like that! An interpretation of life and God which reduces the soul to impotency must be false. A reading of the Bible which cuts the nerve of action is certainly a deadly superstition which all open-eyed lovers of the truth must resist and overcome.

But there is also another error against which we must be on our guard. You to whom I am speaking are in little danger of being captured by the error to which I have referred. Your danger lies in the opposite direction. You know the Lord is not going to drop from heaven with a shout. You do not believe that the end of the world is at hand. You do not believe that Christ is coming in the manner so vividly pictured by traveling evangelists, and therefore you do not believe he is coming at all. You do not look for him soon or late. There is no expectancy in your eyes. There is no leaping hope in your heart. "Maranatha" is not in your vocabulary. You do not rejoice in an anticipated fresh disclosure of God's power. You think that men must do everything alone. No reliance can be put upon the Almighty. If the world is to become a better world it will become better solely through human effort. God will have nothing to do with it. It is for men to devise new schemes and lay out new programs. They should not count on any help from heaven. Whatever progress may be made will be the result of human cleverness and genius. Such is the opinion of many. This is a blighting error. This error, like the former one, cuts the nerve of action. It leaves us dubious and doleful. We are not sure whether our hopes will ever be realized, or whether our dreams will ever come true. We are not certain what man may be able to accomplish. As for God he is a mystery. Christ has come and died and gone, and now we must struggle on alone. If Christ is not at the door, then the spirit of expectation dies. If we cannot say "Maranatha" there is no radiancy of hope. Alas for those who can not face tomorrow with beating hearts eager to see some fresh unfolding of the power of God!

Charles E. Jefferson, D.D.

There is nothing more wonderful in modern science than its spirit of expectancy. The great scientists are all alike in expecting greater things tomorrow than anything known today. They do not prophesy small things but great things, not common things but wonderful things. No matter what marvels have already been achieved still greater marvels are coming. In laboratories all around the world eager groups of men are working, all of them expecting some new manifestation of the power of nature. They are looking among other things for a cure for cancer. They will find it because they are expecting it. The spirit of expectancy is the very breath of the nostrils of the scientific world. The church must catch that spirit if it is to conquer.

We have recently entered on a new year, and what do you expect? Are you saying "Maranatha"? What new thing do you expect God to do in you? What great thing do you expect God to do for you? What marvelous thing do you expect to see accomplished by God's grace in your life before the new year ends? Do you expect anything at all? Or do you expect to go on in the same old rut in which you have long been moving?

What do you expect for your church? What new thing are you looking for? What great thing are you counting on? Are you really expecting any fresh disclosure of God's power and love in your church? Or do you rather expect that the church will continue to travel along the old, drowsy, routine ways, learning nothing wonderfully new and doing nothing

372

startlingly great? What do you expect for your city? Can any new thing take place in your city? What great thing can come to pass by God's help in your city? Or must your city continue to trudge along the old dusty road, repeating endlessly experiences which are monotonous and tame?

What do you expect? In what new form will God appear? What new work do you expect him to perform? With what fresh miracles will he crown this year? "Maranatha!" There is tragic sadness in St. Mark's description of Jesus' experience on his return to his own City of Nazareth. "He could there do no mighty work." And why not? They expected nothing.

THE GOSPEL OF IMMORTALITY

Born at Seaham Harbour, England, in 1892, Dr. Buttrick studied at Victoria University, Manchester, where he was an honor man in philosophy; and at the Lancashire Independent Seminary. All his ministry has been spent in America, two pastorates in the Congregational Church and two in the Presbyterian Church. In 1921 he came to the pulpit of the old First Church of Buffalo, where he had a distinguished ministry; and it is not strange that he was invited to follow Dr. Coffin in the Madison Avenue Church in New York City six years later. All who have followed his rapid rise to the front ranks of the pulpit will look eagerly for his study of *The Parables of Jesus,* now on the press.

No one can say anything new about Easter; no one needs to do so, because Easter itself is always new, like the earth reborn out of winter, like the wonder of the inextinguishable hope in the heart of man. Yet in the sermon by Dr. Buttrick one finds a radiance of faith, and an uncovering of the sources of the ancient, high, heroic faith of man, which fortifies while it inspires. Who can read the last illustration of the shy young Russian priest who answered an atheistic lecturer by giving the Easter salutation, and not feel his heart throb like a drum-beat!

THE GOSPEL OF IMMORTALITY

GEORGE A. BUTTRICK, D.D.

MADISON AVENUE PRESBYTERIAN CHURCH, NEW YORK CITY

If a man die, shall he live again? Job 14: 14.

. . . the appearing of our Savior, Jesus Christ, who abolished death, and brought life and immortality to light. II Timothy 1: 10.

"If a man die"—the question old as death itself and as new as the newest grave! But what a strange way to ask it: *"If* a man die." There is no "if" about death. The "grim reaper" whets his scythe on the day we are born, and soon or late the scythe will cut us down. That is one of the few prophecies we may indulge with certainty concerning this uncertain thing called life.

Since man *must* die, shall he live again? There is nobody into whose field of affection that "reaper" has not come. One moment your friend was there—light in the eyes, speech on the lips, energy in the hands, a warm and living spirit; the next moment—gone. In that fraction of a second what has happened? Everything is as before—eyes, lips, hands—but everything is different. Nothing has been lost except—your loved one! Then are souls blown out like candles? Are those terrible and familiar words

377

George A. Buttrick, D.D.

of Shakespeare the whole truth and nothing but the
truth?—

> Tomorrow and tomorrow and tomorrow,
> Creeps in this petty pace from day to day,
> To the last syllable of recorded time:
> And all our yesterdays have lighted fools
> The way to dusty death. Out, out, brief candle!
> Life's but a walking shadow; a poor player,
> That struts and frets his hour upon the stage,
> And then is heard no more: It is a tale
> Told by an idiot, full of sound and fury,
> Signifying nothing.

The first of these texts asks the inevitable question.
Notice the second text: It speaks of Jesus as bringing immortality to light. Immortality, that is to say,
was in human life before he came, but it was encom-
passed by shadows and doubts. He brought it into
the daylight so that every one might see it. Immortality was like a seed and Jesus was like the sun. He
drew the seed from its dark prison and made it blos-
som gloriously. We may fasten, then, on this truth
first: Immortality has always been in human life.
There is eternity in our nature.

Immortality is in our instincts. In Africa a savage
tribe gathers round the body of a dead king. They
kill his wives and slaves and bury them with him.
He must have company in that other kingdom. In
America in early days the Indians placed weapons
and food in the grave of a chief. He must be
equipped for the "happy hunting grounds." In Italy

378

The Gospel of Immortality

the Etruscans carved a rising sun upon the urns which contained the ashes of their dead: the imperishable instinct gave them hope. In modern England Sir Oliver Lodge loses a son in the war, and writes a book entitled by the son's name, *Raymond,* to assert that his boy has spoken from the dead. The fact that hundreds of thousands bought the book was a better proof of immortality than anything the book contained. Age after age the instinct for immortality endures. Flames cannot scorch it, nor floods drown it, nor bayonets pierce it, nor sorrow conquer it.

In other realms of life instincts are not deceptive. By some sure intuition the birds fly south before the first touch of winter has come. An instinct is their only compass, but it does not play them false:

> I go to prove my soul.
> I see my way as birds their trackless way—
> I shall arrive. What time, what circuit first,
> I ask not: but unless God send his hail,
> Or blinding fireballs, sleet, or stifling snow,
> In some time, his good time, I shall arrive:
> He guides me and the bird.

Likewise, immortality is in our conscience. Have you ever heard a man say, as I once heard a man say in bitter indignation for a wrong done to his child, "If there isn't a hell, there ought to be." It is the voice of conscience, and conscience also says: "If there isn't a heaven, there ought to be." There are too many wrongs unrighted for this to be the only world. I read a short time ago that far less than ten per cent. of all burglaries are requited at the bar of

379

human justice. And what of worse thefts than thefts of money or property? What of those who steal purity? What of those who steal away a child's right to health—steal it away before the child is born? What of those who steal away the good name of a neighbor? Not *one* per cent. of these burglaries are brought to the bar of earthly justice. Is there no cosmic justice? "If there isn't a hell, there ought to be"—not a vindictive hell, but a remedial one in very truth. And look at the credit side of the account. "If there isn't a heaven" . . . There are too many songs unsung before death comes, too many pictures unpainted, too much love thwarted and unsatisfied. . . . "If there isn't a heaven, there ought to be." Chaucer died writing a poem. Haller, the famous physician, died fingering his pulse. Mozart, as the mists gathered about his eyes, asked if he might hear once more the harmonies which had been his solace and delight. Not one of these believed his work was ended. Victor Hugo in his seventieth year said: "Winter is on my head, but Spring is in my heart. For half a century I have been writing, but I feel I have not said a thousandth part of what is in me." What true mother has ever shown a thousandth part of the love that is in her? "If there isn't a heaven there ought to be." Immortality is in our conscience. I do not argue, for the moment, that conscience is in this regard to be trusted. It is a guide in other paths, however, and it points with flaming finger to a world beyond this world.

The Gospel of Immortality

Again, immortality is in our affections. What true affection has ever been content to die? Say of some loved one lost to you that the loss is total and irretrievable, and even as you say the words your spirit will shudder. That shudder is prophetic of eternity. Love will not believe that love is nothing but ashes and tears. In *Aylwin*, a novel by Watts-Dunton, the young hero, Hal, hears his bereaved father declare with yearning conviction:

> Should you ever come to love as I have loved, you will find that materialism is intolerable—is hell itself—to a heart that has known a passion like mine. You will find that it is madness, Hal, madness, to believe in the word "never"! You will find that you dare not leave untried any creed, however wild, that offers the heart a ray of hope.

Once more, immortality is in our sense of God. The feeling for God was in the world before Jesus came. I am speaking now not of the mind's assent to the proposition that God exists. To believe that God is, to believe it as we believe that a straight line is the shortest distance between two given points, proves nothing. It is a piece of almost useless mental furniture. "The devils also believe, and tremble." I am speaking of a knowledge of God which men have had in actual experience—men like Nevarga in that book of Charles Kingsley's, who in the brokenness and defilement of his soul cried out upon God and found him: "Then I spoke right out into the dumb, black air" (Nevarga tells us). "and I said, 'If thou

381

wilt be my God, if thou wilt be on my side, good Lord, who died for me, I will be thine, villain as I am, if thou canst make anything of me.' " When the prayer was offered, the book declares, the desert bushes began to burn with holy fire! Men and women have found God, people like Nevarga, people like Enoch who walked with God, and like Abraham who was called "the friend of God."

Those who have known God cannot think of him as one who would blow out personality as though it were a cheap candle. They cannot think of God as having power to make children capable of longing for immortality yet without power to give them the immortality for which they long, for in that case Death would be the real God and our so-called "God" would be a tinpot monarch ruling by sufferance. Nor can they deem it possible (these who have known God) that he has mocked his children with the dream of eternity, for then he would be not God but a devil with creatures far nobler than he. I am appealing now directly to the religious experience of the race. It is not less valid (it is more valid, I think) than any other kind of experience. The highest religious insight of mankind has not been able to think of God as either a half-God ruling over a vast graveyard or a devil-God mocking his children with false hopes. The saints ever have said: "O taste and see that the Lord is good," "his loving-kindness is better than life," "Yea, though I walk through the valley of the shadow of death, I will fear no evil." They have faced denials as Frederick H. W. Myers faced them:

The Gospel of Immortality

Whoso has felt the Spirit of the Highest,
  Cannot confound him, or doubt him, or deny;
Yea, with one voice, O world, tho' thou deniest,
  Stand thou on that side, for on this stand I.

We are urging the truth that immortality has always been embedded in human life. It has stirred only fitfully, perhaps, but it has never been destroyed. It is in our instincts, our conscience, our love, our sense of God. Death is a cold and stubborn fact. Its stillness is terrifying to the eyes, its silence to the ears, it unresponsiveness to the hands. But which will you believe—your eyes or your conscience, your ears or your heart, your hands or your sense of God? The issue narrows to that question.

To that question—and Jesus! The facts concerning Jesus are that he lived and died and rose again. He lived—as no competent student denies. He died. Nobody need doubt that fact. It is reflected in the utter despair of his disciples. "We trusted this had been he who should have redeemed Israel" . . . but he was not what they had hoped. Such was their mood. Their Messiah, their King, had ended not on a throne but (irony of ironies) on a cross. They remained, the bedraggled survivors of a broken cause. Oh, well, they would know better than to trust the next dreamer. "I go a-fishing," said Peter. Back to the old tasks, sadder but wiser men! Jesus died. Then what happened? Suddenly this same Peter is facing the foes of Jesus with reckless courage. Listen to him as he speaks to them: "Jesus of Nazareth . . .

him ye have taken, and by wicked hands have crucified and slain. Whom God hath raised up, having
loosed the bonds of death, because it was not possible
that death could hold him!"

What had happened? We must concentrate on the
primary and central fact. The rolling away of a
stone is not primary. The manner in which the tomb
was robbed of its corpse is not the primary fact. The
problem of the resurrection appearances of Jesus is
perplexing and important, but not primary. This is
the primary fact: As it might have been on Good
Friday the disciples of Jesus were downcast in tragic
loss, and as it might have been on Easter Sunday
they were thrilling with victory. Why did these
cowering men suddenly rise from their bemoanings
and with light on their faces fairly spring on the
world with the message of a living Saviour for whom
they were willing to suffer any persecution? Read
the New Testament, and see if there are any "In
Memoriam" tendencies in it. It is filled with the
sense of the abiding, empowering presence of Jesus.
Why?

Delusion, suggests somebody. Oh, no! Figs do
not grow on thistles, and the fervor that quickened
a dead world did not grow on the stalk of a delusion.
The noble army of martyrs did not embrace death
by faggot and sword for the sake of a delusion.
Churches named after this crucified Jesus did not
spring up like flowers in a wilderness all because of a
delusion. Our hymn books are not crammed with
devotion to a living Jesus because the best men and
women for two thousand years have fed on the ashes

of a delusion. Mighty events demand a commensurate cause. There is only one commensurate cause
and Peter proclaimed it: "Whom God hath raised up,
having loosed the bonds of death, for it was not possible that death could hold him."

He has brought life and immortality to light. It
was in our conscience, but our conscience was sadly
blemished. It was in our love, but our love at best
was selfish. It was in our sense of God, but our
sense of God was dim. Then he came. He was all
conscience—a holiness passionately pure; he was all
love—a compassion self-forgetting even unto death;
he was all sense of God—walking in God as in an
atmosphere, vital with God as a pulse is vital within
the blood. We must reverently honor his own claim:
"I and my Father are one." The immortality which
has stirred fitfully within our shadowy humanity
shone radiant in him: "He brought it to light." What
had he to do with death? How is it conceivable that
a few chemical changes in his flesh could extinguish
his soul? "It was not possible that death could hold
him."

I return to the question: Will you believe your
eyes or your conscience, your ears or your heart,
your hands or your sense of God? Nay, I ask you
rather: Will you believe your eyes, or *his* conscience,
his heart, *his* sense of God? Which will you trust: a
hole in the ground—or Jesus?—Jesus, and the hope
that quickened the world with gladness on that first
Easter morning?

The other day a lecturer in Russia attacked Christianity as an obsolete faith, a capitalistic product

DATE DUE